Cooking for Beginners

Publisher's Note: Raw or semi-cooked eggs should not be consumed by babies, toddlers, pregnant or breastfeeding women, the elderly or those suffering from a chronic illness.

Publisher & Creative Director: Nick Wells
Senior Project Editor: Catherine Taylor
Art Director: Mike Spender
Layout Design: Mike Spender
Digital Design & Production: Chris Herbert
Proofreader: Siobhan O'Connor

Special thanks to Gina Steer for her continued help and contributions, and to Chris Herbert and William Greaves.

This is a **FLAME TREE** Book

FLAME TREE PUBLISHING
Crabtree Hall, Crabtree Lane
Fulham, London SW6 6TY
United Kingdom
www.flametreepublishing.com

Flame Tree is part of The Foundry Creative Media Company Limited

First published 2010

ISBN: 978-1-84786-698-1

Printed in China

All images © The Foundry Creative Media Co., except the following. Courtesy of Fotolia: 74 © Monkey Business. Courtesy of Cephas Picture Library and © the following photographers: 69 Dean Skip, 71 James Jackson, 73 Jean-Paul Boyer. Courtesy of Shutterstock and © the following photographers: 14 vgstudio; 15 Pete Saloutos; 16l Kellie L. Folkerts; 16r Mike Flippo; 17bl DRGill; 17tr, 66, 41t Robyn Mackenzie; 18r erkanupan; 18l, 21br mates; 19tl Aga & Miko (arsat); 19r Ljupco Smokovski; 20bl Alistair Cotton; 20tr Paul Cowan; 24bl hsintzu; 24r ZTS; 25 arenacreative; 28 RookCreations; 29 Steve Lovegrove; 31t Sandra Cunningham; 31b Svetlana Lukienko; 32, 49, 22l Monkey Business Images; 33 silabob; 34br Colour; 34tl Natalia Klenova; 35 Birdy68; 36 Justin Paget; 37t 3445128471; 38 & 48t Joe Gough; 41b fotogiunta; 42 Zamula Artem; 43 Andi Berger; 44t Eugene Berman; 44b SergioZ; 46l ason; 46r Elena Elisseeva; 48b Khorkova Olga; 50 Tatuasha; 53 anlogin; 56l Robert Anthony; 59 Eaststeel; 60 RexRover; 62t Girish Menon; 62b Kateryna Dyellalova; 63 Paul Turner; 64 olszphoto; 65b Elena Schweitzer; 67 viki2win; 68 moonbeam; 81t ilker canikligil; 81b Richard Griffin; 85 Newton Page; 87 Terence Mendoza; 88 Ingrid Balabanova; 89b Kruglov_Orda; 89t LockStockBob.

Cooking for Beginners

Quick and Easy, Proven Recipes

FLAME TREE
PUBLISHING

Contents

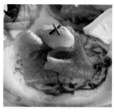

Soups & Starters 94

Soups such as rustic Bread & Tomato Soup and Classic Minestrone offer a reassuring and tasty route into *Cooking for Beginners*, while dishes such as Honey & Ginger Prawns and Potato Pancakes with Smoked Salmon, in turn, present an opportunity to display your growing confidence in the kitchen by creating dishes for a starter course.

Fish & Seafood 136

Delicious *and* healthy, fish and seafood offer a tempting choice for the novice chef. With dishes including Tuna Cannelloni and Ratatouille Mackerel, this chapter is bursting with diverse recipes. There's never been an easier – or tastier – way to get your share of omega-3 fatty acids and other necessary nutrients.

Meat suggestion: Sausage & Redcurrant Pasta Bake, page 214

Meat...180

Hungry carnivores have a mouthwatering choice of meaty dishes to prepare – from the simple yet elegant Fillet Steaks with Tomato & Garlic Sauce to the homely and traditional Shepherd's Pie, you'll find dealing with meat in its many forms is nothing to fear. Why not try something a little different and yet so easy you'll be making it again and again, such as Pork Cabbage Parcels?

Poultry 222

Chicken is one of those foods that you must make sure is thoroughly cooked before serving, but you will be able to test this in no time, going on to create tempting and juicy recipes, from the one-pot style Aromatic Chicken Curry or the satisfying Chicken Pie with Sweet Potato Topping, to the fun Cheesy Chicken Burgers or the more adventurous Stir-fried Duck with Cashews.

Vegetables & Vegetarian..................................264

We all need to eat more vegetables, but it can be hard to fit enough of them into our diet. This section will reveal a plethora of tasty dishes that can be created from the wide variety of vegetables out there – as well as the fact that they are so easy to prepare, from roasting to stir-frying. Try the sweet yet refreshing Vegetables in Coconut Milk or the moreish classic, Melanzane Parmigiana.

Starter suggestion: Mixed Satay Sticks, page 115

Meat suggestion: Traditional Lasagne, page 187

Poultry suggestion: Spicy Chicken Skewers with Mango Tabbouleh, page 230

Desserts & Cakes

Let's not forget that once you've mastered your favourite savoury dishes, if you have a little extra time you may want to try your hand at dessert, or at baking a cake for a real treat. Try classic Rice Pudding – the ultimate in nostalgic comfort food – or, if you're in need of a change, Stir-fried Bananas & Peaches with Rum Butterscotch Sauce would be a great end to a more exotic main course.

Introduction

So you have never cooked – no problem. If you can read, you can cook. Following a recipe is not difficult; cooking is much easier than you might think. In fact, it is people who make cooking hard because they can make it look complicated and daunting. However, as long as you have a little patience and time, you will easily be able to produce a delicious meal for you, your family and friends in a relatively short time.

Maybe you have been put off by the many and differing cookery programmes that are dished up on our screens night after night. Here, celebrity chefs demonstrate their skills so easily and so very quickly that it is almost impossible to see what they are preparing and cooking. This can make even the most experienced cooks doubt their abilities, let alone a beginner. My advice is *switch off*. Remember that all the TV chefs have a small team of experts behind the scenes to peel and chop, fry and boil, thicken or clear – doing many of the jobs for the chef, while you have just yourself ... So do not be put off, switch off.

As with all skills, time is required to learn the basic steps and terminology. Once these are mastered, you will start gaining confidence. Having the correct tools for the different tasks ahead is an essential part of learning to cook. This cookbook aims to take you every step of the way, first explaining in clear, simple terms what tools and equipment you will require and exactly what each tool does, from inexpensive items such as a zester to more pricey pieces such as a free-standing food mixer. The information given will clearly show which items are essential and which may not be necessary but would make life in the kitchen much easier.

A comprehensive explanation of cookery terminology, which can often baffle even the most experienced, is also provided – there is no use being able to read a recipe if you do not know the difference between beating and folding, for instance. As with many things in life, new, more modern terms are being introduced all the time and this simply helps to spread confusion and mayhem.

Next comes an invaluable conversion chart for weights, measures and temperatures,

followed by reams of information on store-cupboard essentials, essential hygiene practices, nutrition, cooking eggs and the varieties and cooking techniques for rice, pasta, herbs and spices, meat, poultry, seafood and vegetables.

So, before you do anything else, make sure that you read through all this essential advice and information in order to get off to the best start on your culinary journey. Of course, practice is the only way to develop your skills, so get stuck in – each recipe in this book has very clear and easy-to-follow step-by-step instructions, often with photography revealing tricky techniques. Remember to read through the whole of a recipe before beginning to make sure that you do not stumble across any surprises halfway through. And do not forget – you learn from your mistakes as well as from your successes. Good luck!

Tools and Equipment

In this section I have listed the tools and equipment you will need in order to start cooking. Some of the tools and equipment are absolutely essential and I would recommend that you invest in these first. Other less essential tools and equipment can also be reasonably expensive, so they might be good ideas to suggest as either birthday or Christmas presents.

Essential Tools

Knives Knives are perhaps the most important tools in the kitchen. It is advisable to have a good selection. First, when buying, make sure that any knife sits comfortably in your hand. You will need a small knife (often called a 'paring' knife) for all the little jobs, such as deseeding a chilli and cutting fruits and vegetables into small pieces. At least a further three or four additional knives would be good: a large chef's knife, which has a long wide blade, is ideal for chopping both meat and fish, as well as fresh herbs; a carving knife; a bread knife, with or without a serrated edge; and a medium-size all-purpose knife for all other jobs. Make sure that the knives are a reputable brand and easy to sharpen – a good knife will last a long while, perhaps for ever.

Wooden spoons I feel that you can never have too many wooden spoons! Although they will not last for ever, looked after and washed properly they should last for at least one to two years, depending on what you use them for. I would recommend buying one of the sets that are so readily available. These usually come in different lengths – the shorter one is super for sauces and the other two for stirring food, such as meat that is being sealed in a pan, as well as for mixing cakes and batters. Although they wash perfectly well, it is a good idea to keep some spoons for sweet dishes and others for savoury dishes. Then there are the wooden spatulas, which are perfect for omelettes or frying meats such as chops because the flat, wider area makes turning food over so much easier.

Kitchen utensils with rack These are usually stainless steel and, although it is not 100 per cent necessary to have the rack fixed to the wall, it is a good idea, especially if close to the cooker. These racks usually contain at least five utensils, all of which play an important part in cooking.

Large spoons These can be a plain spoon ideal for stirring or dishing out casseroles, stews and vegetables, or a slotted draining spoon – this refers to the gaps in the bowl of the spoon, which allow any liquid to drain back into the pan, for example, when removing meat after sealing it for a stew or casserole.

Measuring spoons These ensure that the correct amount of ingredients is used. This is especially useful when either following a specific diet (for example, where oil and butter intake needs to be measured) or for use with a thickening agent such as cornflour, or with spices, where too much could completely ruin the dish.

Vegetable peeler Using a peeler makes the job easier and will ensure that you get an even look to the peeled fruit or vegetable, such as peeling pears for cooking in wine or peeling potatoes. I prefer the swivel-blade peeler, as it removes only a very thin layer and this will mean that, as many of the nutrients are just below the skin, they are preserved. However, it is a matter of personal choice, so when buying try imitating the peeling action and see which fits most comfortably with your needs.

Grater For grating cheese, carrots and other root vegetables, fresh root ginger, chocolate, citrus zest and nutmeg – the last two should be done on the finest side of the grater.

Oven thermometer Especially useful if you plan to make cakes and desserts. Many ovens vary in temperature and pastry and baked goods need to be cooked at the correct temperature in order to achieve good results.

Timer Again, if planning to bake pastries and cakes, time is critical and it is so easy to get distracted. A timer will ensure that you know when it is time to test to see whether the cake or pastry is cooked. Many ovens have timers built in.

Scissors A pair of serrated-edge kitchen scissors are so useful for all the little jobs, such as snipping a few fresh herbs, chopping bacon or dried fruits into small pieces, removing unwanted fat from chicken portions or steaks, cutting out liners for cake tins … the list is endless.

Garlic press A handy alternative to crushing or mincing garlic with a knife. This removes the need to peel the garlic, a clove is simply placed in the bowl and a small handle is pulled over, then the garlic comes out of the tiny holes. A garlic press can also double up as a cherry stoner.

Extra Tools

Fish slice Also known as a spatula, this is not the more ornate, usually silver utensil that is used when serving fish in front of guests, but the plastic or steel utensil that is superb for turning food over and for removing cooked food from hot baking trays or roasting tins – I like to have at least two. A fish slice may be included in your set of utensils plus rack as discussed earlier (third along from the right in the picture).

Ladle Perfect for hot soups, casseroles, stews and any other hot liquids that need transferring or serving.

Potato masher You would be quite stuck without this if you wanted to make mashed potatoes. It is super for mashing all manner of vegetables, from potatoes to parsnips, carrots, yams or sweet potatoes.

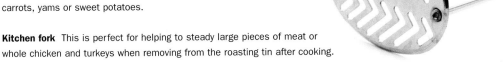

Kitchen fork This is perfect for helping to steady large pieces of meat or whole chicken and turkeys when removing from the roasting tin after cooking.

Chopper/meat cleaver Good for chopping herbs and vegetables, as well as meat and poultry.

Kebab sticks and skewers Either metal or wooden, kebab sticks are for cooking both savoury and sweet kebabs, koftas and satays, and skewering fish or chicken into 'spatchcock' shape – this is where the food is split almost in half, then skewered prior to cooking so that it keeps its shape and lies 'flat'. Remember that wooden kebab sticks or bamboo skewers need first to be soaked in cold water for at least 30 minutes and both ends wrapped in kitchen foil to prevent the ends burning during cooking – and the cook burning her or his fingers.

Of course skewers are also available in metal. Metal skewers can be used for kebabs, but are also perfect for testing whether cakes are cooked in the middle or if poultry is completely cooked through – especially when cooking a whole turkey, as the very long skewers will go right through the thickest part straight to the centre cavity.

Pastry brushes These have a variety of uses, including brushing pans and dishes lightly with oil prior to cooking, brushing the sides of the grater with a clean dry brush to remove any remaining cheese or fruit zest after grating and brushing a glaze or warmed jam over a dessert or cake. You could use them for basting, too, but they are not specially designed to cope with the heat of foods you will be basting and the bristles may curl up, so a spoon, special basting brush or baster pipette would be better for that particular task.

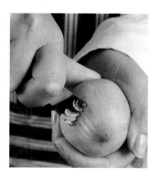

Piping bags and nozzles Used mainly for cake decoration, these are for the more adventurous cook. The nozzles come in two sizes: large, which are referred to as 'potato pipes' (for that is what they are often used for, as well as for meringue dishes such as pavlovas), and the smaller pipes which are called 'icing pipes'.

Tongs Good for lifting raw and cooked foods when turning over during cooking or placing on plates or dishes.

Zester This is for removing long thin strands of outer lemon, orange or lime rind (zest) to use for decoration purposes.

Whisks Used for whisking or whipping cream, eggs and sauces in order to create a smooth consistency and incorporate air. They are usually formed from interlocking wires and are available in various types, most commonly the balloon whisk of varying shapes and sizes, the mechanically hand-operated rotary whisk and a flat whisk. All work well, but take longer than one powered by electricity – see 'Extra Equipment'.

Basic Equipment

Certain pieces of equipment are essential when cooking. There is no need to go out and spend a fortune, as most of the equipment is relatively cheap. However, what I would recommend is that you buy good-quality pans, ones that will not buckle from the heat after being used a couple of times. Nonstick pans can also make life a lot easier when it comes to the washing up. Below is a list of equipment that will start the beginner cook on their way and can easily be added to after a little time and some experience are gained.

Chopping boards Essential for any job that involves cutting. Look for the colour-coordinated boards, so that you can use a different colour for different types of food (that is, to keep meat, especially chicken, separate from vegetables, for example). That way there will be no cross-contamination of food. Make sure that you wash them thoroughly after use, washing in the dishwasher if you have one.

Measuring jugs These are available in three different sizes and again can be bought as glass Pyrex jugs or in plastic. Both do the job well and both have the measurements marked down the side of the jug.

Scales These are essential, especially when baking. Although it is possible to buy measuring cups in the UK, we usually measure ingredients in grams or

storing, creaming butter and sugar for cakes, pastry making, melting chocolate, whipping cream and whisking egg whites.

Pans Perhaps the most expensive investment when first beginning to cook. I would recommend that you buy a set of saucepans, usually there are three to five of differing sizes and these should be adequate to begin with. It would also be a good idea to have a milk pan for making sauces as well as boiling milk, plus a good frying pan, preferably with a lid to increase its versatility.

Colander and sieve Used for sifting flours and straining ingredients to remove any lumps, a sieve is usually made of fine-mesh wire, while a colander tends to be rather bigger, with bigger holes or slots, and is used for draining cooked pasta and vegetables. The latter come in plastic and metal versions.

ounces. Most scales, whether digital or conventional, measure in both types of measurement and all have a bowl in which to place the ingredients to be weighed.

Mixing bowls Ideally, you will have at least three – in small, medium and large. These can be Pyrex glass or similar, and are essential for many jobs in the kitchen, including soaking,

Baking trays These have many varied uses. Dishes such as lasagne can be set on baking trays so that they are easy to place in the oven, as well as remove. They are also good for baking such items as scones, meringues and cookies and for reheating dishes. Other baking equipment can be bought as it is required; to begin with I would suggest that you keep it to the minimum with one or two baking trays.

Extra Equipment

Food processor A very versatile piece of equipment and one that I would recommend investing in. It will chop vegetables, fruit, nuts and herbs, and shred vegetables, as well as blend soups and make pastry dough and even cakes (though you run the risk overmixing cakes). Available at different prices.

Blender or liquidiser Very similar to a food processor, this has a jug rather than a bowl. It blends and chops, but does not do all the jobs that a food processor will do. You can also get hand-held or stick blenders, useful for puréeing soups and the like.

Food mixer These can be free-standing and perform many jobs in the kitchen from whipping cream, whisking egg whites and creaming butter and sugar for baking cakes, to making dough for bread and rubbing butter into flour for pastry, or where all the ingredients are simply put in the bowl and mixed. Smaller versions are available, but these are hand-held. Free-standing mixers, on the other hand, can be left to mix on their own. Either way, some form of food mixer will be greatly appreciated if making cakes – hand whisking and beating can be tiring!

Ice cream maker Useful if you love ice cream and very easy to use, producing creamy delicious ice cream straight from the bowl. Be wary, however – such items run the risk of languishing unused at the back of a cupboard … The same goes for smoothie machines (see below).

Smoothie machine Although a blender or liquidiser will make smoothies, the results are not as smooth as those made in a smoothie machine.

Electric carving knife A bit of a luxury, but useful for carving small joints that do not stand very well and especially good for a whole turkey, as beautifully thin slices can be achieved.

Trivet A mat, rack or tripod-like structure, made out of metal, wood, ceramic, fabric, silicone or cork, and ideal for standing hot casseroles and saucepans on after cooking – in order to prevent your work surface being scorched.

Culinary Terms

Over the years the language of cooking has developed and now there are many new words and expressions that perhaps 25 years ago no one would have dream of using in connection with cooking. Below are some of the words you are likely to come across and what is meant by them.

Baking Cooking foods in the oven. This usually applies primarily to cakes, breads, pastries and puddings, but can refer to anything cooked in the dry heat of the oven. 'Baking' is often used interchangeably with 'roasting', but a distinction can arguably be drawn by saying that 'roasting' implies greater heat and more pronounced browning. 'Roasting' is also the preferred term for meat, poultry and vegetables, while 'baking' tends to be reserved for fish, seafood and the items mentioned above.

Basting Brushing or drizzling meat or fish with its own juices, oil or a prepared sauce, while roasting or grilling, to add flavour and prevent the food drying out.

Beating Using a wooden spoon to mix together ingredients until smooth, such as when making batter for pancakes or Yorkshire pudding.

Blanching Pouring boiling water over fresh green vegetables (or immersing them into boiling water for a short time) in order to preserve the colour. They are then typically plunged into cold water to halt the cooking process. This is done when vegetables are either to be frozen or added to a dish towards the end of cooking. It will also speed up their cooking time.

Bruising Slightly crushing an ingredient, usually with the flat side of a chef's knife or cleaver, in order to release its flavour.

Creaming Beating together butter or margarine with sugar until lighter in colour and soft and creamy in texture. This applies to cake making.

Coulis A trendy word for a strained fruit or vegetable sauce that is generally served with the finished dish.

Drizzling Another trendy word used to signify pouring a little sauce or oil over food, but taking care not to swamp it.

Folding in This applies to stirring another ingredient into an uncooked mixture such as a meringue or sponge cake mixture. Care must be taken that the mixture is not overmixed, as this will remove the air that has been whisked in, thus preventing a good rise or the required light texture.

Frying Cooking fresh foods in, usually, a frying pan or, sometimes, a deep fat fryer, cooking the food to a certain stage or cooking the food completely. Foods are usually fried in a certain amount of fat, such as butter or oil.

Sautéing This simply means frying, usually fairly quickly, and refers mainly to the cooking of meat and vegetables in a frying pan when first starting to cook in order to seal in the meat juices and help to preserve their nutrients and flavour.

Steaming A method of cooking food with steam, rather than directly in the water. Vegetables are especially good when steamed, as most of the nutrients are preserved and not lost into the water as happens when they are boiled. Food is placed in a container that will allow the steam to pass through and sits on top of a pan of gently simmering water. The steamer is covered with a lid.

Whipping This is when whipping or double cream is beaten with a whisk until soft peaks are formed in the thickened cream. Can be whipped either by machine or by a hand-held whisk such as a balloon whisk.

Whisking Beating a liquid with a whisk, either in a food mixer or using a hand-held whisk. To whisk egg whites, whisk until stiff and dry (this means that the bowl of whisked egg whites can be tipped upside down and the egg white does not move).

Zest What is the difference between 'zest' and 'rind'? 'Zest' is the outermost part of the 'rind' of a citrus fruit, as opposed to the white 'pith' underneath, but in a cooking context can refer to the long thin strips of zest made with a 'zester' (which are used for decoration only because, if eaten, they will give a bitter taste) or to grated zest (sometimes referred to as 'grated rind'), which is made by rubbing the unpeeled but washed or scrubbed fruit up and down the fine side of a grater, giving very fine pieces or shreds. As these are finer than zest strips, they can be used to flavour dishes.

Useful Conversions

Temperature Conversion

−4°F	−20°C	68°F	20°C
5°F	−15°C	77°F	25°C
14°F	−10°C	86°F	30°C
23°F	−5°C	95°F	35°C
32°F	0°C	104°F	40°C
41°F	5°C	113°F	45°C
50°F	10°C	122°F	50°C
59°F	15°C	212°F	100°C

Oven Temperatures

Bear in mind that, if using a fan oven, you should reduce the stated temperature by around 20°C. Check the manufacturer's instructions for guidance.

110°C	225°F	Gas Mark ¼	Very slow oven
120/130°C	250°F	Gas Mark ½	Very slow oven
140°C	275°F	Gas Mark 1	Slow oven
150°C	300°F	Gas Mark 2	Slow oven
160/170°C	325°F	Gas Mark 3	Moderate oven
180°C	350°F	Gas Mark 4	Moderate oven
190°C	375°F	Gas Mark 5	Moderately hot oven
200°C	400°F	Gas Mark 6	Moderately hot oven
220°C	425°F	Gas Mark 7	Hot oven
230°C	450°F	Gas Mark 8	Hot oven
240°C	475°F	Gas Mark 9	Very hot oven

Dry Weights

Metric/Imperial

10 g	¼ oz	50 g	2 oz	165 g	5½ oz	300 g	10 oz
15 g	½ oz	65 g	2½ oz	175 g	6 oz	325 g	11 oz
20 g	¾ oz	75 g	3 oz	185 g	6½ oz	350 g	12 oz
25 g	1 oz	90 g	3½ oz	200 g	7 oz	375 g	13 oz
40 g	1½ oz	100 g	3½ oz	225 g	8 oz	400 g	14 oz
		125 g	4–4½ oz	250 g	9 oz	425 g	15 oz
		150 g	5 oz	275 g	9½ oz	450 g	1 lb

Liquid Measures

Metric, Imperial (UK) and US Cups/Quarts

2.5 ml	½ tsp	-	-
5 ml	1 tsp	-	-
15 ml	1 tbsp	-	-
25 ml	1 fl oz	⅛ cup	2 tbsp
50 ml	2 fl oz	¼ cup	3–4 tbsp
65 ml	2½ fl oz	⅓ cup	5 tbsp
75–85 ml	3 fl oz	⅓ cup	6 tbsp
100 ml	3½ fl oz	⅓ cup	7 tbsp
120 ml	4 fl oz	½ cup	8 tbsp
135 ml	4½ fl oz	½ cup	9 tbsp
150 ml	5 fl oz	¼ pint	⅔ cup
175 ml	6 fl oz	⅓ pint	scant ¾ cup
200 ml	7 fl oz	⅓ pint	¾ cup
225 ml	8 fl oz	⅜ pint	1 cup
240 ml	8 fl oz	⅜ pint	1 cup
250 ml	8 fl oz	⅜ pint	1 cup
275 ml	9 fl oz	½ pint	1⅛ cups
300 ml	10 fl oz	½ pint	1¼ cups
350 ml	12 fl oz	⅔ pint	1½ cups
400 ml	14 fl oz	⅝ pint	1⅔ cups
450 ml	15 fl oz	¾ pint	1¾ cups
475 ml	16 fl oz	⅞ pint	scant 2 cups
500 ml	18 fl oz	⅞ pint	2 cups
600 ml	20 fl oz	1 pint	2½ cups
750 ml	26 fl oz	1¼ pints	3¼ cups
900 ml	-	1½ pints	scant 1 quart

1.1 litres	-	2 pints	1¼ quarts
1.2 litres	-	2 pints	1¼ quarts
1.25 litres	-	2¼ pints	1⅓ quarts
1.3 litres	-	2⅓ pints	1⅓ quarts
1.4 litres	-	2½ pints	1½ quarts
1.5 litres	-	2½ pints	1⅔ quarts
1.6 litres	-	2¾ pints	1¾ quarts
1.7 litres	-	3 pints	1¾ quarts
1.8 litres	-	3⅛ pints	1⅞ quarts
1.9 litres	-	3⅓ pints	2 quarts
2 litres	-	3½ pints	2 quarts
2.25 litres	-	4 pints	2⅜ quarts
2.5 litres	-	4½ pints	2⅔ quarts
2.75 litres	-	5 pints	3 quarts

Store–cupboard Essentials

The first food shopping trip should be focused on setting up a well-targeted store cupboard. There are a lot of ingredients that you can expect to use again and again, but which you should not have to buy on a frequent basis – you do not use much at a time and they should keep reasonably well. The store cupboard should also be a source of foods that can make a meal when you have run out of fresh ingredients at the end of the week.

It is worth making a trip to a speciality grocery shop to source more 'exotic' ingredients. Our society's growing interest in recent years with travel and food from around the world has led us to seek out alternative ingredients with which to experiment and to incorporate into our cooking. As a consequence, even supermarket chains have had to broaden their product range and will often have a specialist range of imported ingredients from around the world.

If your local grocer or supermarket carries only a limited choice of products, do not despair. The Internet now offers freedom to food lovers. There are some fantastic food sites (both local and international) where food can be purchased and delivery arranged online.

When thinking about essentials, think of flavour, something that is going to add to a dish without increasing its fat content. It is worth spending a bit more money on these products so that you can make flavoursome dishes that will help to stop the urge to snack on fatty foods.

What to Stock in Your Store Cupboard

There are many different types of store-cupboard ingredients readily available – including myriad varieties of rice and pasta, which can provide much of the carbohydrate required in our daily diets. Store the ingredients in a cool, dark place and remember to rotate them. The ingredients will be safe to use for six months.

Herbs and spices These are a must, so it is worth taking a look at the section on pages 62–67 for more information. Often it is preferable to use fresh herbs, but the dried varieties have their merits and dried herbs and spices keep well. Using herbs

when cooking at home should reduce the temptation to buy ready-made sauces. Often these types of sauces contain large amounts of salt, sugar and additives.

Pasta It is good to have a mixture of wholemeal and plain pasta, as well as a wide variety of flavoured pastas. Whether fresh (it can also be frozen) or dried, pasta is a versatile ingredient with which to provide the body with slow-release energy. It comes in many different sizes and shapes; from the tiny tubettini (which can be added to soups to create a more substantial dish), to penne, fusilli, rigatoni and conchiglie, up to the larger cannelloni and lasagne sheets. (*See also* pages 56–61.)

Noodles Also very useful and can accompany Chinese, Japanese or Southeast Asian dishes. Noodles are low in fat and can be made with or without egg, in flours ranging from wheat and buckwheat to rice and even mung beans. Rice noodles are especially suitable for people who need a gluten-free diet; like pasta, they provide slow-release energy to the body.

Rice Long-grain basmati and Thai fragrant rice are especially well suited to Thai and Indian curries, as the fine grains absorb the sauce and their delicate creaminess balances the pungency of the spices. Arborio is the most commonly available type of risotto rice – but there is also Carnaroli and Vialone Nano, which vary in grain size and texture. When cooked, rice swells to create a substantial low-fat dish. Easy-cook American rice, both plain and brown, is great for casseroles and for stuffing meat, fish and vegetables, as it holds its shape and firmness. Short-grain pudding rice can be used in a variety of ways to create an irresistible dessert. (*See also* pages 50–55.)

Couscous Now available in instant form, couscous just needs to be covered with boiling water, then the grains fluffed up with a fork. Couscous is a precooked wheat semolina. Traditional couscous needs to be steamed and is available from health-food stores. This type of couscous contains more nutrients than the instant variety, but needs a far longer cooking time.

Bulghur wheat A cracked wheat that is often used in tabbouleh. Bulghur wheat is a good source of complex carbohydrate.

Pot and pearl barley Pot barley is the complete barley grain, whereas pearl barley has the outer husk removed. Useful as part of a high-cereal diet, which can help to prevent bowel disorders and diseases.

Pulses Vital ingredients for the store cupboard, pulses are easy to store, have a very high nutritional value and are great when added to soups, casseroles, curries and hotpots. Pulses also act as a thickener, whether flavoured or on their own. They come in two forms: either dried (in which case they generally need to be soaked overnight, then cooked before use – it is important to follow the instructions on the back of the packet) or canned, which is a convenient timesaver because the preparation of dried pulses can take a while. If buying canned pulses, try to buy the variety in water with no added salt or sugar. These simply need to be drained and rinsed before being added to a dish.

Kidney, borlotti, cannellini, butter and flageolet beans, split peas and lentils all make tasty additions to any dish. Baked beans are a favourite with everyone and many shops now stock organic varieties, which have no added salt or sugar, but are sweetened with fruit juice instead.

When boiling previously dried pulses, remember that salt should not be added, as this will make the skins tough and inedible.

Puy lentils are a smaller variety of lentil. They often have mottled skins and are particularly good for cooking in slow dishes because they hold their shape and firm texture particularly well.

Dried fruit The ready-to-eat variety are particularly good, as they are plump and juicy, and do not need to be soaked. They are fantastic when puréed into a compote, added to water and heated to make a pie filling and when added to stuffing mixtures. They are also good cooked with meats, rice or couscous.

Flours A useful addition (particularly cornflour, which can be used to thicken sauces). It is worth mentioning that wholemeal flour should not be stored for too long at room temperature, as the fats may turn rancid. While not strictly a flour, cornmeal is a very versatile low-fat ingredient that can be used when making dumplings and gnocchi.

Stock Good-quality stock is a must in low-fat cooking, as it provides a good flavour base for many dishes. Many supermarkets now carry a variety of fresh and organic stocks, which, although they need refrigeration, are probably one of the most time- and effort-saving ingredients available. There is also a fairly large range of dried stock, perhaps the best being bouillon, a high-quality form of stock (available in powder or liquid form) which can be added to any dish whether it be a sauce, casserole, pie or soup.

Sauce ingredients Many people favour meals that can be prepared and cooked in 30–45 minutes, so helpful ingredients that kick-start a sauce are great. A good-quality passata or canned plum tomatoes can act as the foundation for any sauce, as can a good-quality green or red pesto. Other handy store-cupboard additions include tapenade, mustard and anchovies. These have very distinctive tastes and are particularly flavoursome. Roasted red pepper sauce and sun-dried tomato paste, which tends to be sweeter and more intensely flavoured than regular tomato purée, are also very useful.

Vinegar This is another worthwhile store-cupboard essential, and with so many uses it is worth splashing out on really good-quality balsamic and wine vinegars. Herbs and spices are a must, so it is worth taking a look at the section on pages 62–67. Using herbs when cooking at home should reduce the temptation to buy ready-made sauces. Often these types of sauces contain large amounts of salt, sugar and additives.

Yeast extract This is also a good store-cupboard ingredient. It can pep up sauces, soups and casseroles, and adds a little substance, particularly to vegetarian dishes.

Other oils and flavours Chinese and Southeast Asian flavours offer a lot of scope where low-fat cooking is concerned. Flavourings such as fish sauce, soy sauce, Thai red and green curry paste and Chinese rice wine all provide mouthwatering low-fat flavour. For those who are incredibly short on time, or who rarely shop, it is now possible to purchase a selection of readily prepared freshly minced garlic, ginger and chilli (available in jars or tubes that can be kept in the refrigerator).

Hygiene in the Kitchen

It is well worth remembering that many foods can carry some form of bacteria. In most cases, the worst it will lead to is a bout of food poisoning or gastroenteritis, although for certain groups of people this can be more serious. The risk can be reduced or eliminated by good food hygiene and proper cooking.

Do not buy food that is past its sell-by date and do not consume any food that is past its use-by date. When buying food, use the eyes and nose. If the food looks tired, limp or a bad colour or it has a rank, acrid or simply bad smell, do not buy or eat it under any circumstances.

Regularly clean, defrost and clear out the refrigerator or freezer – it is worth checking the packaging to see exactly how long each product is safe to freeze.

Dish cloths and tea towels must be washed and changed regularly. Ideally, use disposable cloths, which should be replaced on a daily basis. More durable cloths should be left to soak in bleach, then washed in the washing machine on a boil wash.

Always keep your hands, cooking utensils and food preparation surfaces clean and never allow pets to climb onto any work surfaces.

Buying

As we have seen, avoid bulk buying where possible, especially fresh produce such as meat, poultry, fish, fruit and vegetables unless buying for the freezer. Fresh foods lose their nutritional value rapidly, so buying a little at a time minimises loss of nutrients. It also eliminates a packed refrigerator, which reduces the effectiveness of the refrigeration process. When buying frozen foods, ensure that they are not heavily iced on the outside. Place in the freezer as soon as possible after purchase.

Preparation

Make sure that all work surfaces and utensils are clean and dry. Separate chopping boards should be used for raw and cooked meats, fish and vegetables. It is worth washing all fruits and vegetables regardless of whether they are going to be eaten raw or lightly cooked. Do not reheat food more than once.

All poultry must be thoroughly thawed before cooking. Leave the food in the refrigerator until it is completely thawed. Once defrosted, the chicken should be cooked as soon as possible. The only time food can be refrozen is when the food has been thoroughly thawed, then cooked. Once the food has cooled, it can then be frozen again for one month.

All poultry and game (except for duck) must be cooked thoroughly. When cooked the juices will run clear.

Other meats such as minced meat and pork should be cooked right the way through. Fish should turn opaque, be firm in texture and break easily into large flakes.

Storing, Refrigerating and Freezing

Meat, poultry, fish, seafood and dairy products should all be refrigerated. The temperature of the refrigerator should be between 1° and 5°C/34° and 41°F, while the freezer temperature should not rise above −18°C/−0.4°F. When refrigerating cooked food, allow it to cool completely before refrigerating. Hot food will raise the temperature of the refrigerator and possibly affect or spoil other food stored in it.

Food within the refrigerator and freezer should always be covered. Raw and cooked food should be stored in separate parts of the refrigerator. Cooked food should be kept on the top shelves of the refrigerator, while raw meat, poultry and fish should be placed on bottom shelves to avoid drips and cross-contamination.

High-risk Foods

Certain foods may carry risks to people who are considered vulnerable such as the elderly, the ill, pregnant women, babies and those suffering from a chronic illness. It is advisable to avoid those foods that belong to a higher-risk category.

Eggs

There is a slight chance that some eggs carry the bacterium salmonella. Cook the eggs until both the yolk and the white are firm to eliminate this risk. Sauces including hollandaise, mayonnaise, mousses, soufflés and meringues all use raw or lightly cooked eggs, as do custard-based dishes, ice creams and sorbets. These are all considered high-risk foods to the vulnerable groups mentioned above.

Meat and Poultry

Certain meats and poultry also carry the potential risk of salmonella and so should be cooked thoroughly until the juices run clear and there is no pinkness left.

Unpasteurised Products

Unpasteurised products such as milk, cheese (especially soft cheese), pâté and meat (both raw and cooked) all have the potential risk of the bacterium listeria and should be avoided.

Seafood

When buying seafood, buy from a reputable source. Fish should have bright clear eyes, shiny skin and bright pink or red gills. The fish should feel stiff to the touch, with a slight smell of sea air and iodine. The flesh of fish steaks and fillets should be translucent with no signs of discoloration. Avoid any molluscs that are open or do not close when tapped lightly. Univalves such as cockles or winkles should withdraw into their shells when lightly prodded. Squid and octopus should have firm flesh and a pleasant sea smell.

Care is required when freezing seafood. It is imperative to check whether the fish has been frozen before. If it has been, it should not be frozen again under any circumstances.

Nutrition

A healthy and well-balanced diet is the body's primary energy source. In children, it constitutes the building blocks for future health as well as providing lots of energy. In adults, it encourages self-healing and regeneration within the body. A well-balanced diet will provide the body with all the essential nutrients it needs. This can be achieved by eating a variety of foods, demonstrated in the pyramid shown here.

Fats

Fats fall into two categories: saturated and unsaturated fats. It is very important that a healthy balance is achieved within the diet. Fats are an essential part of the diet and a source of energy, and provide essential fatty acids and fat-soluble vitamins. The right balance of fats should boost the body's immunity to infection and keep muscles, nerves and arteries in good condition.

Saturated Fats

Saturated fats are of animal origin and are hard when stored at room temperature. They can be found in dairy produce, meat, eggs, margarines and hard white cooking fat (lard), as well as in manufactured products such as pies, biscuits and cakes. A high intake of saturated fat over many years has been proven to increase heart

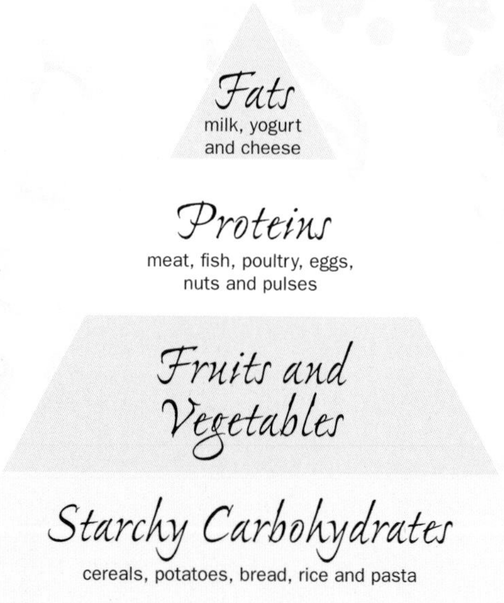

Fats
milk, yogurt
and cheese

Proteins
meat, fish, poultry, eggs,
nuts and pulses

Fruits and Vegetables

Starchy Carbohydrates
cereals, potatoes, bread, rice and pasta

disease and high blood cholesterol levels, and often leads to weight gain. The aim of a healthy diet is to keep the fat content low in the foods that we eat. Lowering the amount of saturated fat that we consume is very important, but this does not mean that it is good to consume lots of other types of fat.

Unsaturated Fats

There are two kinds of unsaturated fats: poly-unsaturated fats and monounsaturated fats. Polyunsaturated fats include the following oils: safflower oil, soyabean oil, corn oil and sesame oil. Within the polyunsaturated group are omega oils. The omega-3 oils are of significant interest because they have been found to be particularly beneficial to coronary health and can encourage brain growth and development. Omega-3 oils are mainly derived from oily fish such as salmon, mackerel, herring, pilchards and sardines. It is recommended that we should eat these types of fish

at least once a week. However, for those who do not eat fish or who are vegetarians, liver oil supplements are available in most supermarkets and health-food shops. It is suggested that these supplements should be taken on a daily basis.

The most popular oils that are high in monounsaturates are olive oil, sunflower oil and groundnut (peanut) oil. The Mediterranean diet, which is based on a diet high in monounsaturated fats, is recommended for heart health. Also, monounsaturated fats are known to help reduce the levels of LDL (the bad) cholestrol.

Proteins

Composed of amino acids (proteins' building bricks), proteins perform a wide variety of essential functions for the body including supplying energy and building and repairing tissues. Good sources of proteins are eggs, milk, yogurt, cheese, meat, fish, poultry, nuts and pulses. (See the second level of the pyramid.) Some of these foods, however, contain saturated fats. To strike a nutritional balance, eat generous amounts of vegetable protein foods such as soya, beans, lentils, peas and nuts.

Fruits and Vegetables

Not only are fruits and vegetables the most visually appealing foods, but also they are extremely good for us, providing essential vitamins and minerals essential for growth, repair and protection in the human body. Fruits and vegetables are low in calories and are responsible for regulating the body's metabolic processes and controlling the composition of its fluids and cells.

Minerals

Calcium Important for healthy bones and teeth, nerve transmission, muscle contraction, blood clotting and hormone function. Calcium promotes a healthy heart, improves skin, relieves aching muscles and bones, maintains the correct acid–alkaline balance and reduces menstrual cramps. Good sources are dairy products, small bones of small fish, nuts, pulses, fortified white flours, breads and green leafy vegetables.

Chromium Part of the glucose tolerance factor, chromium balances blood sugar levels, helps to normalise hunger and reduce cravings, improves lifespan, helps protect DNA and is essential for heart function. Good sources are brewer's yeast, wholemeal bread, rye bread, oysters, potatoes, green peppers, butter and parsnips.

Iodine Important for the manufacture of thyroid hormones and for normal development. Good sources of iodine are seafood, seaweed, milk and dairy products.

Iron As a component of haemoglobin, iron carries oxygen around the body. It is vital for normal growth and development. Good sources are liver, corned beef, red meat, fortified breakfast cereals, pulses, green leafy vegetables, egg yolks and cocoa and cocoa products.

Magnesium Important for efficient functioning of metabolic enzymes and development of the skeleton. Magnesium promotes healthy muscles by helping them to relax and is therefore good for PMS. It is also important for heart muscles and the nervous system. Good sources are nuts, green vegetables, meat, cereals, milk and yogurt.

Phosphorus Forms and maintains bones and teeth, builds muscle tissue, helps to maintain the body's pH and aids metabolism and energy production. Phosphorus is present in almost all foods.

Potassium Enables nutrients to move into cells, while waste products move out; promotes healthy nerves and muscles; maintains fluid balance in the body; helps secretion of insulin for blood sugar control to produce constant energy; relaxes muscles; maintains heart functioning and stimulates gut movement to encourage proper elimination. Good sources are fruit, vegetables, milk and bread.

Selenium Antioxidant properties help to protect against free radicals and carcinogens. Selenium reduces inflammation, stimulates the immune system to fight infections, promotes a healthy heart and helps vitamin E's action. It is also required for the male reproductive system and is needed for metabolism. Good sources are tuna, liver, kidney, meat, eggs, cereals, nuts and dairy products.

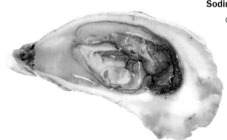

Sodium Important in helping to control body fluid and balance, preventing dehydration. Sodium is involved in muscle and nerve function, and helps to move nutrients into cells. All foods are good sources, but processed, pickled and salted foods are richest in sodium.

Zinc Important for metabolism and the healing of wounds. It also aids ability to cope with stress, promotes a healthy nervous system and brain, especially in the growing foetus, aids bones and teeth formation and is essential for constant energy. Good sources are liver, meat, pulses, wholegrain cereals, nuts and oysters.

Vitamins

Vitamin A Important for cell growth and development, and for the formation of visual pigments in the eye. Vitamin A comes in two forms: retinol and beta-carotenes. Retinol is found in liver, meat and meat products and whole milk and its products. Beta-carotene is a powerful antioxidant and is found in red and yellow fruits and vegetables such as carrots, mangoes and apricots.

Vitamin B_1 Important in releasing energy from carbohydrate-containing foods. Good sources are yeast and yeast products, bread, fortified breakfast cereals and potatoes.

Vitamin B_2 Important for metabolism of proteins, fats and carbohydrates to produce energy. Good sources are meat, yeast extracts, fortified breakfast cereals and milk and its products.

Vitamin B_3 Required for the metabolism of food into energy production. Good sources are milk and milk products, fortified breakfast cereals, pulses, meat, poultry and eggs.

Vitamin B_5 Important for the metabolism of food and energy production. All foods are good sources, but especially fortified breakfast cereals, wholegrain bread and dairy products.

Vitamin B_6 Important for metabolism of protein and fat. Vitamin B_6 may also be involved in the regulation of sex hormones. Good sources are liver, fish, pork, soya beans and peanuts.

Vitamin B_{12} Important for the production of red blood cells and DNA. It is vital for growth and the nervous system. Good sources are meat, fish, eggs, poultry and milk.

Biotin Important for metabolism of fatty acids. Good sources of biotin are liver, kidney, eggs and nuts. Microorganisms also manufacture this vitamin in the gut.

Vitamin C Important for healing wounds and the formation of collagen, which keeps skin and bones strong. It is an important antioxidant. Good sources are fruit, particularly soft summer fruits, and vegetables.

Vitamin D Important for absorption and handling of calcium to help build bone strength. Good sources are oily fish, eggs, whole milk and milk products, margarine and of course sufficient exposure to sunlight, as vitamin D is made in the skin.

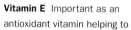

Vitamin E Important as an antioxidant vitamin helping to protect cell membranes from damage. Good sources are vegetable oils, margarines, seeds, nuts and green vegetables.

Folic acid Critical during pregnancy for the development of the brain and nerves. It is always essential for brain and nerve function, and is needed for utilising protein and red blood cell formation. Good sources are wholegrain cereals, fortified breakfast cereals, green leafy vegetables, oranges and liver.

Vitamin K Important for controlling blood clotting. Good sources are cauliflower, Brussels sprouts, lettuce, cabbage, beans, broccoli, peas, asparagus, potatoes, corn oil, tomatoes and milk.

Carbohydrates

Carbohydrates are an energy source and come in two forms: starch and sugar carbohydrates. Starch carbohydrates are also known as complex carbohydrates and they include all cereals, potatoes, breads, rice and pasta. (See the fourth level of the pyramid). Eating wholegrain varieties of these foods also provides fibre. Diets high in fibre are believed to be beneficial in helping to prevent bowel cancer and can also keep cholesterol down. High-fibre diets are also good for those concerned about weight gain. Fibre is bulky, so fills the stomach, therefore reducing hunger pangs.

Sugar carbohydrates, which are also known as fast-release carbohydrates (because of the quick fix of energy they give to the body), include sugar and sugar-sweetened products such as jams and syrups. Milk provides lactose, which is a milk sugar, and fruits provide fructose, which is a fruit sugar.

Cooking Eggs

Boiled Eggs

Eggs should be boiled in gently simmering water. Remove the egg from the refrigerator at least 30 minutes before cooking. Bring a pan of water to the boil, then, once boiling, reduce the heat to a simmer. Gently lower the egg into the water and cook for 3 minutes for lightly set, or 4 minutes for a slightly firmer set. Remove and lightly tap to stop the egg continuing to cook. Hard-boiled eggs should be cooked for 10 minutes, then plunged into cold water and left until cold before shelling. Serve lightly boiled eggs with toast or buttered bread cut into fingers to use as dippers.

Fried Eggs

Put a little sunflower oil or butter in a frying pan. Break an egg into a cup or small jug. Carefully slip into the pan. Cook, spooning the hot oil or fat over the egg, for 3–4 minutes until set to personal preference. Remove with a palette knife or fish slice. Serve with freshly grilled bacon or sausages, or on toast with baked beans and tomatoes.

Poached Eggs

Half-fill a frying pan with water. Bring to a gentle boil, then reduce the heat to a simmer. Add either a little salt or a few drops of vinegar or lemon juice – this will help the egg to retain its shape. Break the egg into a cup or small jug and carefully slip into the simmering water. Lightly oiled round plain pastry cutters can be used to contain the eggs, if preferred. Cover the pan with a lid and cook for 3–4 minutes until set to personal preference. Once cooked, remove by draining with a slotted spoon or fish slice, and serve. Alternatively, special poaching pans are available, if preferred. With these, half-fill the pan with water and place the tray with the egg containers on top. Put a little butter in the cups and bring to the boil. Swirl the melted butter around and carefully slip in the eggs. Cover with the lid and cook for 3–4 minutes. Serve either on hot buttered toast or on top of sliced ham or freshly cooked spinach.

Scrambled Eggs

Melt 1 tablespoon butter in a small pan. Allowing 2 eggs per person, break the eggs into a small bowl and add

1 tablespoon milk and seasoning to taste. Whisk until blended with a fork, then pour into the melted butter. Cook over a gentle heat, stirring with a wooden spoon, until set and creamy. Serve on hot buttered toast with smoked salmon or stir in some freshly snipped chives or chopped tomatoes.

Omelettes

For a basic omelette, allow 2 eggs per person. Break the eggs into a small bowl, add seasoning to taste and 1 tablespoon milk. Whisk with a fork until frothy. Heat 2 teaspoons olive oil in a frying pan and, when hot, pour in the egg mixture. Cook gently, using a wooden spoon to bring the mixture from the edges of the pan to the centre and letting the uncooked egg mixture flow to the edges. When the egg has set, cook without moving for an extra minute before folding the omelette into three and gently turning out onto a warmed serving plate. Take care not to overcook.

Cheese Omelette

Proceed as before, then sprinkle 25–40 g/1–1½ oz grated mature Cheddar cheese on top of the lightly set omelette. Cook for a further 2 minutes, or until the cheese starts to melt. If liked, place under a preheated grill for 2–3 minutes or until golden. Fold and serve.

Tomato Omelette

Proceed as for a plain omelette. After 2 minutes of cooking time, add 1 chopped tomato on top of the omelette. Cook as above until set.

Fine Herbs Omelette

Stir 1 tablespoon finely chopped fresh mixed herbs into the beaten eggs before cooking. Proceed as for a plain omelette.

Mushroom Omelette

Wipe and slice 50 g/2 oz button mushrooms. Heat 1 tablespoon butter in a small pan and cook the mushrooms for 2–3 minutes. Drain and reserve. Cook the omelette as above, adding the mushrooms once set.

Rice

Varieties

Rice is the staple food of many countries throughout the world. Every country and culture has its own repertoire of rice recipes – India, for example, has the aromatic biryani, Spain has the saffron-scented paella, and Italy has the creamy risotto. Rice is grown on marshy, flooded land where other cereals cannot thrive and, because it is grown in so many different areas, there is a huge range of rice types.

Long-grain white rice Probably the most widely used type of rice. Long-grain white rice has been milled so that the husk, bran and germ are removed. Easy-cook long-grain white rice has been steamed under pressure before milling. Pre-cooked rice, also known as parboiled or converted rice, is polished white rice that is half-cooked after milling, then dried again. It is quick to cook, but has a bland flavour.

Long-grain brown rice Where the outer husk is removed, leaving the bran and germ behind. This retains more of the fibre, vitamins and minerals. It has a nutty, slightly chewy texture and takes longer to cook than white rice.

Basmati rice This slender long-grain rice, which may be white or brown, is grown in the foothills of the Himalayas. After harvesting, it is allowed to mature for a year, giving it a unique aromatic flavour, hence its name, which means 'fragrant'.

Risotto rice Grown in the north of Italy, this is the only rice that is suitable for making risotto. The grains are plump and stubby, and have the ability to absorb large quantities of liquid without becoming too soft, cooking to a creamy texture with a slight bite. There are two grades of risotto rice: superfino and fino. Arborio rice is the most widely sold variety of the former, but you may also find Carnaroli, Roma and Baldo in Italian delicatessens. Fino rice such as Vialone Nano has a slightly shorter grain, but the flavour is still excellent.

Valencia rice Traditionally used for Spanish paella, Valencia rice is soft and tender when ready. The medium-size grains break down easily, so should be left unstirred during cooking to absorb the flavour of the stock and other ingredients.

Jasmine rice Also known as Thai fragrant rice, this long-grain rice has a delicate, almost perfumed aroma and flavour, and has a soft, sticky texture.

Japanese sushi rice This is similar to glutinous rice in that it has a sticky texture. When mixed with rice vinegar, it is easy to roll up with a filling inside to make sushi.

Pudding rice This rounded short-grain rice is ideal for rice desserts. The grains swell and absorb large quantities of milk during cooking, giving puddings a rich, creamy consistency.

Wild rice This is an aquatic grass grown in North America rather than a true variety of rice. The black grains are long and slender, and after harvesting and cleaning they are toasted to remove the chaff and intensify the nutty flavour and slight chewiness. It is often sold as a mixture with long-grain rice.

Rice flour Raw rice can be finely ground to make rice flour, which may be used to thicken sauces (1 tablespoon will thicken 300 ml/ ½ pint liquid) or in Asian desserts. It is also used to make rice noodles.

Buying and Storing Rice

Rice will keep for several years if kept in sealed packets. However, it is at its best when fresh. To ensure freshness, always buy rice from reputable shops with a good turnover and buy in small quantities. Once opened, rice should be stored in an airtight container in a cool, dry place to keep out moisture. Most rice (but not risotto rice) benefits from washing before cooking – tip into a sieve and rinse under cold running water until the water runs clear. This removes any starch still clinging to the grains.

Cooked rice will keep for up to two days if cooled and stored in a covered bowl in the refrigerator. If eating rice cold, serve within 24 hours – after this time it should be thoroughly reheated.

Cooking Techniques

There are countless ways to cook rice, but much depends on the variety of rice being used, the dish being prepared and the desired results. Each variety of rice has its own characteristics. Some types of rice cook to light, separate grains, some to a rich, creamy consistency and some to a consistency where the grains stick together. Different types of rice have different powers of absorption. Long-grain rice will absorb three times its weight in water, whereas 25 g/1 oz short-grain pudding rice can soak up a massive 300 ml/½ pint liquid.

Cooking Long-grain Rice

The simplest method of cooking long-grain rice is to add it to plenty of boiling, salted water in a large saucepan. Allow 50 g/ 2 oz rice per person when cooking as an accompaniment. Rinse under cold running water until clear, then tip into rapidly boiling water. Stir once, then, when the water returns to the boil, reduce the heat and simmer uncovered. Allow 10–12 minutes for white rice and 30–40 minutes for brown – check the packet for specific timings. The easiest way to test if rice is cooked is to bite a couple of grains – they should be tender but still firm. Drain immediately, then return to the pan with a little butter and herbs, if liked. Fluff up the grains with a fork and serve. To keep the rice warm, put it in a bowl and place over a pan of barely simmering water. Cover the top of the bowl with a tea towel until ready to serve.

Absorption Method

Cooking rice using the absorption method is also simple. Weigh out the quantity, then measure it by volume in a measuring jug – you will need 150 ml/¼ pint for two people. Rinse the rice, then tip into a large saucepan. If liked, cook the rice in a little butter or oil for 1 minute. Pour in two parts water or stock to one part rice, season with salt and bring to the boil. Cover, then simmer gently until the liquid is absorbed and the rice is tender. White rice will take 15 minutes to cook, whereas brown rice will take 35 minutes. If there is still a little liquid left when the rice is tender, uncover and cook for 1 minute until evaporated. Remove from the heat and leave, covered, for 4–5 minutes, then fluff up the grains with a fork before serving. This method is good for cooking jasmine and Valencia rice.

Oven-baked Method

The oven-baked method works by absorption, too, but takes longer than cooking on the hob. For oven-baked rice for two, fry a chopped onion in 1 tablespoon olive oil in a 1.2 litre/2 pint flameproof casserole until soft and golden. Add 75 g/3 oz long-grain rice and cook for 1 minute, then stir in 300 ml/½ pint stock – add a finely pared strip of lemon zest or a bay leaf if liked. Cover and bake in a preheated oven at 180°C/350°F/Gas Mark 4 for 40 minutes, or until the rice is tender and all the stock has been absorbed. Fluff up before serving.

Cooking in the Microwave

Put rinsed long-grain rice in a large, heatproof bowl. Add boiling water or stock, allowing 300 ml/½ pint for 100 g/3½ oz rice and 500 ml/18 fl oz for 225 g/8 oz rice. Add a pinch salt and a knob of butter, if desired. Cover with pierced clingfilm and cook on high for 3 minutes. Stir, re-cover and cook on medium for 12 minutes for white rice and 25 minutes for brown. Leave, covered, for 5 minutes before fluffing up and serving.

Cooking in a Pressure Cooker

Follow the quantities given for the absorption method and bring to the boil in the pressure cooker. Stir, cover and bring to a high 6.8 kg/15 lb pressure. Reduce the heat and cook for 5 minutes for white rice and 8 minutes for brown.

Cooking in a Rice Cooker

Follow the quantities given for the absorption method. Put the rice, salt and boiling water or stock in the cooker, return to the boil and cover. When all the liquid has been absorbed, the cooker will turn off automatically.

Health and Nutrition

Rice is low in fat and high in complex carbohydrates, which are absorbed slowly and help to maintain blood sugar levels. It is also a reasonable source of protein and provides many B vitamins and the minerals potassium and phosphorus. It is a gluten-free cereal, making it suitable for coeliacs. Brown rice is richer in nutrients and fibre than refined white rice.

Pasta

How to Make Pasta

Home-made pasta has a light, almost silky texture and is different from the fresh pasta that you can buy vacuum-packed in supermarkets. It is also easy to make and little equipment is needed – just a rolling pin and a sharp knife. If you make pasta regularly, it is perhaps worth investing in a pasta machine.

Basic Egg Pasta Dough

225 g/8 oz type '00' pasta flour, plus
    extra for dusting
1 tsp salt
2 eggs, plus 1 egg yolk
1 tbsp olive oil
1–3 tsp cold water

 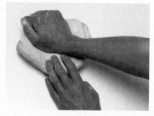

Sift the flour and salt into a mound on a work surface and make a well in the middle, keeping the sides high so that the egg mixture will not trickle out when added. Beat together the eggs, egg yolk, oil and 1 teaspoon water. Add to the well, then gradually work in the flour, adding extra water if needed, to make a soft but not sticky dough. Knead on a lightly floured work surface for 5 minutes, or until the dough is smooth and elastic. Wrap in clingfilm and leave for 20 minutes at room temperature.

Using a Food Processor

Sift the flour and salt into a food processor fitted with a metal blade. Add the eggs, egg yolk, oil and water, and pulse-blend until mixed and the dough begins to come together, adding extra water if needed. Knead for 1–2 minutes, then wrap and rest as before.

Rolling Pasta by Hand

Unwrap the pasta dough and cut in half. Work with just half at a time and keep the other half wrapped in clingfilm. Place the dough on a lightly floured work surface, then flatten and roll out. Always roll away from you. Start from the centre, giving the dough a quarter turn after each rolling. Sprinkle a little more flour over the dough if it starts to get sticky. Continue rolling and turning until the dough is as thin as possible, ideally 3 mm/⅛ inch thick.

Rolling Pasta by Machine

Always refer to the manufacturer's instructions before using. Clamp the machine securely and attach the handle. Set the rollers at their widest setting and sprinkle with flour. Cut the pasta dough into four pieces. Wrap three of them in clingfilm and reserve. Flatten the unwrapped dough slightly, then feed it through the rollers. Fold the strip of dough in three, rotate and feed through the rollers a second time. Continue to roll the dough, narrowing the roller setting by one notch every second time and flouring the rollers if the dough starts to get sticky. Fold the dough only the first time it goes through each roller width. If it is hard to handle, cut the strip in half and work with one piece at a time. Fresh pasta should be dried before cutting. Drape over a wooden pole for 5 minutes or place on a tea towel sprinkled with a little flour for 10 minutes.

Shaping up

For shaping freshly made pasta, have several lightly floured tea towels ready.

Farfalle Use a fluted pasta wheel to cut the pasta sheets into rectangles 2.5 x 5 cm/1 x 2 inches. Pinch the long sides of each rectangle in the middle to make a bow. Spread on a floured tea towel. Leave for 15 minutes.

Lasagne Trim the pasta sheets until neat and cut into lengths. Spread the sheets on a tea towel sprinkled with flour.

Noodles If using a pasta machine, use the cutter attachment to produce tagliatelle or use a narrower one for spaghetti. To make by hand, sprinkle the rolled-out pasta with flour, then roll up like a Swiss roll and cut into thin slices. Unravel immediately after cutting. Leave over a wooden pole for 5 minutes to dry.

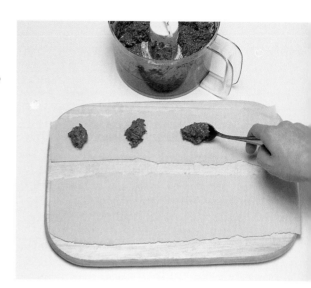

Ravioli Cut the rolled-out sheet of dough in half widthways. Cover one half. Brush the other sheet of dough with beaten egg. Place 1 teaspoon filling in even rows, at 4 cm/1½ inch intervals. Remove the clingfilm from the reserved pasta sheet and, using a rolling pin, lift over the dough with the filling. Press down between the pockets to push out any air. Cut into squares. Leave on a floured tea towel for 45 minutes before cooking.

Variations

Flavoured pastas are simple and there are many ways to change the flavour and colour of pasta.

Chilli Add 2 teaspoons crushed dried red chillies to the egg mixture.

Herb Stir 3 tablespoons chopped fresh herbs into the flour.

Olive Blend 2 tablespoons black olive paste with the egg mixture and omit the water.

Porcini Soak 15 g/½ oz dried porcini mushrooms in boiling water for 20 minutes. Drain and squeeze out as much water as possible, then chop finely. Add to the egg mixture.

Spinach Finely chop 75 g/3 oz cooked fresh spinach. Add to the egg mixture.

Dried Pasta Varieties

Buckwheat A gluten-free pasta made from buckwheat flour.

Coloured and flavoured pasta Varieties are endless, the most popular being spinach and tomato. Others include beetroot, herb, garlic, chilli, mushroom and black ink.

Durum wheat pasta Most readily available and may be made with or without eggs. Look for 'durum wheat' or '*pasta di semola di grano duro*' on the packet, as pastas made from soft wheat tend to become soggy when cooked.

Wholemeal pasta Made with wholemeal flour, this has a higher fibre content than ordinary pasta. Wholemeal pasta takes longer to cook than the refined version.

Pasta Shapes

Long Pasta

Spaghetti Probably the best known type of pasta, spaghetti derives its name from the word *spago* meaning 'string', which describes its round, thin shape perfectly.

Tagliatelle Most common type of ribbon noodle pasta. It is traditionally from Bologna, where it accompanies bolognese sauce (rather than spaghetti). Fettuccine is the Roman version of tagliatelle and is cut slightly thinner.

Short Pasta

There are two types of short pasta: *secca* is factory-made from durum wheat and water and *pasta all'uovo* is made with eggs. There are numerous different shapes and some of the most popular ones are listed below.

Conchiglie Pasta shapes resembling conch shells. Sizes vary from tiny to large. They may be smooth or ridged (conchiglie rigate).

Eliche and fusilli These are twisted into the shape of a screw.

Farfalle Bow- or butterfly-shaped, often with crinkled edges.

Macaroni Known as elbow macaroni or maccheroni in Italy. A thin, quick-cook variety is also available.

Penne Slightly larger than macaroni, the ends of these tubes are cut and pointed like quills.

Pipe Curved, hollow pasta and often sold ridged as 'pipe rigate'.

Rigatoni Substantial, chunky, tubular pasta often used for baking.

Rotelle Thin, wheel-shaped pasta, often sold in packets of two or three colours.

Stuffed Pasta

Tortellini The most common variety, consisting of tiny, stuffed pieces of pasta. Larger ones are called tortelloni.

Cappelletti, ravioli and agnolotti These are sometimes sold dried, but are more often available fresh.

Fresh Pasta

Fresh pasta can be found in supermarkets and specialist shops. It is generally available in the same shapes as dried pasta.

How to Cook Perfect Pasta

Follow a few simple rules to ensure that your pasta is cooked to perfection every time:

1 Choose a large saucepan – there needs to be plenty of room for the pasta to move around so that it does not stick together.

2 Cook the pasta in a large quantity of fast-boiling well-salted water, ideally 4 litres/7 pints water and 1½–2 tablespoons salt for every 350–450 g/12 oz–1 lb pasta.

3 Tip in the pasta all at once, stir and cover. Return to a rolling boil, then remove the lid. Once it is boiling, reduce the heat to medium-high and cook the pasta for the required time. It should be *al dente*, or tender but still firm to the bite.

4 Drain, reserving a little of the cooking water to stir into the drained pasta. This helps to thin the sauce, if necessary, and helps prevent the pasta sticking together as it cools.

Serving Quantities

As an approximate guide, allow 75–100 g/3–3½ oz uncooked pasta per person. The amount will depend on whether the pasta is being served for a light or main meal and the type of sauce that it is being served with.

Herbs and Spices

In a culture where fast food, ready-made meals and processed foods are popular, home-made food can sometimes taste bland by comparison, due to the fact that the palate can quickly become accustomed to additives and flavour enhancers. The use of herbs and spices, however, can make all the difference in helping to make delicious homemade dishes.

Herbs are easy to grow and a garden is not needed, as they can easily thrive on a small patio, in a window box or even on a windowsill. It is worth the effort to plant a few herbs, as they do not require much attention or nurturing. The reward will be a range of fresh herbs available whenever needed and fresh flavours that cannot be beaten to add to any dish that is being prepared.

While fresh herbs should be picked or bought as close as possible to the time of use, freeze-dried and dried herbs and spices will usually keep for around six months.

The best idea is to buy little and often, and to store the herbs in airtight jars in a cool, dark cupboard. Fresh herbs tend to have a milder flavour than dried and equate to around 1 level tablespoon fresh to 1 level teaspoon dried. As a result, quantities used in cooking should be altered accordingly. A variety of herbs and spices and their uses are listed below.

Allspice The dark allspice berries come whole or ground, and have a flavour similar to that of cinnamon, cloves and nutmeg. Although not the same as mixed spice, allspice can be used with pickles, relishes, cakes and milk puddings, or whole in meat and fish dishes.

Aniseed Comes in whole seeds or ground. It has a strong aroma and flavour, and should be used sparingly in baking and salad dressings.

Basil Best fresh but also available in dried form, basil can be used raw or cooked, and works well in many dishes. It is particularly well suited to tomato-based dishes and sauces, salads and Mediterranean dishes.

Bay leaves Available in fresh or dried form as well as ground. Bay leaves make up part of a bouquet garni and are particularly delicious when added to meat and poultry dishes, soups, stews, vegetable dishes and stuffing. They also impart a spicy flavour to milk puddings and egg custards.

Caraway seeds These have a warm, sweet taste and are often used in breads and cakes, but are also delicious with cabbage dishes and pickles.

Cayenne The powdered form of a red chilli pepper said to be native to Cayenne. It is similar in appearance to paprika and can be used sparingly to add a fiery kick to many dishes.

Cardamom Has a distinctive sweet, rich taste. Can be bought whole in the pod, in seed form or ground. This sweet aromatic spice is delicious in curries, rice, cakes and biscuits, and is great served with rice pudding and fruit. Pods come in green and brown ('black') varieties, the former being more usual.

Chervil Reminiscent of parsley and available either in fresh or dried form, chervil has a faintly sweet, spicy flavour and is particularly good in soups, cheese dishes, stews and with eggs.

Chilli Available whole, fresh, dried and in powdered form. Red chillies tend to be sweeter in taste than their green counterparts. They are particularly associated with Spanish, Mexican, South and Southeast Asian dishes, but are also delicious with pickles, dips, sauces and in pizza toppings.

Chives Best used when fresh, but also available in dried form, this member of the onion family is ideal for use when a delicate onion flavour is required. Chives are good with eggs, cheese, fish and vegetable dishes. They also work well as a garnish for soups, meat and vegetable dishes.

Cinnamon Comes in the form of reddish-brown sticks of bark from an evergreen tree and has a sweet, pungent aroma. Either whole or ground, cinnamon is delicious in cakes and milk puddings, particularly with apple, and is used in mulled wine and for preserving.

Cloves Mainly used whole, although available ground, cloves have a very warm, sweet, pungent aroma and can be used to stud roast ham and pork, in mulled wine and punch, and when pickling fruit. When ground, they can be used in making mincemeat and in Christmas puddings and biscuits.

Coriander Coriander seeds have an orangey flavour and are available whole or ground. Coriander is particularly delicious (whole or roughly ground) in curries, casseroles and as a pickling spice. Coriander leaves are used both to flavour spicy aromatic dishes and as a garnish.

Cumin Also available ground or as whole seeds, cumin has a strong, slightly bitter flavour. It is one of the main ingredients in curry powder and complements many fish, meat and rice dishes.

Dill These leaves are available fresh or dried, and have a mild flavour, while the seeds are slightly bitter. Dill is particularly good with salmon, new potatoes and in sauces. The seeds are good in pickles and vegetable dishes.

Fennel As whole seeds or ground, fennel has a fragrant, sweet aniseed flavour and is sometimes known as the fish herb because it complements fish dishes so well.

Ginger Comes in many forms, but primarily as a fresh root and in dried ground form, which can be used in baking, curries, pickles, sauces and Chinese and other Asian cooking.

Lemon grass Available fresh and dried, with a subtle, aromatic, lemony flavour, lemon grass is essential to Thai and other Southeast Asian cooking. It is also delicious when added to soups, poultry and fish dishes.

Mace The outer husk of nutmeg has a milder nutmeg flavour and can be used in pickles, cheese dishes, stewed fruits, sauces and hot punch.

Marjoram Often dried, marjoram has a sweet, slightly spicy flavour, which tastes fantastic when added to stuffing, meat or tomato-based dishes.

Mint Available fresh or dried, mint has a strong, sweet aroma that is delicious in a sauce or jelly to serve with lamb. It is great with fresh peas and new potatoes and an essential part of Pimm's.

Nutmeg The large whole seeds have a warm, sweet taste and complement custards, milk puddings, cheese dishes, parsnips and creamy soups.

Oregano Available fresh and dried; similar to marjoram. The more strongly flavoured dried leaves are used extensively in Italian and Greek cooking.

Paprika Often comes in two varieties. One is quite sweet and mild, and the other has a slight bite to it. Paprika is made from the fruit of the sweet pepper and is good in meat and poultry dishes, as well as a garnish. The rule of buying herbs and spices little and often applies particularly to paprika, as unfortunately it does not keep particularly well.

Parsley The stems as well as the leaves of parsley can be used to complement most savoury dishes, as they contain the most flavour. They can also be used as a garnish.

Poppy seeds These small, grey-black coloured seeds impart a sweet, nutty flavour when added to biscuits, vegetable dishes, dressings and cheese dishes.

Rosemary Delicious fresh or dried, these small, needle-like leaves have a sweet aroma that is particularly good with lamb, stuffing and vegetables dishes. Also delicious when added to charcoal on the barbecue to give a piquant flavour to both meat and corn on the cob.

Saffron Deep orange in colour, saffron is traditionally used in paella, rice and cakes, but is also delicious with poultry. Saffron is the most expensive of all spices.

Sage These fresh or dried leaves have a pungent, slightly bitter taste that is delicious with pork and poultry, sausages, stuffing and with stuffed pasta, such as ravioli, when tossed in a little butter and fresh sage.

Sesame Sesame seeds have a nutty taste, especially when toasted, and are delicious in baking, on salads or with Chinese and other East Asian cooking.

Tarragon The fresh or dried leaves of tarragon have a sweet aromatic taste that is particularly good with poultry, seafood, fish, creamy sauces and stuffing.

Thyme Available fresh or dried, thyme has a pungent flavour and is included in bouquet garni. It complements many meat and poultry dishes and stuffing.

Turmeric Obtained from the root of a lily from Southeast Asia. This root is ground and has a brilliant yellow colour. It has a bitter, peppery flavour and is often used in curry powder and mustard, and is delicious in pickles, relishes and dressings. It can also be used fresh, rather like ginger.

Meat

Both home-grown and imported meat is readily available from supermarkets, butchers, farm shops and markets. In the UK, home-grown meat is usually more expensive than imported meat, often brought into the country frozen. Meat also varies in price depending on the cut. The more expensive and tender meats are usually those cuts that less exercised by the animal. They need a minimal amount of cooking and are suitable for roasting, grilling, griddling, frying and stir-frying. The cheaper cuts need longer, slower cooking and are used in casseroles and for stewing. Meat plays an important part in most people's diet, offering an excellent source of protein, B vitamins and iron.

When choosing meat, it is important to buy from a reputable source and to choose the correct cut for the cooking method. Look for meat that is lean without an excess of fat, is a good colour and has no unpleasant odour. If in doubt about the suitability of a cut, ask the butcher, who should be happy to advise.

If buying frozen meat, allow to thaw before using. This is especially important for both pork and poultry. It is better to thaw meat slowly, lightly covered on the bottom shelf of the refrigerator. Use within 2–3 days of thawing, providing it has been kept in the refrigerator. If buying meat to freeze, do not freeze large joints in a home freezer, as it will not be frozen quickly enough.

Store thawed or fresh meat out of the supermarket wrappings, on a plate, lightly covered with greaseproof or baking paper, then wrapped with clingfilm if liked. Do not secure the paper tightly round the meat, as it needs to breathe. Ensure that the raw meat juices do not drip onto cooked foods. The refrigerator needs to be at a temperature of 5°C/40°F. Fresh meat such as joints, chops and steaks can be stored for up to 3 days. Minced meats, sausages and offal should be stored for only 1 day.

Different cultures and religion affect the way the meat has been killed and the carcass cut. The following is a description of different cuts of meat. They may be called by different names depending on where you live.

Beef

When choosing beef, look for meat that is a good colour, with creamy yellow fat. There should be small flecks of fat (marbling) throughout, as this helps the meat to be tender. Avoid meat with excess gristle. Bright red beef means that the animal has been butchered recently, whereas meat that has a dark, almost purple tinge is from meat that has been hung in a traditional manner. The darker the colour, especially with roasting joints, the more tender and succulent the beef will be.

Rib or fore rib ① Suitable for roasting. Sold either on or off the bone. Look for meat that is marbled for tenderness and succulence.

Topside ② Suitable for pot roasting, roasting or braising. A lean, tender cut from the hindquarter.

Sirloin Suitable for roasting, grilling, frying or barbecuing. Sold boned or off the bone. A lean and tender cut from the back.

T-bone steak Suitable for grilling, griddling, barbecuing or roasting. A tender, succulent cut from the fillet end of the sirloin.

Top rib Suitable for pot roasting or braising. Sold on or off the bone.

Fillet steak Suitable for grilling, frying, barbecuing or griddling. A whole fillet is used to make Chateaubriand, some say the best of all cuts. The most tender and succulent cut with virtually no fat. Comes from the centre of the sirloin.

Rump ③ Suitable for grilling, frying, griddling or barbecuing. Not as tender as fillet of sirloin, but reputed to have more flavour.

Silverside ④ Suitable for boiling and pot roasts. Used to be sold ready-salted, but is now usually sold unsalted.

Flash-fry steaks ⑤ Suitable for grilling, griddling or frying. Cut from the silverside, thick flank or topside.

Braising steak ⑥ Chuck, blade or thick rib, ideal for all braising or stews. Sold either in pieces or ready-diced.

Flank ⑦ Suitable for braising or stewing. A boneless cut from the mid- to hindquarter.

Minute steaks Suitable for grilling or griddling. Cut from the flank, a thin steak and beaten to flatten.

Skirt Suitable for stewing or making into mince. A boneless, rather gristly cut.

Brisket Suitable for slow or pot roasting. Sold boned and rolled, and can be found salted.

Minced beef Suitable for meat sauces such as bolognese, and also burgers, shepherd's pie and moussaka. Usually cut from clod, skirt, neck, thin rib or flank. Can be quite fatty. Steaks can also be minced to give a leaner result, if it is preferred.

Ox kidney Suitable for using in casseroles and stews. Strong flavour with hard central core that is discarded.

Oxtail Suitable for casseroles or braising. Usually sold cut into small pieces.

Lamb

Lamb is probably at its best in the spring, when the youngest lamb is available. It is tender to eat, with a delicate flavour, and its flesh is a paler pink than the older lamb, where the flesh is more red. The colour of the fat is also a good indication of age: young lamb fat is a very light, creamy colour. As the lamb matures, the fat becomes whiter and firmer. In the UK, imported lamb also has firmer, whiter fat. Lamb can be fatty, so take care when choosing. It used to be possible to buy mutton (lamb that is at least one year old), but this now tends to be available only in specialist outlets, halal butchers and areas with Afro-Caribbean populations. It has a far stronger, almost gamey flavour and the joints tend to be larger.

Leg ① Suitable for roasting. Often sold as half legs and steaks cut from the fillet end. These can be grilled, griddled or barbecued. Steaks are very lean and need a little additional oil to prevent the meat from drying out.

Shank Suitable for braising. A cut off the leg.

Shoulder ② Suitable for roasting. Can be sold boned, stuffed and rolled. Is fattier than the leg and has more flavour.

Loin ③ Suitable for roasting. Sold on or off the bone. Can be stuffed and rolled. Can also be cut into chops, often as double loin chops – suitable for grilling, griddling and barbecuing.

Noisette Suitable for grilling, griddling or barbecuing. A small boneless chop cut from the loin.

Valentine steak Suitable for grilling, griddling or barbecuing. Cut from a loin chop.

Chump chop ④ Suitable for grilling, griddling or barbecuing. Larger than loin chops and can be sold boneless.

Best end of neck ⑤ Suitable for roasting, grilling or griddling. Sold as a joint or cutlets.

Neck fillet Suitable for grilling or griddling. Sold whole or diced.

Middle and scrag end ⑥ Suitable for pot roasting, braising or stewing. A cheaper cut with a high ratio of fat and bone.

Breast ⑦ Suitable for pot roast if boned, stuffed and rolled. Can be marinated and grilled or barbecued.

Mince Suitable for burgers, pies, meatballs and for stuffing vegetables such as peppers. From various cuts and is often fatty.

Liver Suitable for pan-frying or grilling. Milder than ox or pig liver and cheaper than calves' liver.

Kidney Suitable for grilling, pan-frying or casseroles. Milder than ox or pig liver and usually sold encased in suet, which is discarded.

Pork

Pork should be pale pink in colour and slightly marbled with small flecks of fat. There should be a layer of firm white fat with a thin elastic skin (rind), which can be scored before roasting to provide crackling. All cuts of pork are tender, as the pigs are slaughtered at an early age and are reared to be lean rather than fatty. Pork used to be well cooked, if not overcooked, due to the danger of the parasite trichina. This no longer applies, however, and it is now recommended that the meat is cooked less to keep it moist and tender.

Leg ① Suitable for roasting. Sold either on the bone or boned. Can be cut into chunks and braised or casseroled.

Steaks ② Suitable for grilling, frying, griddling or barbecuing. A lean cut from the leg or the shoulder. Very tender, but can be dry.

Fillet Sometimes called tenderloin and suitable for roasting, pan-frying, griddling or barbecuing. A tender cut, often sold already marinated.

Loin ③ Suitable for roasting as a joint or cut into chops. Often sold with the kidney intact.

Shoulder ④ Suitable for roasting. Often referred to as 'hand and spring', and sold cubed for casseroles and stews. A fatty cut.

Spare ribs Suitable for barbecuing, casseroles and roasting. Sold either as 'Chinese', where thin ribs are marinated then cooked, or 'American style' ribs, which are larger.

Escalope Suitable for grilling, frying, griddling or barbecuing. Very lean and tender, and requires very little cooking.

Minced pork Suitable for burgers, meatballs or similar recipes. Often from the cheaper cuts and can be fatty.

Belly ⑤ Suitable for grilling or roasting. Can be salted before cooking. Is generally used to provide streaky bacon and is perhaps the fattiest cut of all.

Liver Suitable for casseroles or frying. Stronger than lamb or calves' liver.

Kidney Suitable for casseroles or frying. Often sold as part of a loin chop. Stronger than lambs' kidneys.

Poultry and Game

Poultry relates to turkey, chicken, duck and geese. Most is sold plucked, drawn and trussed. Due to extensive farming since the war, chicken in particular offers a good source of cheap meat. However, there is a growing movement to return to the more traditional methods of farming. Organically grown chickens offer a far more succulent bird with excellent flavour, although they tend to be more expensive. Both home-grown and imported poultry, fresh and frozen, are available. When buying fresh poultry, look for plump birds with a flexible breast bone, and no unpleasant odour or green tinge.

Frozen poultry should be rock hard with no ice crystals, as this could mean that the bird has thawed and been re-frozen. Avoid any produce where the packaging is damaged. When thawing, place in the refrigerator on a large plate and ensure that none of the juices drip on to other foods.

Once the bird thawed, remove all packaging, remove the giblets, if any, and reserve separately. Place on a plate and cover. Use within two days and ensure that the meat is thoroughly cooked and the juices run clear. Rest for 10 minutes before carving.

When storing fresh poultry, place on a plate and cover lightly, allowing air to circulate. Treat as thawed poultry: store for no longer than two days in the refrigerator, storing the giblets separately, and ensure that it is thoroughly cooked. Use within two days of cooking.

Poultry and game are low in saturated fat and provide a good source of protein as well as selenium, an antioxidant mineral. Remove the skin from poultry before eating if following a low-fat diet.

Poultry

Turkey Whole birds are suitable for roasting and traditionally served at Christmas and Thanksgiving. Various turkey cuts are eaten throughout the year, ranging from breast steaks, diced thigh and escalopes to small whole breast fillets, drumsticks, wings and minced turkey. Specific cuts include:

> **Crown** The whole bird with the legs removed.
> **Saddle** Two turkey breast fillets, boned with the wings inserted.
> **Butterfly** The two breast fillets.
> **Breast roll** Boned breast meat, rolled and tied or contained in a net.

Chicken Suitable for all cooking: roasting, grilling, griddling, stewing, braising, frying and barbecuing. Also available in many different breeds and varieties, offering a good choice to the consumer. There are many cuts of chicken readily available: breast, wing and leg quarters, which are still on the bone, drumsticks, thighs, breast fillets, escalopes (boneless skinless portions), diced and stir-fry strips, as well as minced chicken. There are also several types of chicken:

Capon Suitable for roasting. These are young castrated cockerels and are usually bred for their excellent flavour.

Broilers These are older chickens that would be too tough to roast. Usually quite small birds, about 1.6 kg/3½ lb.

Poussin Suitable for roasting, grilling or casseroles. These are spring chickens and are 4–6 weeks old. They can be bought whole or spatchcocked – this is where the bird is split through the breast, opened up and secured on skewers. One bird usually serves two people if small (450 g/1 lb) or one if larger (900 g/2 lb).

Guinea fowl Suitable for roasting or casseroles. Available all year round, with a slightly gamey flavour. Most are sold ready for the table. When roasting, use plenty of fat or bacon, as they can be dry.

Goose Suitable for roasting and often served as an alternative to turkey. Once dressed for the table, a goose will weigh around 4.5 kg/10 lb, but there is not much meat and this will serve six to eight people. It is very fatty, so pierce the skin well and roast on a trivet so that the fat can be discarded or used for other cooking. Goose has a rich flavour, slightly gamey and a little like duck. Goose liver is highly prized and is used for foie gras.

Duck Suitable for roasting, grilling, griddling and casseroles. Ducklings between six weeks and three months old are usually used for the table; adult ducks are not usually eaten. Duck has an excellent flavour, but it is a fatty bird, so cook on a trivet as for goose. Available fresh or frozen, and on average weighs 1.75–2.75 kg/4–6 lb. Also available in cuts, as boneless breast fillets, ideal for grilling or griddling, and leg portions, suitable for casseroles. The meat is also used to make pâté. There are quite a few domestic varieties available, with perhaps the most well known being the Aylesbury. Long Island, Peking and Barbary are also popular varieties.

Game

Game describes birds or animals that are hunted, not farmed, although some, such as pheasant, quails and rabbits, are now being reared domestically. Most game has a stronger flavour than poultry and some is at its best when 'high' and smelling quite strong. Game is not as popular as most meat or poultry and is an acquired taste. When buying game, it is important to know its age, as this dictates the method of cooking. Usually sold oven-ready, it is best bought from a reputable source who can guarantee the quality.

Pigeon Suitable for casseroles or stews, although the breast from young pigeons can be fried or grilled. Sometimes classified as poultry. Not widely available, mainly from licensed game sources.

Pheasant Suitable for roasting or casseroles. Breast, which can be grilled, is also available. Pheasant needs to be well hung to give the best flavour.

Rabbit Suitable for casseroles, stews and can be roasted or, if young, fried. Also makes excellent pies and fricassée. Sold whole or in portions, both with and without the bone, and available both fresh and frozen. Frozen rabbit often comes from China. If a milder flavour is preferred, soak in cold salted water for 2 hours before using. Generally regarded as country food and not served as haute cuisine.

Hare Suitable for casseroles. The most well-known recipe is jugged hare, where the blood is used to thicken the dish. Has a strong, gamey flavour. If a milder flavour is preferred, soak in cold water for up to 24 hours. Available from reputable game dealers.

Venison Suitable for roasting, grilling, casseroles or making into sausages. The saddle, haunch and shoulder are best for roasting, although the loin and fillet can also be used. All cuts benefit from marinating to help tenderise.

Other game Less widely available are partridge, grouse, quail, snipe and boar.

Fish and Seafood

Preparing and Cooking Seafood

Requiring only minimal cooking, all fish is an excellent choice for speedy and nutritious meals. There are two categories of fish: white and oily (*see* page 81–85). Seafood can be divided into three categories: shellfish, crustaceans and molluscs (*see* page 85–87).

Both types of fish are sold fresh or frozen as small whole fish, fillets or cutlets. Store as soon as possible in the refrigerator. Remove from the wrappings, place on a plate, cover lightly and store towards the top. Use within 1 day of purchase. If using frozen, thaw slowly in the refrigerator and use within 1 day of thawing.

Seafood should be eaten as fresh as possible. Live seafood gives the best flavour, as long as it is consumed on the day of purchase. If live is not available, buy from a reputable source and eat on the day of purchase, refrigerating until required. Clean all seafood thoroughly and, with mussels and clams, discard any that do not close when tapped lightly before cooking. After cooking, discard any that have not opened.

Cleaning Fish

When cleaning whole fish, first remove the scales. Using a round-bladed knife, gently scrape the knife along the fish, starting from the tail and moving towards the head. Rinse frequently. To clean round fish, make a slit along the abdomen from the gills to the tail using a small, sharp knife and scrape out the innards. Rinse thoroughly.

For flat fish, open the cavity under the gills and remove the innards. Rinse. Remove the gills and fins and, if preferred, the tail and head. Rinse thoroughly in cold water and pat dry. Cutlet and fillets simply need lightly rinsing in cold water and patting dry.

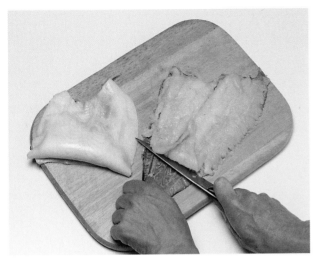

Skinning Fish

For whole flat fish, clean and remove the fins as before. Make a small cut on the dark side of the fish across the tail and slip your thumb between the skin and flesh. Loosen the skin along the side. Holding the fish firmly with one hand, rip off the skin with the other. The white skin can be removed in the same way.

Round fish are usually cooked with the skin on but, if you do wish to skin them, start from the head and cut a narrow strip of skin along the backbone. Cut below the head and loosen the skin with the point of the knife. Dip your fingers in salt for a better grip and gently pull the skin down towards the tail. Take care not to break the flesh.

Filleting Fish

To fillet flat fish, use a sharp knife and make a cut along the line of bones. Insert the knife under the flesh and carefully cut it with long, sweeping strokes. Cut the first fillet from the left-hand side, working from head to tail. Turn the fish around and repeat, this time cutting from tail to head. Turn the fish over and repeat on this side.

For round fish, cut along the centre of the back to the bone, then cut along the abdomen. Cleanly remove the flesh with short, sharp strokes from the head downwards, pressing the knife against the bones. Turn the fish over and repeat. This is suitable for larger fish such as salmon.

To fillet herring and mackerel, discard the head, tail and fins, and clean, reserving any roe if applicable. Place on a chopping board and gently press along the backbone to open fully and loosen the bone. Turn the fish over, ease the backbone up and remove, taking as many of the small bones as possible at the same time.

Basic Fish Recipes

Poached Fish

Clean the fish, remove scales if necessary and rinse thoroughly. Place in a large frying pan with 1 small peeled and sliced onion, 1 small peeled and sliced carrot, 1 bay leaf, 5 black peppercorns and a few parsley stalks. Pour over sufficient cold water to barely cover, then bring to the boil over a medium heat. Reduce the heat to a simmer, cover and cook gently for 8–10 minutes for fillets and 10–15 minutes for whole fish.

This method is suitable for fillets and small whole fish. When the fish is cooked, the flesh should yield easily when pierced with a round-bladed knife, and the fish should look opaque.

Grilled Fish

Line a grill rack with kitchen foil and preheat the grill to medium high just before grilling. Lightly rinse the fish, pat it dry and place on the foil-lined grill rack. Season with salt and pepper, and brush lightly with a little oil. Cook under the grill for 8–10 minutes until cooked, turning the heat down if the fish is cooking too quickly. Sprinkle with herbs or pour over a little melted butter or herb-flavoured olive oil to serve.

This method is suitable for fresh fish fillets (not smoked), sardines and other small whole fish. Make three slashes across whole fish before grilling.

Griddled Fish

Rinse the fish fillet, pat dry and, if desired, marinate in a marinade of your choice for 30 minutes. Heat a griddle pan until smoking and add the fish, skin-side down. Cook for 5 minutes, pressing the fish down with a fish slice. Turn the fish over and continue to cook for a further 4–5 minutes until cooked to personal preference.

Types of Fish and Other Seafood

White Fish

White fish, such as cod, haddock, plaice or coley, is an excellent source of protein and has a low fat content. It also contains vitamin B_{12} and niacin, plus important minerals such as phosphorous, iodine, selenium and potassium.

Bass Sea fish. Suitable for grilling or frying. Large bass can be poached whole. Has very white flesh. At its best from May to August.

Sea bream Sea fish. Suitable for grilling, poaching and frying, can also be stuffed and baked, or poached. Has firm white flesh with a delicate flavour. At its best from June to December.

Brill Sea fish. Suitable for grilling, baking or poaching, and serving cold. Has firm flesh with a slight yellow tinge. At its best from April to August, but available all year.

Cod Sea fish. Also available smoked. Suitable for all types of cooking. Perhaps the most popular and versatile of all fish, with white flesh and a very delicate flavour. At its best from October to May, but available all year round.

Coley Sea fish. Suitable for all types of cooking. One of the cheaper varieties of fish. Has a greyish-coloured flesh which turns slightly white on cooking. Available all year round.

Haddock Sea fish. Also available smoked. Suitable for all types of cooking. Has a firm white flesh with a slightly stronger flavour than cod. At its best from September to February, but available all year round.

Hake Sea fish. Suitable for all methods of cooking. Has a firm, close-textured white flesh and is considered to have a better flavour than cod. At its best from June to January, but available all year round.

Halibut Sea fish. Suitable for all methods of cooking except deep-frying. A large flat fish with excellent flavour. At its best from August to April, but available all year round.

John Dory Sea fish. Suitable for poaching or baking whole, or fillets can be cooked as for sole. Has a firm white flesh with good flavour. Can be difficult to find. At its best from October to December.

Monkfish Sea fish. Suitable for all methods of cooking including roasting. A firm white fish with 'meaty' texture. A good substitute for lobster. Only the tail is eaten – the central bone is usually discarded and the two fillets are used. Available all year round.

Plaice Sea fish. The whole fish is suitable for grilling and pan-frying, whilst fillets can be steamed, stuffed and rolled, or used as goujons. A flat fish with distinctive dark grey/black skin with red spots. Has soft white flesh with a very delicate flavour. Available all year round.

Red mullet Sea fish. Suitable for grilling, frying or baking. Has a firm white flesh and red skin. At its best from May to September.

Skate Sea fish. Suitable for grilling, frying or poaching. Only the wings are eaten and the bones are soft and gelatinous. A white fish with a delicate flavour. At its best from September to April.

Sole Sea fish. Suitable for frying or grilling. Has a firm yet delicate white skin with a delicious flavour. Available all year round. Dover sole is recognised by its dark grey/black skin and is considered by many to be the finest of the sole varieties. Lemon sole, which is more pointed, Witch and Torbay soles have the same qualities, but the flavour is not as good.

Turbot Sea fish. Suitable for grilling or baking. Usually sold in cutlets, it has a creamy white flesh with a delicious flavour, which is reputed to be the best of all flat fish. At its best from March to August.

Whiting Sea fish. Suitable for all methods of cooking. Cooked whole or in fillets, it has a white, delicately flavoured flesh. Available all year round.

Oily Fish

Oily fish, such as sardines, mackerel, salmon and herring, has a higher fat content than white fish, but is an excellent source of omega-3 polyunsaturated fatty acids, important in fighting heart disease, cancers and arthritis. Oily fish also contains niacin, B_6, B_{12} and D vitamins and selenium, iodine, potassium and phosphorus minerals. The flavour is stronger and more robust, enabling stronger flavours such as chilli and garlic to be used. It is recommended that at least one portion of oily fish should be eaten each week.

Herring Sea fish. Suitable for frying, grilling or preserving in vinegar to make rollmops. A small fish with creamy-coloured flesh and fairly strong flavour, herring contain many bones. At its best from June to December

Mackerel Sea fish. Suitable for grilling and frying, whilst whole fish can be stuffed or baked. Has a distinctive bluish-coloured skin with blue/black lines and a creamy underside. At its best from April to June.

Pilchard Sea fish. Usually sold canned but fresh pilchards are sometimes available. Similar to herring but smaller. Caught off the Cornish coast all year round.

Salmon Freshwater fish. The whole fish is suitable for poaching or baking to serve hot or cold. Fillets or cutlets can be fried, grilled, baked, steamed or barbecued. Farmed salmon has a milder flavour than wild, and the deep pink flesh is not as firm as that of wild salmon. The smaller wild salmon is much paler in colour, with a far-superior flavour and texture. Nowadays farmed salmon is available all year round – wild salmon is at its best from February to August.

Sardine Sea fish. Suitable for grilling or frying. Sardines are young pilchards, sprats or herrings. Available all year round.

Sprat Sea fish. Suitable for frying or grilling. A small fish similar to herring and at its best from November to March.

Brown trout Freshwater fish. Suitable for grilling or frying. The darker pink/red flesh is considered to be better than that of rainbow trout. At its best from March to September.

Rainbow trout Freshwater fish. Suitable for grilling, frying, poaching and baking. Can be cooked whole or in fillets. Has a delicate pale pink flesh. Available all year round.

Salmon trout Freshwater fish. Suitable for poaching or baking whole. Cutlets or fillets can be fried, grilled or griddled. At its best from March to August. Treat as for salmon. Has a pinker flesh than salmon and the flavour is not as good.

Tuna Sea fish (mostly). Suitable for all methods of cooking. Does not count as an oily fish when canned. Available all year round. Due to overfishing concerns, it is advisable to avoid bluefin and ideally yellowfin too, sticking to skipjack, preferably pole-and-line-caught.

Seafood

Crustaceans, such as lobsters, have hard shells that they shed and replace during their lifetime. Molluscs are animals that have hinged shells, such as scallops, or single shells, such as whelks. This term also includes cephalopods such as squid, cuttlefish and octopus.

Clams Available all year round, but best in September. Usually eaten raw like oysters, or cook as for mussels.

Cockles Available all year round, but best in September. Usually eaten cooked. Eat plain with vinegar or use in recipes such as paella.

Crab Best from May to August, but also available canned and frozen. Usually sold ready-cooked either whole or as dressed crab.

Crawfish Also known as langoustines. Available all year round, usually imported frozen. Has no claws and is the size of a small lobster.

Crayfish Available from September to April. Resembles a mini-lobster and has a delicate flavour.

Dublin Bay prawns Available all year round. Sold live or cooked. Other large prawns are often confused for them.

Mussels Best from September to March, but available most of the year due to farming. Usually sold live and can be eaten raw or cooked.

Oysters Available from September to April. Usually eaten raw on day of purchase, but can be cooked. Must be eaten absolutely fresh.

Shrimp/prawns Available all year round, fresh or frozen. Shrimp are the smaller of the two and are not used as much in everyday cooking. Shrimp are brown in colour prior to cooking and prawns are grey, both tuning pink once cooked.

Scallops Best from October to March, but available frozen all year. Usually sold live on the shell, but can be bought off the shell, often frozen. Scallops have a bright orange roe, called 'coral', which is edible. Serve cooked.

Squid/octopus Available all year round, sold fresh but previously frozen. Their black ink is often used in sauces, and is also used to make black pasta.

Tiger prawns Available all year round, raw or cooked. Just one of many varieties of large prawns that are now imported. They are grey when raw and turn pink once cooked. Use within 1 day of purchasing if live or thawed.

Whelks Best from September to February. Usually sold cooked and shelled, and served with vinegar.

Winkles Best from October to May. Can be sold cooked or raw. Usually served cooked and with vinegar.

Vegetables and Salads

Vegetables add colour, texture, flavour and valuable nutrients to a meal. They play an important role in the diet, providing necessary vitamins, minerals and fibre. Vegetables are versatile: they can be served as an accompaniment to other dishes – they go well with meat, poultry and fish – or they can be used as the basis for the whole meal.

There is a huge range of fresh vegetables on sale today in supermarkets, greengrocers and local markets. Also available is a growing selection of fresh organic produce, plus a wide variety of seasonal pick-your-own vegetables from specialist farms. For enthusiastic gardeners, a vast range of vegetable seeds are available. In addition, the increase of ethnic markets has introduced an extensive choice of exotic vegetables, such as chayote and breadfruit. With improved refrigeration and transport networks, vegetables are now flown around the world, resulting in year-round availability.

Vegetables are classified into different groups: leaf vegetables; roots and tubers; beans, pods and shoots; bulb vegetables; fruit vegetables; brassicas; cucumbers and squashes; sea vegetables; and mushrooms.

Leaf Vegetables

This includes lettuce and other salad leaves, such as oakleaf, frisée, radicchio, lamb's lettuce and lollo rosso, as well as rocket, spinach, Swiss chard and watercress. These are available all year round, as most are now grown under glass. Many leaf vegetables, such as watercress and spinach, are delicious cooked and made into soups.

Roots and Tubers

This group includes beetroot, carrots, celeriac, daikon, Jerusalem artichokes, parsnips, potatoes, radish, salsify, scorzonera, sweet potatoes, swede, turnip and yam. Most are available all year round.

Beans, Pods and Shoots

This category includes all the beans, such as broad beans, French/green beans, mangetout peas and runner beans, as well as peas and sweetcorn, baby corn and okra. Shoots include asparagus, bamboo shoots, celery, chicory, fennel, globe artichokes and palm hearts. The majority are available all year round.

Bulb Vegetables

This is the onion family and includes all the different types of onion, from the common brown-skinned globe onion, Italian red onion and Spanish onion to shallots, pickling onions, pearl onions and spring onions. This category also includes leeks, chives and garlic. All are available throughout the year.

Fruit Vegetables

Grown mainly in hot climates such as the Mediterranean, this group includes aubergines, avocados, chillies, sweet peppers and tomatoes. These are available all year round, but are more plentiful in the summer.

Brassicas

This is the cabbage family and includes all the different types of cabbage, broccoli, Brussels sprouts, cauliflower, curly kale, Chinese cabbage, pak choi and purple sprouting broccoli. Some of the cabbages are only seasonal, such as Savoy cabbage and red cabbage, while summer cabbages are available only during the summer months.

Cucumbers and Squashes

These vegetables are members of the gourd family and include cucumbers, gherkins, pumpkins and other squashes. There are two types of squash: summer squashes, which include courgettes, marrows and pattypan squashes, and winter squashes such as pumpkins and butternut, acorn, gem and spaghetti squashes. Courgettes and cucumbers are available all through the year, but pumpkins and other winter squashes and marrow are seasonal.

Sea Vegetables

The vegetables from this group may be quite difficult to find in supermarkets. The most readily available are seaweed (usually available dried) and sea kale.

Mushrooms and Fungi

This category includes all the different types of mushroom: the cultivated button mushrooms, chestnut mushrooms, large portobello or flat mushrooms, oyster and shiitake mushrooms, as well as wild mushrooms such as ceps, morels, chanterelles and truffles. Cultivated mushrooms are available throughout the year, but wild ones are around only from late summer. If you collect your own wild mushrooms, make sure that you correctly identify them before picking, as some are very poisonous and can be fatal if eaten. Dried mushrooms are also available, including ceps, morels and oyster mushrooms. They add a good flavour to a dish, but need to be reconstituted before use.

Buying and Storage

When buying fresh vegetables, always look for ones that are bright and feel firm to the touch, and avoid any that are damaged or bruised. Choose onions and garlic that are hard and not sprouting, and avoid ones that are soft, as they may be damaged. Salad leaves and other leaf vegetables should be fresh, bright and crisp – do not buy any that are wilted, look limp or have yellow leaves. Vegetables such as peas and beans do not keep for very long, so try to eat them as soon as possible after buying or picking. Most vegetables can be stored in a cool, dry place that is frost-free, such as a larder or garage. Green vegetables, fruit vegetables and salad leaves should be kept in the salad drawer of the refrigerator, while root vegetables, tuber vegetables and winter squashes should be kept in a cool, dark place. Winter squashes can be kept for several months if stored correctly.

Preparation

Always clean vegetables thoroughly before using. Brush or scrape off any dirt and wash well in cold water. Wash lettuce and other salad leaves gently under cold running water and tear rather than cut the leaves. Dry thoroughly in a salad spinner or on absorbent kitchen paper before use, otherwise the leaves tend to wilt. Spinach should be washed thoroughly to remove all traces of dirt. Cut off and discard any tough stalks and damaged leaves. Wash leaf vegetables and salad leaves well, then pull off and discard any tough stalks or outer leaves. Leeks need to be thoroughly cleaned before use to remove any grit and dirt. Most mushrooms just need wiping with a damp cloth. Prepare the vegetables just before cooking, as once peeled they lose nutrients. Do not leave them in water, as valuable water-soluble vitamins will be lost.

Cooking Techniques

Vegetables can be cooked in a variety of different ways, such as baking, barbecuing, blanching, boiling, braising, deep-frying, grilling, roasting, sautéing, steaming and stir-frying.

Boiling Always cook vegetables in a minimum amount of water and do not overcook, or valuable nutrients will be lost. It is best to cut vegetables into even-size pieces and briefly cook them in a small amount of water.

Blanching and parboiling These terms mean lightly cooking raw vegetables for a brief period of time, whether parboiling potatoes before roasting or cooking cabbage before braising or cooking leaf vegetables such as spinach. Spinach should be cooked for 2–3 minutes until wilted, in only the water clinging to its leaves. Blanching is also used to remove skins easily from tomatoes. Cut a small cross in the base of the tomato and place in a heatproof bowl. Cover with boiling water and leave for a few seconds, then drain and peel off the skin.

Braising This method is a slow way of cooking certain vegetables, notably cabbage and leeks. The vegetable is simmered for a long period of time in a small amount of stock or water.

Deep-frying This method is suitable for most vegetables except leafy ones. The vegetables can be cut into small pieces, coated in batter, then deep-fried briefly in hot oil.

Grilling For peppers, aubergines and tomatoes, brush them with a little oil first, as they quickly dry out. To remove the skins from peppers, cut them in half lengthways and deseed. Place them skin-side up on the grill rack under a preheated hot grill and cook until the skins are blackened and blistered. Remove with tongs and place in a polythene bag, which will retain moisture. Seal and leave until the peppers are cool enough to handle. Once cool, remove from the bag and carefully peel away the blackened skin.

Roasting Suitable for vegetables such as fennel, courgettes, pumpkin, squash, peppers, garlic, aubergines and tomatoes. Cut the vegetables into even-size chunks. Heat some oil in a roasting tin

in a preheated oven at 200°C/400°F/Gas Mark 6. Put the vegetables in the hot oil, baste and roast in the oven for 30 minutes. Garlic can be split into separate cloves or whole heads can be roasted. It is best not to peel them until cooked.

Steaming This is a great way to cook vegetables such as broccoli, cauliflower, beans, carrots, parsnips and peas. Fill a large saucepan with about 5 cm/2 inches water. Cut the vegetables into even-size pieces, put in a metal steamer basket and lower into the saucepan, then cover and steam until tender. Alternatively, use a plate standing on a trivet in the pan. Do not let the water boil – it should just simmer. Once tender, refresh under cold running water. Asparagus is traditionally cooked in an asparagus steamer.

Health and Nutrition

Vegetables contain many essential nutrients and are especially high in vitamins A, B and C. They contain important minerals, in particular iron and calcium, and are also low in fat, high in fibre and have low cholesterol value. Red and orange vegetables, such as peppers and carrots, and dark green vegetables, such as broccoli, contain excellent anti-cancer properties, as well as helping to prevent heart disease. Current healthy eating guidelines suggest that at least five portions of fruit and vegetables should be eaten per day, with vegetables being the more essential.

Soups & Starters

Tuna Chowder

SERVES 4

2 tsp vegetable oil
1 onion, peeled and
   finely chopped
2 celery stalks, trimmed
   and finely sliced
1 tbsp plain flour

600 ml/1 pint semi-
   skimmed milk
200 g/7 oz can tuna in water
320 g/11 oz can sweetcorn in
   water, drained
2 tsp freshly chopped thyme

salt and freshly ground
   black pepper
pinch cayenne pepper
2 tbsp freshly
   chopped parsley

Heat the oil in a large heavy-based saucepan. Add the onion and celery, and gently cook for about 5 minutes, stirring from time to time, until the onion is softened.

Stir in the flour and cook for about 1 minute to thicken.

Draw the pan off the heat and gradually pour in the milk, stirring throughout.

Add the tuna and its liquid, the drained sweetcorn and the thyme.

Mix gently, then bring to the boil. Cover and simmer for 5 minutes.

Remove the pan from the heat and season to taste with salt and pepper.

Sprinkle the chowder with the cayenne pepper and chopped parsley. Divide among four soup bowls and serve immediately.

TASTY TIP

This creamy soup also works well using equivalent amounts of canned crab meat instead of the tuna.

Clear Chicken
& Mushroom Soup

SERVES 4

2 large chicken legs, about 450 g/1 lb total weight
1 tbsp groundnut oil
1 tsp sesame oil
1 onion, peeled and very thinly sliced
2.5 cm/1 inch piece fresh root ginger, peeled and

very finely chopped
1.1 litres/2 pints clear chicken stock
1 lemon grass stalk, bruised
50 g/2 oz long-grain rice
75 g/3 oz button mushrooms, wiped and finely sliced

4 spring onions, trimmed, cut into 5 cm/2 inch pieces and shredded
1 tbsp dark soy sauce
4 tbsp dry sherry
salt and freshly ground black pepper

Skin the chicken legs and remove any fat. Cut each in half to make 2 thigh and 2 drumstick portions and reserve. Heat the groundnut and sesame oils in a large saucepan. Add the sliced onion and cook gently for 10 minutes, or until soft but not beginning to colour.

Add the chopped ginger to the saucepan and cook for about 30 seconds, stirring all the time to prevent it sticking, then pour in the stock. Add the chicken pieces and the lemon grass, cover and simmer gently for 15 minutes. Stir in the rice and cook for a further 15 minutes, or until the chicken is cooked through.

Remove the chicken from the saucepan and leave until cool enough to handle. Finely shred the flesh, then return to the saucepan with the mushrooms, spring onions, soy sauce and sherry. Simmer for 5 minutes, or until the rice and mushrooms are tender. Remove the lemon grass.

Season the soup to taste with salt and pepper. Ladle into warmed serving bowls, making sure each has an equal amount of shredded chicken and vegetables, and serve immediately.

Creamy Caribbean Chicken & Coconut Soup

SERVES 4

6–8 spring onions
2 garlic cloves
1 red chilli
175 g/6 oz cooked chicken, shredded or diced
2 tbsp vegetable oil
1 tsp ground turmeric

300 ml/½ pint coconut milk
900 ml/1½ pints chicken stock
50 g/2 oz small soup pasta or spaghetti, broken into small pieces
½ lemon, sliced

salt and freshly ground black pepper
1–2 tbsp freshly chopped coriander
fresh coriander sprigs, to garnish

Trim the spring onions and thinly slice; peel the garlic and finely chop. Cut off the top from the chilli, slit down the side and remove seeds and membrane, then finely chop and reserve.

Remove and discard any skin or bones from the cooked chicken and shred using two forks and reserve.

Heat a large wok, add the oil and when hot add the spring onions, garlic and chilli and stir-fry for 2 minutes, or until the onion has softened. Stir in the turmeric and cook for 1 minute.

Blend the coconut milk with the chicken stock until smooth, then pour into the wok. Add the soup pasta or spaghetti with the lemon slices and bring to the boil.

Simmer, half-covered, for 10–12 minutes until the pasta is tender; stir occasionally.

Remove the lemon slices from the wok and add the chicken. Season to taste with salt and pepper and simmer for 2–3 minutes until the chicken is heated through thoroughly.

Stir in the chopped coriander and ladle into warmed soup bowls. Garnish with fresh coriander sprigs and serve immediately.

HELPFUL HINT

Be careful handling chillies. Either wear rubber gloves or scrub your hands thoroughly, using plenty of soap and water. Avoid touching eyes or any other sensitive areas.

Carrot & Ginger Soup

SERVES 4

1 tsp yeast extract
4 slices bread, crusts
    removed, cut into squares
2 tsp olive oil
1 onion, peeled
    and chopped
1 garlic clove, peeled
    and crushed

½ tsp ground ginger
450 g/1 lb carrots, peeled
    and chopped
1 litre/1¾ pints
    vegetable stock
2.5 cm/1 inch piece root
    ginger, peeled and
    finely grated

salt and freshly ground
    black pepper
1 tbsp lemon juice

To garnish:
chives
lemon zest

Preheat the oven to 180°C/350°F/Gas Mark 4. Dissolve the yeast extract in 2 tablespoons warm water and mix with the bread.

Spread the bread cubes over a lightly oiled baking tray and bake for 20 minutes, turning halfway through. Remove from the oven and reserve.

Heat the oil in a large saucepan. Gently cook the onion and garlic for 3–4 minutes. Stir in the ground ginger and cook for 1 minute to release the flavour.

Add the chopped carrots, then stir in the stock and the fresh ginger. Simmer gently for 15 minutes.

Remove from the heat and allow to cool a little. Blend until smooth, then season to taste with salt and pepper. Stir in the lemon juice. Garnish with the chives and lemon zest, and serve immediately.

TASTY TIP

Lightly grill thick slices of ciabatta bread on both sides. While still warm rub the top of the bruschetta with a peeled garlic clove and drizzle with a little olive oil.

Bread & Tomato Soup

SERVES 4

900 g/2 lb very
   ripe tomatoes
4 tbsp olive oil
1 onion, peeled and
   finely chopped
1 tbsp freshly chopped basil

3 garlic cloves, peeled
   and crushed
¼ tsp hot chilli powder
salt and freshly ground
   black pepper
600 ml/1 pint chicken stock

175 g/6 oz stale white bread
50 g/2 oz cucumber, cut into
   small dice
4 whole basil leaves

Make a small cross in the bottom of each tomato, then place in a bowl and cover with boiling water. Allow to stand for 2 minutes, or until the skins have started to peel away, then drain, remove the skins and seeds, and chop into large pieces.

Heat 3 tablespoons of the olive oil in a saucepan and gently cook the onion until softened. Add the skinned tomatoes, chopped basil, garlic and chilli powder and season to taste with salt and pepper. Pour in the stock, cover the saucepan, bring to the boil and simmer gently for 15–20 minutes.

Remove the crusts from the bread and break into small pieces. Remove the tomato mixture from the heat and stir in the bread. Cover and leave to stand for 10 minutes, or until the bread has blended with the tomatoes. Season to taste. Serve warm or cold with a swirl of olive oil on the top, garnished with a spoonful of chopped cucumber and basil leaves.

TASTY TIP

This soup is best made when fresh tomatoes are in season. If making it at other times of the year, use two 400 g cans peeled plum tomatoes instead and cook the soup for 5–10 minutes longer.

Roasted Red Pepper, Tomato & Red Onion Soup

SERVES 4

fine spray of oil
2 large red peppers,
    deseeded and
    roughly chopped
1 red onion, peeled and
    roughly chopped

350 g/12 oz tomatoes,
    halved
1 small crusty French loaf
1 garlic clove, peeled
600 ml/1 pint
    vegetable stock

salt and freshly ground
    black pepper
1 tsp Worcestershire sauce
4 tbsp fromage frais

Preheat the oven to 190°C/375°F/Gas Mark 5. Spray a large roasting tin with the oil and arrange the peppers and onion in the bottom. Cook in the oven for 10 minutes. Add the tomatoes and cook for a further 20, minutes or until the peppers are soft.

Cut the bread into 1 cm/½ inch slices. Cut the garlic clove in half and rub the cut edge of the garlic over the bread.

Place all the bread slices on a large baking tray, and bake in the preheated oven for 10 minutes, turning halfway through, until golden and crisp.

Remove the vegetables from the oven and allow to cool slightly, then blend in a food processor until smooth. Strain the vegetable mixture through a large nylon sieve into a saucepan, to remove the seeds and skin. Add the stock, season to taste with salt and pepper, and stir to mix. Heat the soup gently until piping hot.

In a small bowl beat together the Worcestershire sauce and fromage frais.

Pour the soup into warmed bowls and swirl a spoonful of the fromage frais mixture into each bowl. Serve immediately with the garlic toasts.

HELPFUL HINT

You really need a food processor or blender for this soup. Add one to your birthday wish list!

Potatoes, Leek & Rosemary Soup

SERVES 4

50 g/2 oz butter
450 g/1 lb leeks, trimmed
and finely sliced
700 g/1½ lb potatoes,
peeled and roughly
chopped

900 ml/1½ pints
vegetable stock
4 fresh rosemary sprigs
450 ml/¾ pint
full-cream milk
2 tbsp freshly

chopped parsley
2 tbsp crème fraîche
salt and freshly ground
black pepper
wholemeal rolls,
to serve

Melt the butter in a large saucepan, add the leeks and cook gently for 5 minutes, stirring frequently. Remove 1 tablespoon of the cooked leeks and reserve for garnishing.

Add the potatoes, vegetable stock, rosemary sprigs and milk. Bring to the boil, then reduce the heat, cover and simmer gently for 20–25 minutes until the vegetables are tender. Cool for 10 minutes.

Discard the rosemary, then pour into a food processor or blender, and blend well to form a smooth-textured soup.

Return the soup to the rinsed-out saucepan and stir in the chopped parsley and crème fraîche. Season to taste with salt and pepper. If the soup is too thick, stir in a little more milk or water. Reheat gently without boiling, then ladle into warmed soup bowls. Garnish the soup with the reserved leeks and serve immediately with wholemeal rolls.

HELPFUL HINT

If you don't have a food processor or blender you could use a potato masher and muscle power to mash the vegetables together as much as possible, to create a more rustic, chunky soup.

Italian Bean Soup

SERVES 4

2 tsp olive oil	75 g/3 oz green beans,	1 litre/1¾ pints
1 leek, trimmed and	trimmed and cut into	vegetable stock
chopped	bite-size pieces	8 cherry tomatoes
1 garlic clove, peeled	410 g/14 oz can cannellini	salt and freshly ground
and crushed	beans, drained and rinsed	black pepper
2 tsp dried oregano	75 g/3 oz small pasta shapes	3 tbsp freshly shredded basil

Heat the oil in a large saucepan. Add the leek, garlic and oregano, and cook gently for 5 minutes, stirring occasionally.

Stir in the green beans and the cannellini beans. Sprinkle in the pasta and pour in the stock. Bring the stock mixture to the boil, then reduce the heat to a simmer.

Cook for 12–15 minutes until the vegetables are tender and the pasta is cooked to *al dente*. Stir occasionally.

In a heavy-based frying pan, dry-fry the tomatoes over a high heat until they soften and the skins begin to blacken.

Gently crush the tomatoes in the pan with the back of a spoon and add to the soup.

Season to taste with salt and pepper. Stir in the shredded basil and serve immediately.

HELPFUL HINT

In general, if you decide to use dried herbs when fresh are required, remember that they are much more pungent: 1 teaspoon dried herbs equals roughly 1 tablespoon fresh herbs.

Classic Minestrone

SERVES 6-8

25 g/1 oz butter
3 tbsp olive oil
3 rashers streaky bacon
1 large onion, peeled
1 garlic clove, peeled
1 celery stalk, trimmed
2 carrots, peeled

400 g can chopped tomatoes
1.1 litres/2 pints chicken stock
175 g/6 oz green cabbage, finely shredded
50 g/2 oz French beans, trimmed and halved
3 tbsp frozen petits pois

50 g/2 oz spaghetti, broken into short pieces
salt and freshly ground black pepper
Parmesan cheese shavings, to garnish
crusty bread, to serve

Heat the butter and olive oil together in a large saucepan. Chop the bacon and add to the saucepan. Cook for 3–4 minutes, then remove with a slotted spoon and reserve.

Finely chop the onion, garlic, celery and carrots, and add to the saucepan, one ingredient at a time, stirring well after each addition. Cover and cook gently for 8–10 minutes until the vegetables are softened.

Add the chopped tomatoes, with their juice, and the stock, bring to the boil, then cover the saucepan with a lid. Reduce the heat and simmer gently for about 20 minutes.

Stir in the cabbage, beans, peas and spaghetti pieces. Cover and simmer for a further 20 minutes, or until all the ingredients are tender. Season to taste with salt and pepper.

Return the cooked bacon to the saucepan and bring the soup to the boil. Serve the soup immediately with Parmesan cheese shavings sprinkled on the top and plenty of crusty bread to accompany it.

TASTY TIP

There are many variations of minestrone. You can add drained canned cannellini beans either in place of or as well as the spaghetti, or use small soup pasta shells.

107

Potato Pancakes with Smoked Salmon

SERVES 4

450 g/1 lb floury potatoes, peeled and quartered
1 large egg
1 large egg yolk
25 g/1 oz butter
25 g/1 oz plain flour
150 ml/¼ pint double cream

salt and freshly ground black pepper
2 tbsp freshly chopped parsley
5 tbsp crème fraîche
1 tbsp horseradish sauce
225 g/8 oz smoked

salmon, sliced
salad leaves, to serve

To garnish:
lemon slices
snipped chives

Cook the potatoes in a saucepan of lightly salted boiling water for 15–20 minutes until tender. Drain thoroughly, then mash until free of lumps. Beat in the whole egg and egg yolk, together with the butter. Beat until smooth and creamy. Slowly beat in the flour and cream, then season to taste with salt and pepper. Stir in the chopped parsley.

Beat together the crème fraîche and horseradish sauce in a small bowl, cover with clingfilm and reserve.

Heat a lightly oiled heavy-based frying pan over a medium-high heat. Place a few spoonfuls of the potato mixture in the hot pan and cook for 4–5 minutes until cooked and golden, turning halfway through cooking time. Remove from the pan, drain on absorbent kitchen paper and keep warm. Repeat with the remaining mixture.

Arrange the pancakes on individual serving plates. Place the smoked salmon on the pancakes and spoon over a little of the horseradish sauce. Serve with salad and the remaining horseradish sauce, garnished with lemon slices and chives.

HELPFUL HINT

Commercially made sauces vary in hotness, so it is best to add a little at a time to the crème fraîche and taste until you have the desired flavour.

Pea & Prawn Risotto

SERVES 6

450 g/1 lb whole raw prawns
125 g/4 oz butter
1 red onion, peeled
    and chopped
4 garlic cloves, peeled

and finely chopped
225 g/8 oz Arborio rice
150 ml/¼ pint dry
    white wine
1.1 litres/2 pints vegetable

or fish stock
375 g/13 oz frozen peas
4 tbsp freshly chopped mint
salt and freshly ground
    black pepper

Peel the prawns and reserve the heads and shells. Remove the black vein from the back of each prawn, then wash and dry on absorbent kitchen paper. Melt half the butter in a large frying pan, add the prawns' heads and shells, and fry, stirring occasionally for 3–4 minutes until golden. Strain the butter, discard the heads and shells, and return the butter to the pan.

Add a further 25 g/1 oz of the butter to the pan and fry the onion and garlic for 5 minutes until softened but not coloured. Add the rice and stir the grains in the butter for 1 minute until they are coated thoroughly. Add the white wine and boil rapidly until the wine is reduced by half.

Bring the stock to a gentle simmer, and add to the rice, a ladleful at a time. Stir constantly, adding the stock as it is absorbed, until the rice is creamy, but still has a bite in the centre.

Melt the remaining butter and stir-fry the prawns for 3–4 minutes. Stir into the rice, along with all the pan juices and the peas. Add the chopped mint and season to taste with salt and pepper. Cover the pan and leave the prawns to infuse for 5 minutes before serving.

FOOD FACT

Frying the prawn shells and heads before cooking the dish adds a great deal of flavour to the rice.

Crispy Prawns with Chinese Dipping Sauce

SERVES 4

450 g/1 lb medium-size
  raw prawns, peeled
¼ tsp salt
6 tbsp groundnut oil
2 garlic cloves, peeled and
  finely chopped
2.5 cm/1 inch piece fresh

root ginger, peeled
  and finely chopped
1 green chilli, deseeded and
  finely chopped
4 fresh coriander sprigs,
  leaves and stalks
  roughly chopped

For the chinese dipping sauce:
3 tbsp dark soy sauce
3 tbsp rice wine vinegar
1 tbsp caster sugar
2 tbsp chilli oil
2 spring onions,
  finely shredded

Using a sharp knife, remove the black vein along the back of the prawns. Sprinkle the prawns with the salt and leave to stand for 15 minutes. Pat dry on absorbent kitchen paper.

Heat a wok or large frying pan, add the groundnut oil, and when hot, add the prawns and stir-fry in two batches for about 1 minute until they turn pink and are almost cooked. Using a slotted spoon, remove the prawns from the wok or pan, and keep warm in a low oven.

Drain the oil from the wok or pan, leaving 1 tablespoon. Add the garlic, ginger and chilli, and cook for about 30 seconds. Add the coriander, return the prawns and stir-fry for 1–2 minutes until the prawns are cooked through and the garlic is golden. Turn into a warmed serving dish.

For the dipping sauce, using a fork, beat together the soy sauce, rice vinegar, caster sugar and chilli oil in a small bowl. Stir in the spring onions. Serve immediately with the hot prawns.

TASTY TIP

You must cook raw prawns thoroughly, but it is equally important not to overcook them or they will be tough and chewy. Stir-fry them until pink and opaque, constantly moving them around the pan.

Honey & Ginger Prawns

SERVES 4

1 carrot
50 g/2 oz bamboo shoots
4 spring onions
1 tbsp clear honey
1 tbsp tomato ketchup
1 tsp soy sauce
2.5 cm/1 inch piece fresh
 root ginger, peeled and

finely grated
1 garlic clove, peeled
 and crushed
1 tbsp lime juice
175 g/6 oz peeled prawns,
 thawed if frozen
2 heads little gem
 lettuce leaves

2 tbsp freshly chopped
 coriander
salt and freshly ground
 black pepper

To garnish:
fresh coriander sprigs
lime slices

Cut the carrot into matchstick-size pieces, roughly chop the bamboo shoots and finely slice the spring onions. Combine the bamboo shoots with the carrot matchsticks and spring onions.

In a wok or large frying pan gently heat the honey, tomato ketchup, soy sauce, ginger, garlic and lime juice with 3 tablespoons water. Bring to the boil.

Add the carrot mixture and stir-fry for 2–3 minutes until the vegetables are hot. Add the prawns and continue to stir-fry for 2 minutes. Remove the wok or frying pan from the heat and reserve until cooled slightly.

Divide the little gem lettuce into leaves and rinse lightly.

Stir the chopped coriander into the prawn mixture and season to taste with salt and pepper. Spoon into the lettuce leaves and serve immediately garnished with fresh coriander sprigs and lime slices.

Thai Fish Cakes

SERVES 4

1 red chilli, deseeded
   and roughly chopped
4 tbsp roughly chopped
   fresh coriander
1 garlic clove, peeled
   and crushed
2 spring onions, trimmed

and roughly chopped
1 lemon grass stalk, outer
   leaves discarded,
   roughly chopped
75 g/3 oz prawns,
   thawed if frozen
275 g/10 oz cod fillet,

skinned, pin bones
   removed and cubed
salt and freshly ground
   black pepper
sweet chilli dipping sauce,
   to serve

Preheat the oven to 190°C/375°F/Gas Mark 5. Put the chilli, coriander, garlic, spring onions and lemon grass in a food processor and blend together.

Pat the prawns and cod dry with absorbent kitchen paper. Add to the food processor and blend until the mixture is roughly chopped. Season to taste with salt and pepper, and blend to mix.

Dampen the hands, then shape heaped tablespoons of the mixture into 12 little patties. Place the patties on a lightly oiled baking sheet and cook in the preheated oven for 12–15 minutes until piping hot and cooked through. Turn the patties over halfway through the cooking time.

Serve the fish cakes immediately with the sweet chilli sauce for dipping.

Mixed Satay Sticks

SERVES 4

12 large raw prawns
350 g/12 oz beef rump steak
1 tbsp lemon juice
1 garlic clove, peeled
  and crushed
salt
2 tsp soft dark brown sugar
1 tsp ground cumin

1 tsp ground coriander
¼ tsp ground turmeric
1 tbsp groundnut oil
fresh coriander leaves,
  to garnish

For the spicy peanut sauce:
1 shallot, peeled and very

finely chopped
1 tsp demerara sugar
50 g/2 oz creamed
  coconut, chopped
pinch of chilli powder
1 tbsp dark soy sauce
125 g/4 oz crunchy
  peanut butter

Soak eight bamboo skewers in cold water for at least 30 minutes. Peel the prawns, leaving the tails on. Using a sharp knife, remove the black vein along the back of the prawns. Cut the beef into 1 cm/½ inch wide strips. Put the prawns and beef in separate bowls and sprinkle each with ½ tablespoon of the lemon juice.

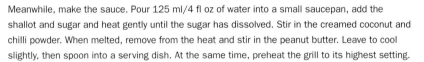

Mix together the garlic, pinch of salt, sugar, cumin, coriander, turmeric and groundnut oil to make a paste. Lightly brush over the prawns and beef. Cover and leave to marinate in the refrigerator for at least 30 minutes, but for longer if possible.

Meanwhile, make the sauce. Pour 125 ml/4 fl oz of water into a small saucepan, add the shallot and sugar and heat gently until the sugar has dissolved. Stir in the creamed coconut and chilli powder. When melted, remove from the heat and stir in the peanut butter. Leave to cool slightly, then spoon into a serving dish. At the same time, preheat the grill to its highest setting.

Thread 3 prawns onto each of four skewers and divide the sliced beef among the remaining skewers. Cook the skewers under the preheated grill for 4–5 minutes, turning occasionally. The prawns should be opaque and pink and the beef browned on the outside, but still pink in the centre. Transfer to warmed individual serving plates, garnish with a few fresh coriander leaves and serve immediately with the warm peanut sauce.

Moo Shi Pork

SERVES 4

175 g/6 oz pork fillet	2 tbsp groundnut oil	cut into fine strips
2 tsp Chinese rice wine	3 medium eggs,	salt and freshly ground
or dry sherry	lightly beaten	black pepper
2 tbsp light soy sauce	1 tsp freshly grated	8 mandarin pancakes,
1 tsp cornflour	root ginger	steamed
25 g/1 oz dried golden	3 spring onions, trimmed	hoisin sauce
needles (a.k.a. tiger	and thinly sliced	sprigs of fresh coriander,
lily buds)	150 g/5 oz bamboo shoots,	to garnish

Soak the golden needles for 30 minutes, drain, rinse and squeeze dry.

Cut the pork across the grain into 1 cm/½ inch slices, then cut into thin strips. Put in a bowl with the Chinese rice wine or sherry, soy sauce and cornflour. Mix well and reserve. Trim off and discard the tough ends of the golden needles, then cut in half and reserve.

Heat a wok or large frying pan, add 1 tablespoon of the groundnut oil and when hot, add the lightly beaten eggs. Cook for 1 minute, stirring all the time, until scrambled. Remove and reserve. Wipe the wok clean with absorbent kitchen paper.

Return the wok to the heat, add the remaining oil and, when hot, transfer the pork strips from the marinade mixture to the wok, shaking off as much marinade as possible (reserve the marinade). Stir-fry for 30 seconds, then add the ginger, spring onions and bamboo shoots and pour in the marinade. Stir-fry for 2–3 minutes until cooked.

Return the scrambled eggs to the wok, season to taste with salt and pepper, and stir for a few seconds until mixed well and heated through. Divide the mixture among the pancakes, drizzle each with 1 teaspoon hoisin sauce and roll up. Garnish and serve immediately.

HELPFUL HINT

About 5 cm/2 inches long, golden needles are strongly fragrant and should be brightly golden. Store in a cool, dark place. Omit them if you prefer and increase the quantity of pork to 225 g/8 oz.

Sticky Braised Spare Ribs

SERVES 4

900 g/2 lb meaty pork spare
    ribs, cut crossways into
    7.5 cm/3 inch pieces
125 ml/4 fl oz apricot nectar
    or orange juice
50 ml/2 fl oz dry white wine
3 tbsp black bean sauce

3 tbsp tomato ketchup
2 tbsp clear honey
3–4 spring onions, trimmed
    and chopped
2 garlic cloves, peeled
    and crushed
grated zest of 1 small orange

salt and freshly ground
    black pepper

To garnish:
spring onion tassels
lemon wedges

Put the spare ribs in the wok and add enough cold water to cover. Bring to the boil over a medium-high heat, skimming off any scum that rises to the surface. Cover and simmer for 30 minutes, then drain and rinse the ribs.

Rinse and dry the wok and return the ribs to it. In a bowl, blend the apricot nectar or orange juice with the white wine, black bean sauce, tomato ketchup and honey until smooth. Stir in the spring onions, garlic and orange zest. Stir well until mixed thoroughly.

Pour the mixture over the spare ribs in the wok and stir gently until the ribs are lightly coated. Place over a medium heat and bring to the boil. Cover then simmer, stirring occasionally, for 1 hour, or until the ribs are tender and the sauce is thickened and sticky. (If the sauce reduces too quickly or begins to stick, add 1 tablespoon water at a time until the ribs are tender.)

Adjust the seasoning to taste, then transfer the ribs to a serving plate and garnish with spring onion tassels and lemon wedges. Serve immediately.

HELPFUL HINT

It's probably best to get your butcher to cut the ribs into pieces for you, as they are quite bony.

Penne with Artichokes, Bacon & Mushrooms

SERVES 6

2 tbsp olive oil
75 g/3 oz pancetta or smoked bacon, chopped
1 small onion, peeled and finely sliced
125 g/4 oz chestnut mushrooms, wiped and sliced
2 garlic cloves, peeled and finely chopped
400 g/14 oz can artichoke hearts, drained and halved (or quartered if large)
100 ml/3½ fl oz dry white wine
100 ml/3½ fl oz chicken stock
3 tbsp double cream
50 g/2 oz freshly grated Parmesan cheese, plus extra, to serve
salt and freshly ground black pepper
450 g/1 lb penne
shredded basil leaves, to garnish

Heat the olive oil in a frying pan and add the pancetta or bacon and the onion. Cook over a medium heat for 8–10 minutes until the bacon is crisp and the onion is just golden. Add the mushrooms and garlic, and cook for a further 5 minutes, or until softened.

Add the artichoke hearts to the mushroom mixture and cook for 3–4 minutes. Pour in the wine, bring to the boil, then simmer rapidly until the liquid is reduced and syrupy.

Pour in the chicken stock, bring to the boil, then simmer rapidly for about 5 minutes until slightly reduced. Reduce the heat slightly, then slowly stir in the double cream and Parmesan cheese. Season the sauce to taste with salt and pepper.

Meanwhile, bring a large pan of lightly salted water to a rolling boil. Add the pasta and cook according to the packet instructions, or until *al dente*.

Drain the pasta thoroughly and transfer to a large warmed serving dish. Pour over the sauce and toss together. Garnish with shredded basil and serve with extra Parmesan cheese.

Gnocchetti with Broccoli & Bacon Sauce

SERVES 6

450 g/1 lb broccoli florets
4 tbsp olive oil
50 g/2 oz pancetta
  or smoked bacon,
  finely chopped
1 small onion, peeled and

finely chopped
3 garlic cloves, peeled
  and sliced
200 ml/7 fl oz milk
450 g/1 lb gnocchetti (little
  elongated ribbed shells)

50 g/2 oz freshly grated
  Parmesan cheese, plus
  extra, to serve
salt and freshly ground
  black pepper

Bring a large pan of salted water to the boil. Add the broccoli florets and cook for 8–10 minutes until very soft. Drain thoroughly, allow to cool slightly, then chop finely and reserve.

Heat the olive oil in a heavy-based pan, add the pancetta or bacon and cook over a medium heat for 5 minutes, or until golden and crisp. Add the onion and cook for a further 5 minutes, or until soft and lightly golden. Add the garlic and cook for 1 minute.

Transfer the chopped broccoli to the pancetta or bacon mixture and pour in the milk. Bring slowly to the boil and simmer rapidly for about 15 minutes until reduced to a creamy texture.

Meanwhile, bring a large pan of lightly salted water to a rolling boil. Add the pasta and cook according to the packet instructions, or until *al dente*.

Drain the pasta thoroughly, reserving a little of the cooking water. Add the pasta and the Parmesan cheese to the broccoli mixture. Toss, adding enough of the reserved cooking water to make a creamy sauce. Season to taste with salt and pepper. Serve immediately with extra Parmesan cheese.

Hoisin Chicken Pancakes

SERVES 4

3 tbsp hoisin sauce
1 garlic clove, peeled
and crushed
2.5 cm/1 inch piece fresh
root ginger, peeled and
finely grated
1 tbsp soy sauce

1 tsp sesame oil
salt and freshly ground
black pepper
4 skinless chicken
thigh fillets
½ cucumber, peeled
(optional)

12 ready-made Chinese
pancakes
6 spring onions, trimmed
and cut lengthways into
fine shreds
sweet chilli dipping sauce,
to serve

Preheat the oven to 190°C/375°F/Gas Mark 5. In a non-metallic bowl, mix the hoisin sauce with the garlic, ginger, soy sauce, sesame oil and seasoning.

Add the chicken thighs and turn to coat in the mixture. Cover loosely and leave to marinate in the refrigerator for 3–4 hours, turning the chicken from time to time.

Remove the chicken from the marinade and place in a roasting tin. Reserve the marinade. Bake in the preheated oven for 30 minutes, basting occasionally with the marinade.

If using, cut the cucumber in half lengthways and remove the seeds by running a teaspoon down the middle to scoop them out. Cut into thin batons.

Place the pancakes in a steamer to warm or heat according to the packet instructions. Thinly slice the hot chicken and arrange on a plate with the shredded spring onions, cucumber and pancakes.

To serve, place a spoonful of the chicken in the middle of each warmed pancake and top with pieces of cucumber (if using), spring onion and a little dipping sauce. Roll up and serve immediately.

Cantonese Chicken Wings

SERVES 4

3 tbsp hoisin sauce
2 tbsp dark soy sauce
1 tbsp sesame oil
1 garlic clove, peeled
   and crushed
2.5 cm/1 inch piece fresh
   root ginger, peeled

and grated
1 tbsp Chinese rice wine
   or dry sherry
2 tsp chilli bean sauce
2 tsp red or white wine
   vinegar
2 tbsp soft light brown sugar

900 g/2 lb large
   chicken wings
50 g/2 oz cashew nuts,
   chopped
2 spring onions, trimmed
   and finely chopped

Preheat the oven to 220°C/425°F/Gas Mark 7, 15 minutes before cooking. Put the hoisin sauce, soy sauce, sesame oil, garlic, ginger, Chinese rice wine or sherry, chilli bean sauce, vinegar and sugar in a small saucepan with 6 tablespoons water. Bring to the boil, stirring occasionally, then simmer for about 30 seconds. Remove the glaze from the heat.

Arrange the chicken wings in a single layer in a roasting tin. Pour over the glaze and stir until the wings are coated thoroughly. Cover the tin loosely with kitchen foil, place in the preheated oven and roast for 25 minutes. Remove the kitchen foil, baste the wings and cook for a further 5 minutes.

Reduce the oven temperature to 190°C/375°F/Gas Mark 5. Turn the wings over and sprinkle with the chopped cashew nuts and spring onions. Return to the oven and cook for 5 minutes, or until the nuts are lightly browned, the glaze is sticky and the wings are tender. Remove from the oven and leave to stand for 5 minutes before arranging on a warmed platter. Serve immediately with finger bowls and plenty of napkins for wiping sticky fingers.

HELPFUL HINT
Though popular in China and Thailand, the wings are often discarded when cutting chickens into portions. So give your butcher advance notice and he will probably sell them to you very cheaply.

Soy–glazed Chicken Thighs

SERVES 6-8

900 g/2 lb chicken thighs
2 tbsp vegetable oil
3–4 garlic cloves, peeled
   and crushed
4 cm/1½ inch piece fresh root
   ginger, peeled and finely

chopped or grated
125 ml/4 fl oz soy sauce
2–3 tbsp Chinese rice wine
   or dry sherry
2 tbsp clear honey
1 tbsp soft brown sugar

2 or 3 dashes hot chilli
   sauce, or to taste
freshly chopped parsley,
   to garnish

Heat a large wok and, when hot, add the oil and heat. Stir-fry the chicken thighs for 5 minutes, or until golden on all sides. Remove and drain on absorbent kitchen paper. You may need to do this in two or three batches.

Pour off the oil and fat and, using absorbent kitchen paper, carefully wipe out the wok. Add the garlic, ginger, soy sauce, Chinese rice wine or sherry, and honey to the wok and stir well. Sprinkle in the sugar with the hot chilli sauce to taste, then place over the heat and bring to the boil.

Reduce the heat to a gentle simmer, then carefully add the chicken thighs. Cover the wok and simmer gently over a very low heat for 30 minutes, or until they are tender and the sauce is reduced and thickened and glazes the chicken thighs. Stir or spoon the sauce over the chicken thighs occasionally and add a little water if the sauce is starting to become too thick.

Arrange in a shallow serving dish, garnish with freshly chopped parsley and serve immediately.

Mozzarella Frittata
with Tomato & Basil Salad

SERVES 6

For the salad:
6 ripe but firm tomatoes
2 tbsp fresh basil leaves
2 tbsp olive oil
1 tbsp fresh lemon juice
1 tsp caster sugar
freshly ground black pepper

For the frittata:
7 medium eggs, beaten
salt
300 g/10 oz mozzarella
    cheese
2 spring onions, trimmed
    and finely chopped

2 tbsp olive oil
warm crusty bread,
    to serve

To make the tomato and basil salad, slice the tomatoes very thinly, tear up the basil leaves and sprinkle over. Make the dressing by whisking together the olive oil, lemon juice and sugar until well combined. Season with black pepper before drizzling the dressing over the salad.

To make the frittata, preheat the grill to a high heat, just before beginning to cook. Put the eggs in a large bowl with plenty of salt, and whisk. Grate the mozzarella and stir into the egg with the finely chopped spring onions.

Heat the oil in a large nonstick frying pan over a medium-low heat and pour in the egg mixture, stirring with a wooden spoon to spread the ingredients evenly over the pan. Cook for 5–8 minutes until the frittata is golden brown and firm on the underside.

Place the whole pan under the preheated grill and cook for 4–5 minutes until the top is golden brown. Slide the frittata on to a serving plate, cut into 6 large wedges and serve immediately with the tomato and basil salad and plenty of warm crusty bread.

HELPFUL HINT

After grating the mozzarella cheese, firmly press between layers of absorbent kitchen paper to remove any excess water that might leak out during cooking.

Courgette & Tarragon Tortilla

SERVES 4

700 g/1½ lb potatoes
3 tbsp olive oil
1 onion, peeled and
   thinly sliced

salt and freshly ground
   black pepper
1 courgette, trimmed
   and thinly sliced

6 medium eggs
2 tbsp freshly chopped
   tarragon
tomato wedges, to serve

Peel the potatoes and thinly slice. Dry the slices in a clean tea towel to get them as dry as possible. Heat the oil in a large heavy-based pan over a medium heat, add the onion and cook for 3 minutes. Add the potatoes with a little salt and pepper, then stir the potatoes and onion lightly to coat in the oil.

Reduce the heat to the lowest possible setting, cover and cook gently for 5 minutes. Turn the potatoes and onion over and continue to cook for a further 5 minutes. Give the pan a shake every now and again to ensure that the potatoes do not stick to the bottom or burn. Add the courgette, then cover and cook for a further 10 minutes.

Beat together the eggs and tarragon, and season to taste with salt and pepper. Pour the egg mixture over the vegetables and return to the heat. Cook over a low heat for 20–25 minutes until there is no liquid egg left on the surface of the tortilla.

Turn the tortilla over by inverting it onto the lid or onto a flat plate. Return the pan to the heat and cook the tortilla for a final 3–5 minutes until the underside is golden brown. If preferred, place the tortilla under a preheated grill for 4 minutes, or until set and golden brown on top. Cut into small squares and serve hot or cold with tomato wedges.

HELPFUL HINT
Use even-size waxy potatoes, which won't break up during cooking – Maris Bard, Charlotte or Pentland Javelin are all good choices of potato.

Potato Skins

SERVES 4

4 large baking potatoes
2 tbsp olive oil
2 tsp paprika
125 g/4 oz pancetta,
   roughly chopped

6 tbsp double cream
125 g/4 oz Gorgonzola
   cheese
1 tbsp freshly
   chopped parsley

To serve:
mayonnaise
sweet chilli dipping sauce
tossed green salad

Preheat the oven to 200°C/400°F/Gas Mark 6. Scrub the potatoes, then prick a few times with a fork or skewer, and place directly on the top shelf of the oven. Bake in the preheated oven for at least 1 hour until tender. The potatoes are cooked when they yield gently to the pressure of your hand. Do not turn off the oven.

Set the potatoes aside until cool enough to handle, then cut in half and scoop the flesh into a bowl and reserve. Preheat the grill to its highest setting and line the grill rack with kitchen foil.

Mix together the oil and the paprika and use half to brush the outside of the potato skins. Place on the grill rack under the preheated hot grill and cook for 5 minutes, or until crisp, turning as necessary.

Heat the remaining paprika-flavoured oil and gently fry the pancetta until crisp. Add to the reserved potato flesh along with the cream, Gorgonzola cheese and parsley. Halve the potato skins and fill with the Gorgonzola filling. Return to the oven for a further 15 minutes to heat through. Sprinkle with a little more paprika and serve immediately with mayonnaise, sweet chilli sauce and a green salad.

Beetroot Risotto

6 tbsp extra-virgin olive oil
1 onion, peeled and
   finely chopped
2 garlic cloves, peeled and
   finely chopped
2 tsp freshly chopped thyme
1 tsp grated lemon zest
350 g/12 oz Arborio rice

150 ml/¼ pint dry
   white wine
900 ml/1½ pints vegetable
   stock, heated
2 tbsp double cream
225 g/8 oz cooked beetroot,
   peeled and finely chopped
2 tbsp freshly chopped

parsley
75 g/3 oz Parmesan cheese,
   freshly grated
salt and freshly ground
   black pepper
fresh thyme sprigs,
   to garnish

Heat half the oil in a large heavy-based frying pan. Add the onion, garlic, thyme and lemon zest. Cook for 5 minutes, stirring frequently, until the onion is soft and transparent but not coloured. Add the rice and stir until it is well coated in the oil.

Add the wine, then bring to the boil and boil rapidly until the wine has almost evaporated. Reduce the heat.

Keeping the pan over a low heat, add a ladleful of the hot stock to the rice and cook, stirring constantly, until the stock is absorbed. Continue gradually adding the stock in this way until the rice is tender; this should take about 20 minutes. You may not need all the stock.

Stir in the cream, chopped beetroot, parsley and half the grated Parmesan cheese. Season to taste with salt and pepper. Garnish with sprigs of fresh thyme and serve immediately with the remaining grated Parmesan cheese.

HELPFUL HINT

If you buy ready-cooked beetroot, choose small ones, which are sweeter. Make sure that they are not doused in vinegar, as this would spoil the flavour of the dish.

Sweetcorn Fritters

SERVES 4

4 tbsp groundnut oil
1 small onion, peeled and
   finely chopped
1 red chilli, deseeded and
   finely chopped
1 garlic clove, peeled
   and crushed

1 tsp ground coriander
325 g/11 oz can sweetcorn
6 spring onions, trimmed
   and finely sliced
1 medium egg, lightly
   beaten
salt and freshly ground

black pepper
3 tbsp plain flour
1 tsp baking powder
spring onion curls,
   to garnish
Thai-style chutney,
   to serve

Heat 1 tablespoon of the groundnut oil in a frying pan, add the onion and cook gently for 7–8 minutes until beginning to soften. Add the chilli, garlic and ground coriander and cook for 1 minute, stirring continuously. Remove from the heat.

Drain the sweetcorn and tip into a mixing bowl. Lightly mash with a potato masher to break down the corn a little. Add the cooked onion mixture to the bowl with the sliced spring onions and beaten egg. Season to taste with salt and pepper, then stir to mix together. Sift the flour and baking powder over the mixture and stir in.

Heat 2 tablespoons of the groundnut oil in a large frying pan. Drop 4 or 5 heaped teaspoonfuls of the sweetcorn mixture into the pan and, using a fish slice or spatula, flatten each to make a 1 cm/½ inch thick fritter.

Fry the fritters for 3 minutes, or until golden brown on the underside, turn over and fry for a further 3 minutes, or until cooked through and crisp.

Remove the fritters from the pan and drain on absorbent kitchen paper. Keep warm while cooking the remaining fritters, adding a little more oil if needed. Garnish with spring onion curls and serve immediately with a Thai-style chutney.

HELPFUL HINT

To make a spring onion curl, trim off the root and some green top to leave 10 cm/ 4 inches. Make several 3 cm/ 1¼ inch cuts down from the top. Soak in iced water for 20 minutes until curled.

Spaghettini with Peas, Spring Onions & Mint

SERVES 6

pinch saffron strands
700 g/1½ lb fresh peas or
    350 g/12 oz frozen petit
    pois, thawed
75 g/3 oz unsalted butter,
    softened

6 spring onions, trimmed
    and finely sliced
salt and freshly ground
    black pepper
1 garlic clove, peeled and
    finely chopped

2 tbsp freshly chopped mint
1 tbsp freshly snipped chives
450 g/1 lb spaghettini
freshly grated Parmesan
    cheese, to serve

Soak the saffron in 2 tablespoons hot water while you prepare the sauce. Shell the peas if using fresh ones.

Heat 50 g/2 oz of the butter in a medium frying pan, add the spring onions and a little salt and cook over a low heat for 2–3 minutes until the onions are softened. Add the garlic, then the peas and 100 ml/3½ fl oz water. Bring to the boil and cook for 5–6 minutes until the peas are just tender. Stir in the mint and keep warm.

Blend the remaining butter and the saffron water in a large warmed serving bowl and reserve.

Meanwhile, bring a large pan of lightly salted water to a rolling boil and add the spaghettini. Cook according to the packet instructions, or until *al dente*.

Drain thoroughly, reserving 2–3 tablespoons of the pasta cooking water. Tip into a warmed serving bowl, add the pea sauce and toss together gently. Season to taste with salt and pepper. Serve immediately with extra black pepper and grated Parmesan cheese.

Tagliatelle with Brown Butter, Asparagus & Parmesan

SERVES 6

450 g/1 lb fresh or dried tagliatelle, such as the white and green variety
350 g/12 oz fresh asparagus, trimmed and cut into short lengths
75 g/3 oz unsalted butter

1 garlic clove, peeled and sliced
25 g/1 oz flaked hazelnuts or whole hazelnuts, roughly chopped
1 tbsp freshly chopped parsley

1 tbsp freshly snipped chives
salt and freshly ground black pepper
50 g/2 oz freshly grated Parmesan cheese, to serve

If using fresh pasta, prepare the dough according to the recipe on page 56. Cut into tagliatelle, wind into nests and reserve on a floured tea towel until ready to cook.

Bring a pan of lightly salted water to the boil. Add the asparagus and cook for 1 minute. Drain immediately, refresh under cold running water and drain again. Pat dry and reserve.

Melt the butter in a large frying pan, then add the garlic and hazelnuts, and cook over a medium heat until the butter turns golden. Immediately remove from the heat and add the parsley, chives and asparagus. Leave for 2–3 minutes until the asparagus is heated through.

Meanwhile, bring a large pan of lightly salted water to a rolling boil, then add the pasta nests. Cook until *al dente*: 2–3 minutes for fresh pasta and according to the packet instructions for dried pasta. Drain the pasta thoroughly and return to the pan. Add the asparagus mixture and toss together. Season to taste with salt and pepper, and tip into a warmed serving dish. Serve immediately with grated Parmesan cheese.

HELPFUL HINT

If you buy loose asparagus, rather than pre-packed, choose stems of similar thickness so that they will all cook in the same time.

Peperonata
(Braised Mixed Peppers)

SERVES 4

2 green peppers
1 red pepper
1 yellow pepper
1 orange pepper
1 onion, peeled
2 garlic cloves, peeled

2 tbsp olive oil
4 very ripe tomatoes
1 tbsp freshly
    chopped oregano
salt and freshly ground
    black pepper

150 ml/¼ pint light chicken or
    vegetable stock
fresh oregano sprigs,
    to garnish
focaccia or flat bread,
    to serve

Halve each pepper lengthways, remove the seeds and membranes and cut into thin strips. Slice the onion into rings and chop the garlic cloves finely.

Heat the olive oil in a frying pan and fry the peppers, onion and garlic for 5–10 minutes until soft and lightly coloured, stirring continuously.

Using a sharp knife, make a small cross in the base of each tomato then place in a bowl and cover with boiling water. Allow to stand for about 2 minutes. Drain, then remove the skins and seeds, and chop the tomato flesh into cubes.

Add the tomatoes and oregano to the peppers and onion, and season to taste with salt and pepper. Cover the pan and bring to the boil. Simmer gently for about 30 minutes until tender, adding the chicken or vegetable stock halfway through the cooking time.

Garnish with oregano sprigs and serve hot with plenty of freshly baked focaccia or alternatively lightly toast slices of flat bread and pile a spoonful of peperonata onto each plate.

Bruschetta with Pecorino, Garlic & Tomatoes

SERVES 4

6 ripe but firm tomatoes
125 g/4 oz pecorino cheese,
    finely grated
1 tbsp oregano leaves
salt and freshly ground
    black pepper

3 tbsp olive oil
3 garlic cloves, peeled
8 slices Italian flatbread,
    such as focaccia
50 g/2 oz mozzarella
    cheese

marinated black olives,
    to serve
mixed bitter salad leaves,
    such as frisée, radicchio
    and rocket, to serve

Preheat the grill to medium and line the grill rack with kitchen foil just before cooking. Using a sharp knife, make a small cross in the base of each tomato, then place in a small bowl and cover with boiling water. Leave to stand for 2 minutes, then drain and remove the skins. Cut into quarters, remove the seeds, and chop the flesh into small dice.

Mix the tomato flesh with the pecorino cheese and 2 teaspoons of the fresh oregano and season to taste with salt and pepper. Add 1 tablespoon of the olive oil and mix thoroughly.

Crush the garlic and spread evenly over the slices of bread. Heat the remaining olive oil in a large frying pan and sauté the bread slices until they are crisp and golden.

Place the fried bread on a lightly oiled baking tray and spoon on the tomato and cheese topping. Place a little mozzarella on top and cook under the preheated grill for 3–4 minutes until golden and bubbling. Garnish with the remaining oregano, then arrange the bruschettas on a serving plate and serve immediately with the olives.

Fish & Seafood

Stir–fried Salmon with Peas

SERVES 4

450 g/1 lb salmon fillet
salt
6 slices streaky bacon
1 tbsp vegetable oil
50 ml/2 fl oz chicken
    or fish stock
2 tbsp dark soy sauce

2 tbsp Chinese rice wine
    or dry sherry
1 tsp sugar
75 g/3 oz frozen peas,
    thawed
1–2 tbsp freshly
    shredded mint

1 tsp cornflour
fresh mint sprigs,
    to garnish
freshly cooked noodles,
    to serve

Wipe and skin the salmon fillet and remove any pin bones. Slice into 2.5 cm/1 inch strips, transfer to a plate and sprinkle with salt (this draws out some of the juices and makes the flesh firmer, so that it remains whole when cooked). Leave for 20 minutes, then pat dry with absorbent kitchen paper and reserve.

Remove and discard any cartilage from the bacon, cut the bacon into small dice and reserve.

Heat a wok or large frying pan over a high heat. Add the oil and, when hot, add the bacon and stir-fry for 3 minutes or until crisp and golden. Push to one side and add the strips of salmon. Stir-fry gently for 2 minutes or until the flesh is opaque.

Pour the chicken or fish stock, soy sauce and Chinese rice wine or sherry into the wok, then stir in the sugar, peas and freshly shredded mint.

Blend the cornflour with 1 tablespoon water to form a smooth paste and stir into the sauce. Bring to the boil, reduce the heat and simmer for 1 minute, or until slightly thickened and smooth. Garnish and serve immediately with noodles.

HELPFUL HINT

Dark soy sauce is used in this recipe because it is slightly less salty than the light version. To reduce the salt content further, cook the noodles in plain boiling water with no added salt.

Salmon Fish Cakes

SERVES 4

450 g/1 lb salmon fillet, skinned	2 medium tomatoes, skinned, deseeded and chopped	cheese, grated
salt and freshly ground black pepper	2 tbsp freshly chopped parsley	2 tbsp plain flour
450 g/1 lb potatoes, peeled and cut into chunks	75 g/3 oz wholemeal breadcrumbs	2 medium eggs, beaten
25 g/1 oz butter	25 g/1 oz Cheddar	3–4 tbsp vegetable oil
1 tbsp milk		

450 g/1 lb salmon fillet, skinned

salt and freshly ground black pepper

450 g/1 lb potatoes, peeled and cut into chunks

25 g/1 oz butter

1 tbsp milk

2 medium tomatoes, skinned, deseeded and chopped

2 tbsp freshly chopped parsley

75 g/3 oz wholemeal breadcrumbs

25 g/1 oz Cheddar

cheese, grated

2 tbsp plain flour

2 medium eggs, beaten

3–4 tbsp vegetable oil

To serve:

ready-made raita

fresh mint sprigs

Put the salmon in a shallow frying pan and cover with water. Season to taste with salt and pepper, and simmer for 8–10 minutes until the fish is cooked. Drain and flake into a bowl.

Boil the potatoes in lightly salted water until soft, then drain. Mash with the butter and milk until smooth. Add the potato to the bowl of fish and stir in the tomatoes and half the parsley. Adjust the seasoning to taste. Chill the mixture in the refrigerator for at least 2 hours to firm up.

Mix the breadcrumbs with the grated cheese and the remaining parsley. When the fish mixture is firm, form into eight flat cakes. First, lightly coat the fish cakes in the flour, then dip into the beaten egg, allowing any excess to drip back into the bowl. Finally, press into the breadcrumb mixture until well coated.

Heat a little of the oil in a frying pan and fry the fish cakes in batches for 2–3 minutes on each side until golden and crisp, adding more oil if necessary. Serve with raita garnished with sprigs of mint.

HELPFUL HINT

To skin the tomatoes, pierce each one with the tip of a sharp knife, then plunge into boiling water and leave for up to 1 minute. Drain, then rinse in cold water – the skins should peel off easily.

Salmon with Herbed Potatoes

SERVES 4

450 g/1 lb baby
new potatoes
salt and freshly ground
black pepper
4 salmon steaks, each
weighing about 175 g/6 oz

1 carrot, peeled and cut
into fine strips
175 g/6 oz asparagus
spears, trimmed
175 g/6 oz sugar snap
peas, trimmed

finely grated zest and
juice 1 lemon
25 g/1 oz butter
4 large fresh parsley sprigs

Preheat the oven to 190°C/375°F/Gas Mark 5, 10 minutes before required. Parboil the potatoes in lightly salted boiling water for 5–8 minutes until they are barely tender. Drain and reserve.

Cut out four pieces of baking paper, measuring 20.5 cm/8 inches square, and place on the work surface. Arrange the parboiled potatoes on top. Wipe the salmon steaks and place on top of the potatoes.

Put the carrot strips in a bowl with the asparagus spears, sugar snap peas and grated lemon zest and juice. Season to taste with salt and pepper. Toss lightly together.

Divide the vegetables evenly among the salmon. Dot the top of each parcel with butter and a sprig of parsley.

To wrap a parcel, lift up two opposite sides of the paper and fold the edges together. Twist the paper at the other two ends to seal the parcel well. Repeat with the remaining parcels.

Put the parcels on a baking tray and bake in the preheated oven for 15 minutes. Place an unopened parcel on each plate and open just before eating.

Pan-fried Salmon with Herb Risotto

SERVES 4

4 x 175 g/6 oz salmon fillets	225 g/8 oz Arborio rice	2 tbsp freshly chopped
3–4 tbsp plain flour	150 ml/¼ pint dry white wine	flat-leaf parsley
1 tsp dried mustard powder	1.4 litres/2½ pints	knob of butter
salt and freshly ground	vegetable or fish stock	
black pepper	50 g/2 oz butter	**To garnish:**
2 tbsp olive oil	2 tbsp freshly	lemon slices
3 shallots, peeled	snipped chives	fresh dill sprigs
and chopped	2 tbsp freshly chopped dill	tomato salad, to serve

Wipe the salmon fillets with a clean, damp cloth. Mix together the flour, mustard powder and seasoning on a large plate and use to coat the salmon fillets and reserve.

Heat half the olive oil in a large frying pan and fry the shallots for 5 minutes until softened but not coloured. Add the rice and stir for 1 minute, then slowly add the wine, bring to the boil and boil rapidly until reduced by half.

Bring the stock to a gentle simmer, then add to the rice, a ladleful at a time. Make sure that the stock is absorbed between each addition before adding more. Cook, stirring frequently, until all the stock has been added and the rice is cooked but still retains a bite. Stir in the butter and freshly chopped herbs and season to taste with salt and pepper.

Heat the remaining olive oil and the knob of butter in a large griddle pan, add the salmon fillets and cook for 2–3 minutes on each side until cooked. Arrange the herb risotto on warmed serving plates and top with the salmon. Garnish with slices of lemon and sprigs of dill and serve immediately with a tomato salad.

HELPFUL HINT

Stirring butter into the risotto at the end is an important step – in Italian it is called *mantecare*. This final addition gives the risotto its fine texture and a beautiful shine. Serve as soon as it is cooked.

Salmon Noisettes with Fruity Sauce

SERVES 4

4 x 125 g/4 oz salmon steaks
grated zest and juice of
   2 lemons
grated zest and juice of
   1 lime
3 tbsp olive oil

1 tbsp clear honey
1 tbsp wholegrain mustard
coarse sea salt and freshly
   ground black pepper
1 tbsp groundnut oil
125 g/4 oz mixed salad

leaves, washed
1 bunch watercress, washed
   and thick stalks removed
250 g/9 oz baby plum
   tomatoes, halved

Using a sharp knife, cut the bone away from each salmon steak to create two salmon fillets. Repeat with the remaining salmon steaks. Shape the salmon fillets into noisettes and secure with fine string.

Mix together the citrus zests and juices, olive oil, honey, wholegrain mustard, salt and pepper in a shallow dish. Add the salmon fillets and turn to coat. Cover and leave to marinate in the refrigerator for 4 hours, turning the salmon occasionally in the marinade.

Heat the wok, then add the groundnut oil and heat until hot. Lift out the salmon noisettes, reserving the marinade. Add the salmon to the wok and cook for 6–10 minutes, turning once during cooking, until cooked and the fish is just flaking. Pour the marinade into the wok and heat through gently.

Mix together the salad leaves, watercress and tomatoes, and arrange on serving plates. Top with the salmon noisettes and drizzle over any remaining warm marinade. Serve immediately.

Seared Salmon & Lemon Linguine

SERVES 4

4 small skinless salmon
fillets, each about 75 g/3 oz
2 tsp sunflower oil
½ tsp mixed or black
peppercorns, crushed
400 g/14 oz linguine

15 g/½ oz unsalted butter
1 bunch spring onions,
trimmed and shredded
300 ml/½ pint sour cream
finely grated zest of 1 lemon
50 g/2 oz freshly grated

Parmesan cheese
1 tbsp lemon juice

To garnish:
fresh dill sprigs
lemon slices

Brush the salmon fillets with the sunflower oil, sprinkle with crushed peppercorns, press on firmly and reserve.

Bring a large pan of lightly salted water to a rolling boil. Add the linguine and cook according to the packet instructions, or until *al dente*.

Meanwhile, melt the butter in a saucepan and cook the shredded spring onions gently for 2–3 minutes until soft. Stir in the sour cream and lemon zest, and remove from the heat.

Preheat a griddle or heavy-based frying pan until very hot. Add the salmon and sear for 1½–2 minutes on each side. Remove from the pan and allow to cool slightly.

Bring the sour cream sauce to the boil and stir in the Parmesan cheese and lemon juice. Drain the pasta thoroughly and return to the pan. Pour over the sauce and toss gently to coat.

Spoon the pasta onto warmed serving plates and top with the salmon fillets. Serve immediately with sprigs of dill and lemon slices.

Farfalle with Smoked Trout in a Dill & Vodka Sauce

SERVES 4

400 g/14 oz farfalle
150 g/5 oz smoked trout
2 tsp lemon juice
200 ml/7 fl oz double cream

2 tsp wholegrain mustard
2 tbsp freshly chopped dill
4 tbsp vodka
salt and freshly ground

black pepper
fresh dill sprigs,
to garnish

Bring a large pan of lightly salted water to a rolling boil. Add the pasta and cook according to the packet instructions, or until *al dente*.

Meanwhile, cut the smoked trout into thin slivers, using scissors. Sprinkle lightly with the lemon juice and reserve.

Put the cream, mustard, chopped dill and vodka in a small pan. Season lightly with salt and pepper. Bring the contents of the pan to the boil and simmer gently for 2–3 minutes until slightly thickened.

Drain the cooked pasta thoroughly, then return to the pan. Add the smoked trout to the dill and vodka sauce, then pour over the pasta. Toss gently until the pasta is coated and the trout evenly mixed.

Spoon into a warmed serving dish or onto individual plates. Garnish with sprigs of dill and serve immediately.

Ratatouille Mackerel

SERVES 4

1 red pepper
1 tbsp olive oil
1 red onion, peeled
1 garlic clove, peeled and
   thinly sliced
2 courgettes, trimmed and
   cut into thick slices

400 g/14 oz can chopped
   tomatoes
sea salt and freshly ground
   black pepper
4 small mackerel, each
   about 275 g/10 oz, cleaned
   and heads removed

spray of olive oil
lemon juice for drizzling
12 fresh basil leaves
couscous or rice mixed with
   chopped parsley, to serve

Preheat the oven to 190°C/375°F/Gas Mark 5. Cut the top off the red pepper, halve lengthways, remove the seeds and membrane, then cut into chunks. Cut the red onion into thick wedges.

Heat the oil in a large pan and cook the onion and garlic for 5 minutes or until beginning to soften.

Add the pepper chunks and courgettes slices, and cook for a further 5 minutes.

Pour in the chopped tomatoes with their juice and cook for a further 5 minutes. Season to taste with salt and pepper, and pour into an ovenproof dish.

Season the fish with salt and pepper, and arrange on top of the vegetables. Spray with a little olive oil and lemon juice. Cover and cook in the preheated oven for 20 minutes.

Remove the cover, add the basil leaves and return to the oven for a further 5 minutes. Serve immediately with couscous or rice mixed with parsley.

FOOD FACT

Ratatouille is a very versatile dish to which many other vegetables can be added. For that extra kick, why not add a little chopped chilli.

Smoked Mackerel & Pasta Frittata

SERVES 4

25 g/1 oz tricolore pasta
   spirals or shells
225 g/8 oz smoked mackerel
6 medium eggs
3 tbsp milk
2 tsp wholegrain mustard
2 tbsp freshly chopped

parsley
salt and freshly ground
   black pepper
25 g/1 oz unsalted butter
6 spring onions, trimmed
   and diagonally sliced
50 g/2 oz frozen

peas, thawed
75 g/3 oz mature Cheddar
   cheese, grated

To serve
green salad
warm crusty bread

Preheat the grill to its highest setting just before cooking. Bring a pan of lightly salted water to a rolling boil. Add the pasta and cook according to the packet instructions, or until *al dente*. Drain thoroughly and reserve.

Remove the skin from the mackerel and break the fish into large flakes, discarding any bones, and reserve.

Put the eggs, milk, mustard and parsley in a bowl and whisk together. Season with just a little salt and plenty of freshly ground black pepper, and reserve.

Melt the butter in a large heavy-based frying pan. Cook the spring onions gently for 3–4 minutes until soft. Pour in the egg mixture, then add the drained pasta, peas and half the mackerel.

Gently stir the mixture in the pan for 1–2 minutes until beginning to set. Stop stirring and cook for about 1 minute until the underneath is golden brown.

Scatter the remaining mackerel over the frittata, followed by the grated cheese. Place under the preheated grill for about 1½ minutes, or until golden-brown and set. Cut into wedges and serve immediately with salad and crusty bread.

Tuna & Mushroom Ragout

SERVES 4

225 g/8 oz basmati
and wild rice
50 g/2 oz butter
1 tbsp olive oil
1 large onion, peeled
and finely chopped
1 garlic clove, peeled
and crushed
300 g/11 oz baby button

mushrooms, wiped
and halved
2 tbsp plain flour
400 g/14 oz can chopped
tomatoes
1 tbsp freshly chopped parsley
dash of Worcestershire sauce
400 g/14 oz can tuna in oil,
drained

salt and freshly ground
black pepper
4 tbsp freshly grated
Parmesan cheese
1 tbsp freshly shredded basil

To serve:
green salad
garlic bread

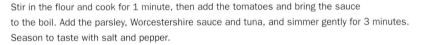

Cook the basmati and wild rice in a saucepan of boiling salted water for 20 minutes, then drain and return to the pan. Stir in half the butter, cover the pan and leave to stand for 2 minutes until all of the butter has melted.

Heat the oil and the remaining butter in a frying pan and cook the onion for 1–2 minutes until soft. Add the garlic and mushrooms, and continue to cook for a further 3 minutes.

Stir in the flour and cook for 1 minute, then add the tomatoes and bring the sauce to the boil. Add the parsley, Worcestershire sauce and tuna, and simmer gently for 3 minutes. Season to taste with salt and pepper.

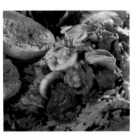

Stir the rice well, then spoon onto four serving plates and top with the tuna and mushroom mixture. Sprinkle each portion with a spoonful of grated Parmesan cheese and some shredded basil and serve immediately with a green salad and chunks of garlic bread.

Seared Tuna with Pernod & Thyme

SERVES 4

4 tuna or swordfish steaks
salt and freshly ground
    black pepper
3 tbsp Pernod

1 tbsp olive oil
zest and juice of 1 lime
2 tsp fresh thyme leaves
4 sun-dried tomatoes

To serve:
freshly cooked mixed rice
tossed green salad

Wipe the fish steaks with a damp cloth or dampened absorbent kitchen paper. Season both sides of the fish to taste with salt and pepper, then place in a shallow bowl and reserve.

Mix together the Pernod, olive oil, lime zest and juice with the fresh thyme leaves. Finely chop the sun-dried tomatoes and add to the Pernod mixture.

Pour the Pernod mixture over the fish and chill in the refrigerator for about 2 hours, occasionally spooning the marinade over the fish.

Heat a griddle or heavy-based frying pan. Drain the fish, reserving the marinade. Cook the fish for 3–4 minutes on each side for a steak that is still slightly pink in the middle. Or, if liked, cook the fish for 1–2 minutes longer on each side if you prefer your fish cooked through.

Put the remaining marinade in a small saucepan and bring to the boil. Pour the marinade over the fish and serve immediately with the mixed rice and salad.

Tuna Cannelloni

SERVES 4

1 tbsp olive oil
6 spring onions, trimmed
    and finely sliced
1 red pepper, deseeded and
    finely chopped
200 g/7 oz can tuna in brine
250 g/7 oz tub ricotta cheese

zest and juice of 1 lemon
1 tbsp freshly
    snipped chives
salt and freshly ground
    black pepper
8 dried cannelloni tubes
1 medium egg, beaten

125 g/4 oz cottage cheese
150 ml/¼ pint plain yogurt
pinch freshly grated nutmeg
50 g/2 oz mozzarella
    cheese, grated
tossed green salad,
    to serve

Preheat oven to 180°C/375°F/Gas Mark 5, 10 minutes before cooking. Heat the olive oil in a frying pan and cook the spring onions and red pepper until soft. Remove from the pan with a slotted spoon and place in large bowl.

Drain the tuna, then stir into the spring onions and pepper mixture. Beat together the ricotta cheese, lemon zest and juice, and snipped chives and until soft and blended. Season to taste with salt and pepper. Add to the tuna and mix together. If the mixture is still a little stiff, add a little extra lemon juice.

With a teaspoon, carefully spoon the mixture into the cannelloni tubes, then lay the filled tubes in a lightly oiled shallow ovenproof dish. Beat together the egg, cottage cheese, yogurt and nutmeg, and pour over the cannelloni. Sprinkle with the grated mozzarella cheese and bake in the preheated oven for 15–20 minutes until the topping is golden brown and bubbling. Serve immediately with a tossed green salad.

HELPFUL HINT

Don't be tempted to part cook the cannelloni tubes before stuffing them; this makes them too slippery to handle. They will cook thoroughly in the sauce while they are baking.

Tuna Fish Burgers

450 g/1 lb potatoes, peeled and cut into chunks
50 g/2 oz butter
2 tbsp milk
400 g/14 oz can tuna in oil
1 spring onion, trimmed and finely chopped
1 tbsp freshly chopped

parsley
salt and freshly ground black pepper
2 medium eggs, beaten
2 tbsp seasoned plain flour
125 g/4 oz fresh white breadcrumbs
4 tbsp vegetable oil

4 sesame seed baps (optional)

To serve:
fat chips
mixed salad
tomato chutney

Put the potatoes in a large saucepan, cover with boiling water and simmer until soft. Drain, then mash with 40 g/1½ oz of the butter and the milk. Turn into a large bowl. Drain the tuna, discarding the oil, and flake into the bowl of potato. Stir well to mix.

Add the spring onion and parsley to the mixture and season to taste with salt and pepper. Add 1 tablespoon of the beaten egg to bind the mixture together. Chill in the refrigerator for at least 1 hour until firm.

Shape the chilled mixture with your hands into four large burgers. First, coat the burgers with seasoned flour, then brush them with the remaining beaten egg, allowing any excess to drip back into the bowl. Finally, coat them evenly in the breadcrumbs, pressing the crumbs on with your hands, if necessary. If time allows, cover the bread-coated burgers with clingfilm and chill in the refrigerator for 30 minutes before cooking so that they are really firm.

Heat a little of the oil in a frying pan and fry the burgers for 2–3 minutes on each side until golden, adding more oil if necessary. Drain on absorbent kitchen paper and serve hot in baps, if using, with chips, mixed salad and chutney.

HELPFUL HINT
Drain the potatoes thoroughly and dry them over a very low heat before mashing with the milk and butter to ensure that the mixture is not too soft to shape.

Seared Pancetta–wrapped Cod

SERVES 4

4 thick cod fillets, each about
    175 g/6 oz
4 very thin slices pancetta
3 tbsp capers in vinegar
1 tbsp vegetable or

sunflower oil
2 tbsp lemon juice
1 tbsp olive oil
freshly ground black pepper
1 tbsp freshly chopped

parsley, to garnish
To serve:
freshly cooked vegetables
new potatoes

Wipe the cod fillets and wrap each one with the pancetta. Secure each fillet with a cocktail stick and reserve.

Drain the capers and soak in cold water for 10 minutes to remove any excess salt, then drain and reserve.

Heat the oil in a large frying pan and sear the wrapped pieces of cod fillet for about 3 minutes on each side, turning carefully with a fish slice so as not to break up the fish. Reduce the heat, then continue to cook for 2–3 minutes until the fish is cooked thoroughly.

Meanwhile, put the reserved capers, lemon juice and olive oil in a small saucepan and grind over the black pepper. Place the saucepan over a low heat and bring to a gentle simmer, stirring continuously for 2–3 minutes.

Once the fish is cooked, garnish with the parsley and serve with the warm caper dressing, freshly cooked vegetables and new potatoes.

Gingered Cod Steaks

SERVES 4

2.5 cm /1 inch piece
fresh root ginger, peeled
4 spring onions
2 tsp freshly
chopped parsley

1 tbsp soft brown sugar
4 thick cod steaks, each
about 175 g/6 oz
salt and freshly ground
black pepper

25 g/1 oz butter
freshly cooked vegetables,
to serve

Preheat the grill and line the grill rack with a layer of kitchen foil. Coarsely grate the piece of ginger. Trim the spring onions and cut into thin strips.

Mix together the spring onions, ginger, chopped parsley and sugar. Add 1 tablespoon water.

Wipe the fish steaks. Season to taste with salt and pepper. Place on four separate 20.5 x 20.5 cm/8 x 8 inch kitchen foil squares.

Carefully spoon the spring onions and ginger mixture over the fish. Cut the butter into small cubes and dot over the fish. Loosely fold the foil over the steaks to enclose the fish and make a parcel.

Place under the preheated grill and cook for 10–12 minutes until cooked and the flesh has turned opaque.

Transfer the fish parcels to individual serving plates. Serve immediately with the freshly cooked vegetables.

HELPFUL HINT

This recipe also works well with other fish steaks. Try salmon, fresh haddock or monkfish fillets. The monkfish fillets may take a little longer to cook.

Spanish Omelette with Smoked Cod

SERVES 3-4

3 tbsp sunflower oil
350 g/12 oz potatoes,
    peeled and cut into 1 cm/
    ½ inch cubes
2 medium onions, peeled
    and cut into wedges
2–4 large garlic cloves,
    peeled and thinly sliced
1 large red pepper,

quartered, deseeded
    and thinly sliced
125 g/4 oz smoked cod
salt and freshly ground
    black pepper
25 g/1 oz butter, melted
1 tbsp double cream
6 medium eggs, beaten
2 tbsp freshly chopped

flat-leaf parsley
50 g/2 oz mature Cheddar
    cheese, grated

To serve:
crusty bread
tossed green salad,
    to serve

Heat the oil in a large nonstick heavy-based frying pan, add the potatoes, onions and garlic. Cook gently for 10–15 minutes until golden brown, then add the red pepper and cook for a further 3 minutes.

Meanwhile, put the fish in a shallow frying pan and cover with water. Season to taste with salt and pepper, and poach gently for 10 minutes. Drain and flake the fish into a bowl, toss in the melted butter and cream, adjust the seasoning and reserve.

When the vegetables are cooked, drain off any excess oil and stir in the beaten egg with the chopped parsley. Pour the fish mixture over the top and cook gently for 5 minutes, or until the eggs become firm.

Sprinkle the grated cheese over the top and place the pan under a preheated hot grill. Cook for 2–3 minutes until the cheese is golden and bubbling. Carefully slide the omelette onto a large plate and serve immediately with plenty of bread and salad.

HELPFUL HINT
For best results, Spanish omelette should be cooked slowly until set. Finishing the dish under the grill gives it a delicious golden look.

Saucy Cod & Pasta Bake

SERVES 4

450 g/1 lb cod fillets, skinned
2 tbsp sunflower oil
1 onion, peeled and
    chopped
4 rashers smoked streaky
    bacon, rind removed,
    chopped
150 g/5 oz baby button
    mushrooms, wiped

2 celery stalks, trimmed and
    thinly sliced
2 small courgettes, halved
    lengthways and sliced
400 g/14 oz can chopped
    tomatoes
100 ml/3½ fl oz fish stock or
    dry white wine
1 tbsp freshly chopped

tarragon
salt and freshly ground
    black pepper

For the pasta topping:
225–275 g/8–10 oz pasta shells
25 g/1 oz butter
4 tbsp plain flour
450 ml/¾ pint milk

Preheat the oven to 200°C/400°F/Gas Mark 6, 15 minutes before cooking. Cut the cod into bite-size pieces and reserve.

Heat the sunflower oil in a large saucepan, add the onion and bacon, and cook for 7–8 minutes. Add the mushrooms and celery, and cook for 5 minutes, or until fairly soft.

Add the courgettes and tomatoes to the bacon mixture and pour in the fish stock or wine. Bring to the boil, then simmer uncovered for 5 minutes, or until the sauce has thickened slightly. Remove from the heat and stir in the cod pieces and the tarragon. Season to taste with salt and pepper, then spoon into a large oiled baking dish.

Meanwhile, bring a large pan of lightly salted water to a rolling boil. Add the pasta shells and cook according to the packet instructions, or until *al dente*. Drain thoroughly.

For the topping, put the butter and flour in a saucepan and pour in the milk. Bring to the boil slowly, whisking until thickened and smooth. Stir the drained pasta into the sauce. Spoon carefully over the fish and vegetables. Bake in the preheated oven for 20–25 minutes until the top is lightly browned and bubbling.

HELPFUL HINT

For a speedier topping, beat together 2 eggs, 3 tablespoons Greek yogurt and 3 tablespoons double cream; season. Add the pasta and mix. Spoon on top of the filling and bake for 15–20 minutes.

Pappardelle with Smoked Haddock & Blue Cheese Sauce

SERVES 4

350 g/12 oz smoked haddock
2 bay leaves
300 ml/½ pint milk
400 g/14 oz pappardelle
    or tagliatelle
25 g/1 oz butter
25 g/1 oz plain flour

150 ml/¼ pint single cream
    or extra milk
125 g/4 oz Dolcelatte cheese
    or Gorgonzola, cut into
    small pieces
¼ tsp freshly grated nutmeg
salt and freshly ground

black pepper
40 g/1½ oz toasted
    walnuts, chopped
1 tbsp freshly
    chopped parsley

Put the smoked haddock in a saucepan with 1 bay leaf and pour in the milk. Bring to the boil slowly, cover and simmer for 6–7 minutes until the fish is opaque. Remove and roughly flake the fish, discarding the skin and any bones. Strain the milk and reserve.

Bring a large pan of lightly salted water to a rolling boil. Add the pasta and cook according to the packet instructions, or until *al dente.*

Meanwhile, put the butter, flour and single cream or milk, if preferred, in a pan and stir to mix. Stir in the reserved warm poaching milk and add the remaining bay leaf. Bring to the boil, whisking all the time until smooth and thick. Gently simmer for 3–4 minutes, stirring frequently. Discard the bay leaf.

Add the Dolcelatte or Gorgonzola cheese to the sauce. Heat gently, stirring until melted. Add the flaked haddock and season with the nutmeg and salt and pepper to taste.

Drain the pasta thoroughly and return to the pan. Add the sauce and toss gently to coat, taking care not to break up the flakes of fish. Tip into a warmed serving bowl, sprinkle with toasted walnuts and parsley, and serve immediately.

Smoked Haddock Rosti

SERVES 4

450 g/1 lb potatoes, peeled and coarsely grated
1 large onion, peeled and coarsely grated
2–3 garlic cloves, peeled and crushed

450 g/1 lb smoked haddock
1 tbsp olive oil
salt and freshly ground black pepper
finely grated zest of ½ lemon
1 tbsp freshly

chopped parsley
2 tbsp crème fraîche
mixed salad leaves, to garnish
lemon wedges, to serve

Dry the grated potatoes in a clean tea towel. Rinse the grated onion thoroughly in cold water, dry in a clean tea towel and add to the potatoes. Stir the garlic into the potato mixture.

Skin the smoked haddock and remove as many of the tiny pin bones as possible. Cut into thin slices and reserve.

Heat the oil in a nonstick frying pan. Add half the potato mixture and press down well in the frying pan. Season to taste with salt and pepper.

Add a layer of fish and a sprinkling of lemon zest, parsley and a little black pepper. Top with the remaining potatoes and press down firmly. Cover with a sheet of kitchen foil and cook over the lowest heat possible for 25–30 minutes.

Preheat the grill 2–3 minutes before the end of cooking time. Remove the foil and place the rosti under the grill to brown. Turn out onto a warmed serving dish, and serve immediately with spoonfuls of crème fraîche, lemon wedges and mixed salad leaves.

HELPFUL HINT

Use smoked haddock fillets. Finnan or Arbroath smokies would be too bony for this dish.

Smoked Haddock Kedgeree

SERVES 4

450 g/1 lb smoked
   haddock fillets
50 g/2 oz butter
1 onion, peeled and
   finely chopped
2 tsp mild curry powder

175 g/6 oz long-grain rice
450 ml/¾ pint fish or
   vegetable stock, heated
2 large eggs, hard-boiled
   and shelled
2 tbsp freshly

chopped parsley
2 tbsp whipping cream
   (optional)
salt and freshly ground
   black pepper
pinch cayenne pepper

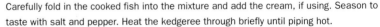

Put the haddock in a shallow frying pan and cover with 300 ml/½ pint water. Simmer gently for 8–10 minutes until the fish is cooked. Drain, then remove and discard all the skin and bones from the fish. Flake the flesh into a dish. Keep warm.

Melt the butter in a saucepan and add the chopped onion and curry powder. Cook, stirring, for 3–4 minutes until the onion is soft, then stir in the rice. Cook for a further minute, stirring continuously, then stir in the hot stock.

Cover and simmer gently for 15 minutes, or until the rice has absorbed all the liquid. Cut the eggs into quarters or eighths, and add half to the mixture with half the parsley.

Carefully fold in the cooked fish into the mixture and add the cream, if using. Season to taste with salt and pepper. Heat the kedgeree through briefly until piping hot.

Transfer the mixture to a large dish and garnish with the remaining quartered eggs and parsley, and serve with a pinch of cayenne pepper sprinkled over the top. Serve immediately.

Chunky Halibut Casserole

50 g/2 oz butter
  or margarine
2 large onions, peeled
  and sliced into rings
1 red pepper, deseeded
  and roughly chopped
450 g/1 lb potatoes, peeled
450 g/1 lb courgettes,

trimmed and thickly sliced
2 tbsp plain flour
1 tbsp paprika
2 tsp vegetable oil
300 ml/½ pint white wine
150 ml/¼ pint fish stock
400 g/14 oz can chopped
  tomatoes

2 tbsp freshly chopped basil
salt and freshly ground
  black pepper
450 g/1 lb halibut fillet,
  skinned and cut into
  2.5 cm/1 inch cubes
fresh basil sprigs, to garnish
freshly cooked rice, to serve

Melt the butter or margarine in a large saucepan, add the onions and red pepper, and cook for 5 minutes, or until softened.

Cut the peeled potatoes into 2.5 cm/1 inch dice, rinse lightly and shake dry, then add them to the onions and pepper in the saucepan. Add the courgettes and cook, stirring frequently, for a further 2–3 minutes.

Sprinkle the flour, paprika and vegetable oil into the saucepan and cook, stirring continuously, for 1 minute. Pour in 150 ml/¼ pint of the wine, all of the stock and the chopped tomatoes, and bring to the boil.

Add the basil to the casserole, season to taste with salt and pepper, and cover. Simmer for 15 minutes, then add the halibut and the remaining wine, and simmer very gently for a further 5–7 minutes until the fish and vegetables are just tender. Garnish with basil sprigs and serve immediately with freshly cooked rice.

Pasta Provençale

SERVES 4

2 tbsp olive oil
1 garlic clove, peeled and crushed
1 onion, peeled and finely chopped
1 small fennel bulb, trimmed, halved and thinly sliced

400 g/14 oz can chopped tomatoes
1 fresh rosemary sprig, plus extra sprig, to garnish
350 g/12 oz monkfish, skinned
2 tsp lemon juice
400 g/14 oz gnocchi pasta

50 g/2 oz pitted black olives
200 g/7 oz can flageolet beans, drained and rinsed
1 tbsp freshly chopped oregano, plus extra sprig, to garnish
salt and freshly ground black pepper

Heat the olive oil in a large saucepan, add the garlic and onion, and cook gently for 5 minutes. Add the fennel and cook for a further 5 minutes. Stir in the chopped tomatoes and rosemary sprig. Half-cover the pan and simmer for 10 minutes.

Cut the monkfish into bite-size pieces and sprinkle with the lemon juice. Add to the tomatoes, cover and simmer gently for 5 minutes, or until the fish is opaque.

Meanwhile, bring a large pan of lightly salted water to a rolling boil. Add the pasta and cook according to the packet instructions, or until *al dente*. Drain the pasta thoroughly and return to the saucepan.

Remove the rosemary from the tomato sauce. Stir in the black olives, flageolet beans and chopped oregano, then season to taste with salt and pepper. Add the sauce to the pasta and toss together gently to coat, taking care not to break up the monkfish. Tip into a warmed serving bowl. Garnish with the extra rosemary and oregano sprigs, and serve immediately.

HELPFUL HINT

Only the tail of the monkfish is eaten and is usually sold skinned. It may still have a tough transparent membrane covering it, which should be carefully removed before cooking.

Mediterranean Fish Stew

SERVES 4-6

4 tbsp olive oil
1 onion, peeled and finely sliced
5 garlic cloves, peeled and finely sliced
1 fennel bulb, trimmed and finely chopped
3 celery stalks, trimmed and finely chopped

400 g/14 oz can chopped tomatoes with Italian herbs
1 tbsp freshly chopped oregano
1 bay leaf
grated zest and juice of 1 orange
1 tsp saffron strands
750 ml/1¼ pints fish stock

3 tbsp dry vermouth
salt and freshly ground black pepper
225 g/8 oz thick haddock fillets
225 g/8 oz sea bass or bream fillets
225 g/8 oz raw tiger prawns, peeled and deveined
crusty bread, to serve

Heat the olive oil in a large saucepan. Add the onion, garlic, fennel and celery, and cook over a low heat for 15 minutes, stirring frequently, until the vegetables are soft and just beginning to turn brown.

Add the canned tomatoes with their juice, oregano, bay leaf, orange zest and juice, and saffron strands. Bring to the boil, then reduce the heat and simmer for 5 minutes. Add the fish stock and vermouth, and season to taste with salt and pepper. Bring to the boil. Reduce the heat and simmer for 20 minutes.

Wipe or rinse the haddock and bass fillets, and remove as many of the bones as possible. Place on a chopping board and cut into 5 cm/2 inch cubes. Add to the saucepan and cook for 3 minutes. Add the prawns and cook for a further 5 minutes. Adjust the seasoning to taste and serve with fresh crusty bread.

HELPFUL HINT

Use the list of fish here as a guideline – any combination of fish and shellfish that you prefer will work well in a stew such as this.

Fish Crumble

SERVES 6

450 g/1 lb whiting or
   halibut fillets
300 ml/½ pint milk
salt and freshly ground
   black pepper
1 tbsp sunflower oil
75 g/3 oz butter or margarine
1 medium onion, peeled
   and finely chopped

2 leeks, trimmed and sliced
1 medium carrot, peeled and
   cut into small dice
2 medium potatoes, peeled
   and cut into small pieces
75 g/3 oz plain flour
300 ml/½ pint fish or
   vegetable stock
2 tbsp whipping cream

1 tsp freshly chopped dill
runner beans, to serve

For the crumble topping:
75 g/3 oz butter or margarine
175 g/6 oz plain flour
75 g/3 oz Parmesan
   cheese, grated
¾ tsp cayenne pepper

Preheat the oven to 200°C/400°F/Gas Mark 6, 15 minutes before cooking. Oil a 1.4 litre/ 2½ pint pie dish. Put the fish in a saucepan with the milk and season to taste with salt and pepper. Bring to the boil, cover and simmer for 8–10 minutes until the fish is cooked. Remove with a slotted spoon, reserving the cooking liquid. Flake the fish into the prepared dish.

Heat the oil and 1 tablespoon of the butter or margarine in a small frying pan and gently fry the onion, leeks, carrot and potatoes for 1–2 minutes. Cover tightly and cook over a gentle heat for a further 10 minutes until softened. Spoon the vegetables over the fish.

Melt the remaining butter or margarine in a saucepan, add the flour and cook for 1 minute, stirring. Whisk in the reserved cooking liquid and the stock. Cook until thickened, then stir in the cream. Remove from the heat and stir in the dill. Pour over the fish.

To make the crumble, rub the butter or margarine into the flour until the mixture resembles breadcrumbs, then stir in the cheese and cayenne pepper. Sprinkle over the dish, and bake in the preheated oven for 20 minutes until piping hot. Serve with runner beans.

Traditional Fish Pie

SERVES 4

450 g/1 lb cod or coley fillets, skinned	900 g/2 lb potatoes, peeled and cut into chunks	198 g/7 oz can sweetcorn, drained
450 ml/¾ pint milk	100 g/3½ oz butter	2 tbsp freshly chopped parsley
1 small onion, peeled and quartered	125 g/4 oz large raw prawns, peeled and deveined	3 tbsp plain flour
salt and freshly ground black pepper	2 large eggs, hard-boiled and quartered	50 g/2 oz Cheddar cheese, grated

Preheat the oven to 200°C/400°F/Gas Mark 6, about 15 minutes before cooking. Put the fish in a shallow frying pan, pour over 300 ml/½ pint of the milk and add the onion. Season to taste with salt and pepper. Bring to the boil and simmer for 8–10 minutes until the fish is cooked. Remove the fish with a slotted spoon and place in a 1.4 litre/2½ pint baking dish. Strain the cooking liquid and reserve.

Boil the potatoes until soft, then mash with 40 g/1½ oz of the butter and 2–3 tablespoons of the remaining milk. Reserve.

Arrange the prawns and sliced eggs on top of the fish, then scatter over the sweetcorn and sprinkle with the parsley.

Melt the remaining butter in a saucepan, stir in the flour and cook gently for 1 minute, stirring. Whisk in the reserved cooking liquid and remaining milk. Cook for 2 minutes, or until thickened, then pour over the fish mixture and cool slightly.

Spread the mashed potato over the top of the pie and sprinkle over the grated cheese. Bake in the preheated oven for 30 minutes until golden. Serve immediately.

TASTY TIP

Any variety of white fish may be used here, including haddock, hake, pollack and whiting. You could also used smoked cod or haddock. After simmering in milk, carefully check and remove any bones.

Coconut Fish Curry

SERVES 4

2 tbsp sunflower oil
1 medium onion, peeled
   and very finely chopped
1 yellow pepper, deseeded
   and finely chopped
1 garlic clove, peeled
   and crushed
1 tbsp mild curry paste
2.5 cm/1 inch piece fresh root
   ginger, peeled and grated

1 red chilli, deseeded and
   finely chopped
400 ml can coconut milk
700 g/1½ lb firm white fish,
   e.g. monkfish fillets, skinned
   and cut into chunks
225 g/8 oz basmati rice
1 tbsp freshly
   chopped coriander
1 tbsp mango chutney

salt and freshly ground
   black pepper

To garnish:
lime wedges
fresh coriander sprigs

To serve:
Greek-style yogurt
warm naan bread

Put 1 tablespoon of the oil into a large frying pan and cook the onion, pepper and garlic for 5 minutes, or until soft. Add the remaining oil, curry paste, ginger and chilli and cook for a further minute.

Pour in the coconut milk and bring to the boil, reduce the heat and simmer gently for 5 minutes, stirring occasionally. Add the monkfish to the pan and continue to simmer gently for 5–10 minutes until the fish is tender, but not overcooked.

Meanwhile, cook the rice in a saucepan of boiling salted water for 15 minutes, or until tender. Drain the rice thoroughly and turn out into a serving dish.

Stir the chopped coriander and chutney gently into the fish curry and season to taste with salt and pepper. Spoon the fish curry over the cooked rice, garnish with lime wedges and coriander sprigs and serve immediately with spoonfuls of Greek yogurt and warm naan bread.

Crispy Prawn Stir-fry

SERVES 4

3 tbsp soy sauce
1 tsp cornflour
pinch sugar
6 tbsp groundnut oil
450 g/1 lb raw peeled and deveined tiger prawns, halved lengthways

125 g/4 oz carrots, peeled and cut into matchsticks
2.5 cm/1 inch piece fresh root ginger, peeled and cut into matchsticks
125 g/4 oz mangetout peas, trimmed and shredded

125 g/4 oz fresh asparagus spears, cut into short lengths
125 g/4 oz beansprouts
¼ head Chinese leaves, shredded
2 tsp sesame oil

Mix together the soy sauce, cornflour and sugar in a small bowl and reserve.

Heat a large wok, then add 3 tablespoons of the oil and heat until almost smoking. Add the prawns and stir-fry for 4 minutes, or until pink all over. Using a slotted spoon, transfer the prawns to a plate and keep warm in a low oven.

Add the remaining oil to the wok and, when just smoking, add the carrots and ginger, and stir-fry for 1 minute, or until slightly softened, then add the mangetout and stir-fry for a further 1 minute. Add the asparagus and stir-fry for 4 minutes, or until softened.

Add the beansprouts and Chinese leaves and stir-fry for 2 minutes, or until the leaves are slightly wilted. Pour in the soy sauce mixture and return the prawns to the wok. Stir-fry over a medium heat until piping hot, then add the sesame oil, give a final stir and serve immediately.

HELPFUL HINT

The long list of ingredients need not be daunting. Good preparation saves a lot of time. Cut everything into small, uniform pieces and have everything ready before starting to cook.

Szechuan Chilli Prawns

SERVES 4

450 g/1 lb raw tiger prawns
2 tbsp groundnut oil
1 onion, peeled and sliced
1 red pepper, deseeded and
   cut into strips
1 small red chilli, deseeded
   and thinly sliced
2 garlic cloves, peeled

and finely chopped
2–3 spring onions, trimmed
   and diagonally sliced
chilli flowers or fresh
   coriander sprigs,
   to garnish
freshly cooked rice or
   noodles, to serve

For the chilli sauce:
1 tbsp cornflour
4 tbsp cold fish stock
   or water
2 tbsp soy sauce
2 tbsp sweet or hot chilli
   sauce, or to taste
2 tsp soft light brown sugar

Peel the prawns, leaving the tails attached if you like. Using a sharp knife, remove the black vein along the back of the prawns. Rinse and pat dry with absorbent kitchen paper.

Heat a wok or large frying pan, add the oil and, when hot, add the onion, red pepper and chilli, and stir-fry for 4–5 minutes until the vegetables are tender but retain a bite. Stir in the garlic and cook for 30 seconds. Using a slotted spoon, transfer to a plate and reserve.

Add the prawns to the wok and stir-fry for 1–2 minutes, or until they turn pink and opaque.

Blend together all the chilli sauce ingredients in a bowl or jug, then stir into the prawns. Add the reserved vegetables and bring to the boil, stirring constantly. Cook for 1–2 minutes until the sauce is thickened and the prawns and vegetables are well coated.

Stir in the spring onions, tip onto a warmed platter and garnish with chilli flowers or coriander sprigs. Serve immediately with freshly cooked rice or noodles.

Cheesy Vegetable & Prawn Bake

SERVES 4

175 g/6 oz long-grain rice
salt and freshly ground
   black pepper
1 garlic clove, peeled
   and crushed
1 large egg, beaten
3 tbsp freshly shredded basil

4 tbsp Parmesan
   cheese, grated
125 g/4 oz fresh baby
   asparagus spears,
   trimmed
150 g/5 oz baby carrots,
   trimmed

150 g/5 oz fine green
   beans, trimmed
150 g/5 oz cherry tomatoes
175 g/6 oz peeled prawns,
   thawed if frozen
125 g/4 oz mozzarella
   cheese, thinly sliced

Preheat the oven to 200°C/400°F/Gas Mark 6, about 10 minutes before required. Cook the rice in lightly salted boiling water for 12–15 minutes until tender; drain. Stir in the garlic, beaten egg, shredded basil and 2 tablespoons of the Parmesan cheese, and season to taste with salt and pepper. Press this mixture into a greased 23 cm/9 inch square ovenproof dish and reserve.

Bring a large saucepan of water to the boil, then drop in the asparagus, carrots and green beans. Return to the boil and cook for 3–4 minutes. Drain and leave to cool.

Quarter or halve the cherry tomatoes and mix them into the cooled vegetables. Spread the prepared vegetables over the rice and top with the prawns. Season to taste with salt and pepper.

Cover the prawns with the mozzarella and sprinkle over the remaining Parmesan cheese. Bake in the preheated oven for 20–25 minutes until piping hot and golden brown in places. Serve immediately.

FOOD FACT

Mozzarella cheese becomes stringy when cooked, so should be sliced as thinly as possible here.

Scallops with Black Bean Sauce

SERVES 4

700 g/1½ lb scallops,
with their coral
2 tbsp vegetable oil
2–3 tbsp Chinese fermented
black beans, rinsed,
drained and coarsely
chopped
2 garlic cloves, peeled and
finely chopped
4 cm/1½ inch piece fresh
root ginger, peeled and
finely chopped
4–5 spring onions, thinly
sliced diagonally
2–3 tbsp soy sauce
1½ tbsp Chinese rice wine
or dry sherry
1–2 tsp sugar
1 tbsp fish stock or water
2 or 3 dashes hot pepper
sauce
1 tbsp sesame oil
freshly cooked noodles,
to serve

Pat the scallops dry with absorbent kitchen paper. Carefully separate the orange coral from the scallop. Peel off and discard the membrane and thickish opaque muscle that attaches the coral to the scallop. Cut any large scallops in half crossways; leave the corals whole.

Heat a wok or large frying pan, add the oil and, when hot, add the white scallop meat and stir-fry for 2 minutes, or until just beginning to colour on the edges. Using a slotted spoon or spatula, transfer to a plate. Reserve.

Add the black beans, garlic and ginger to the wok or pan, and stir-fry for 1 minute. Add the spring onions, soy sauce, Chinese rice wine or sherry, sugar, fish stock or water, hot pepper sauce and the corals and stir until mixed.

Return the scallops and any juices to the wok and stir-fry gently for 3 minutes, or until the scallops and corals are just cooked through. Add a little more stock or water if necessary. Stir in the sesame oil and turn into a heated serving dish. Serve immediately with noodles.

Mussels Arrabbiata

SERVES 4

1.8 kg/4 lb mussels
3–4 tbsp olive oil
1 large onion, peeled
   and sliced
4 garlic cloves, peeled
   and finely chopped

1 red chilli, deseeded and
   finely chopped
3 x 400 g/14 oz cans
   chopped tomatoes
150 ml/¼ pint white wine
175 g/6 oz black olives,

   pitted and halved
salt and freshly ground
   black pepper
2 tbsp freshly
   chopped parsley
warm crusty bread, to serve

Clean the mussels by scrubbing with a small, soft brush, removing the beard and any barnacles from the shells. Discard any mussels that are open or have damaged shells. Put the scrubbed mussels in a large bowl and cover with cold water. Change the water frequently before cooking and leave in the refrigerator until required (for up to 8 hours).

Meanwhile, heat the olive oil in a large saucepan and sweat the onion, garlic and chilli until soft but not coloured. Add the chopped tomatoes and bring to the boil, then simmer for 15 minutes.

Pour the white wine into the tomato sauce, bring the sauce to the boil and add the mussels. Cover and carefully shake the pan. Cook the mussels for 5–7 minutes until the shells have opened.

Add the olives to the pan and cook uncovered for about 5 minutes to warm through. Season to taste with salt and pepper, and sprinkle in the chopped parsley. Discard any mussels that have not opened and serve immediately with lots of warm crusty bread.

Meat

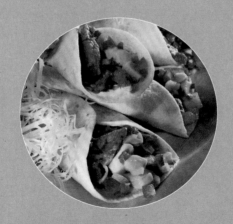

Grilled Steaks with Saffron Potatoes & Roast Tomatoes

SERVES 4

700 g/1½ lb new potatoes, halved
a few saffron strands
300 ml/½ pint vegetable or beef stock
1 small onion, peeled and finely chopped
75 g/3 oz butter
salt and freshly ground black pepper
2 tsp balsamic vinegar
2 tbsp olive oil
1 tsp caster sugar
8 plum tomatoes, halved
4 boneless sirloin steaks, each about 225 g/8 oz
2 tbsp freshly chopped parsley

Cook the potatoes in boiling salted water for 8 minutes and drain well. Return the potatoes to the saucepan, along with the saffron, stock, onion and 25 g/1 oz of the butter. Season to taste with salt and pepper, and simmer, uncovered, for 10 minutes until the potatoes are tender.

Meanwhile, preheat the grill to medium. Mix together the vinegar, olive oil, sugar and seasoning in a small bowl or jug. Arrange the tomatoes cut-side up in a foil-lined grill pan and drizzle over the dressing. Grill for 12–15 minutes, basting occasionally, until tender.

Melt the remaining butter in a frying pan. When it is foaming add the steaks and cook for 4–8 minutes to taste and depending on thickness. (As a rough guide a 2 cm/¾ inch thick steak will take about 2 minutes on each side for rare, 3–4 minutes on each side for medium and 6–7 minutes on each side for well done.)

Arrange the potatoes and tomatoes in the centre of four serving plates. Top with the steaks, along with any pan juices. Sprinkle over the parsley and serve immediately.

HELPFUL HINT

You can tell how well a steak is cooked by lightly pressing on it with your fingertips – the less the resistance, the rarer the meat.

Fillet Steaks with Tomato & Garlic Sauce

SERVES 4

700 g/1½ lb ripe tomatoes
2 tbsp olive oil
2 garlic cloves, peeled and chopped
2 tbsp freshly chopped basil
2 tbsp freshly chopped oregano
2 tbsp red wine
salt and freshly ground black pepper
75 g/3 oz pitted black olives, chopped
4 fillet steaks, each about 175 g/6 oz
freshly cooked vegetables, to serve

Using a sharp knife, make a small cross in the base of each tomato and place in a large bowl. Cover with boiling water and leave for 2 minutes. Using a slotted spoon, remove each tomato and skin carefully. Repeat until all the tomatoes have been skinned. Place on a chopping board, cut into quarters and remove and discard the seeds. Roughly chop the flesh, then reserve.

Heat half the olive oil in a saucepan and cook the garlic for 30 seconds. Add the reserved chopped tomatoes with the basil, oregano and red wine, and season to taste with salt and pepper. Bring to the boil, then reduce the heat, cover and simmer for 15 minutes, stirring occasionally, or until the sauce is reduced and thickened. Stir the olives into the sauce and keep warm while cooking the steaks.

Lightly oil a griddle pan or heavy-based frying pan with the remaining olive oil and cook the steaks for 2 minutes on each side to seal. Continue to cook the steaks for a further 2–4 minutes, depending on personal preference. Serve the steaks immediately with the tomato and garlic sauce and freshly cooked vegetables.

HELPFUL HINT

Raw fillet steak should be a deep mahogany with a good marbling of fat. If the meat is bright red or the fat bright white, the meat has not been aged properly and will probably be quite tough.

Pasta with Beef, Capers & Olives

SERVES 4

2 tbsp olive oil
300 g/11 oz rump steak, trimmed and cut into strips
4 spring onions, trimmed and sliced
2 garlic cloves, peeled and chopped
2 courgettes, trimmed and cut into strips
1 red pepper, deseeded and cut into strips
2 tsp freshly chopped oregano
2 tbsp capers, drained and rinsed
4 tbsp pitted black olives, sliced
400 g/14 oz can chopped tomatoes
salt and freshly ground black pepper
450 g/1 lb fettuccine
1 tbsp freshly chopped parsley, to garnish

Heat the olive oil in a large frying pan over a high heat. Add the steak and cook, stirring, for 3–4 minutes until browned. (Cook it in two batches, so there is plenty of room to move it around the pan.) Remove from the pan using a slotted spoon and reserve.

Reduce the heat, add the spring onions and garlic to the pan and cook for 1 minute. Add the courgettes and red pepper, and cook for 3–4 minutes.

Add the oregano, capers and olives to the pan with the chopped tomatoes. Season to taste with salt and pepper, then simmer for 7 minutes, stirring occasionally. Return the beef to the pan and simmer for 3–5 minutes until the sauce has thickened slightly.

Meanwhile, bring a large pan of lightly salted water to a rolling boil. Add the pasta and cook according to the packet instructions, or until *al dente*.

Drain the pasta thoroughly. Return to the pan and add the beef sauce. Toss gently until the pasta is lightly coated. Tip into a warmed serving dish or onto individual plates. Sprinkle with chopped parsley and serve immediately.

TASTY TIP

It is important that the beef fries rather than steams, giving a beautifully brown and caramelised outside, while keeping the middle moist and tender. Make sure that the oil in the pan is hot.

Spaghetti Bolognese

SERVES 4

1 carrot
2 celery stalks
1 onion
2 garlic cloves
450 g/1 lb lean minced beef
225 g/8 oz smoked streaky
  bacon, chopped

1 tbsp plain flour
150 ml/¼ pint red wine
400 g/14 oz can chopped
  tomatoes
2 tbsp tomato purée
2 tsp dried mixed herbs
salt and freshly ground

black pepper
pinch sugar
350 g/12 oz spaghetti
fresh oregano sprigs,
  to garnish
shavings of Parmesan
  cheese, to serve

Peel and chop the carrot, trim and chop the celery, then peel and chop the onion and garlic. Heat a large nonstick frying pan and sauté the beef and bacon for 5–10 minutes, stirring occasionally, until browned. Add the prepared vegetables to the frying pan and cook for about 3 minutes until softened, stirring occasionally.

Add the flour and cook for 1 minute. Stir in the red wine, chopped tomatoes, tomato purée, mixed herbs, salt and pepper to taste and a pinch of sugar. Bring to the boil, then cover and simmer for 45 minutes, stirring occasionally.

Meanwhile, bring a large saucepan of lightly salted water to the boil and cook the spaghetti for 10–12 minutes until *al dente*. Drain well and divide among four serving plates. Spoon over the sauce, garnish with a few sprigs of oregano and serve immediately with plenty of Parmesan shavings.

Traditional Lasagne

1 tbsp olive oil
450 g/1 lb lean minced beef
175 g/6 oz pancetta or
   smoked streaky bacon,
   chopped
1 large onion, peeled
   and chopped
2 celery stalks, trimmed
   and chopped
125 g/4 oz button
   mushrooms, wiped
   and chopped

2 garlic cloves, peeled
   and chopped
90 g/3½ oz plain flour
300 ml/½ pint beef stock
1 tbsp freeze-dried
   mixed herbs
5 tbsp tomato purée
salt and freshly ground
   black pepper
75 g/3 oz butter
1 tsp English
   mustard powder

pinch freshly grated nutmeg
900 ml/1½ pints milk
125 g/4 oz Parmesan
   cheese, grated
125 g/4 oz Cheddar
   cheese, grated
8–12 precooked lasagne
   sheets

To serve:
crusty bread
fresh green salad leaves

Preheat oven to 200°C/400°F/Gas Mark 6, 15 minutes before cooking. Heat the oil in a frying pan and cook the beef and pancetta or bacon in a large saucepan for 10 minutes, stirring to break up any lumps. Add the onion, celery and mushrooms, and cook for 4 minutes, or until softened slightly. Stir in the garlic and 1 tablespoon of the flour, then cook for 1 minute. Stir in the stock, herbs and tomato purée. Season to taste with salt and pepper. Bring to the boil, then cover, reduce the heat and simmer gently for 45 minutes.

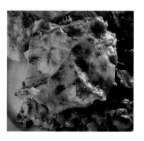

Meanwhile, melt the butter in a small saucepan and stir in the remaining flour, mustard powder and nutmeg until well blended. Cook for 2 minutes. Remove from the heat and gradually blend in the milk until smooth. Return to the heat and bring to the boil, stirring, until thickened. Gradually stir in half the Parmesan and Cheddar cheeses until melted. Season to taste. Spoon half the meat mixture into the bottom of a large ovenproof dish. Top with a single layer of pasta. Spread over half the sauce and scatter with half the cheese. Repeat the layers, finishing with cheese. Bake in the preheated oven for 30 minutes, or until the pasta is cooked and the top is golden brown and bubbly. Serve immediately with crusty bread and a green salad.

Beef Fajitas with Avocado Salsa

SERVES 3-6

2 tbsp sunflower oil
450 g/1 lb beef fillet or rump
   steak, trimmed and cut
   into thin strips
2 garlic cloves, peeled
   and crushed
1 tsp ground cumin
¼ tsp cayenne pepper
1 tbsp paprika

230 g/8 oz can chopped
   tomatoes
215 g/7 oz can red kidney
   beans, drained
1 tbsp freshly
   chopped coriander
1 avocado
1 shallot, peeled and
   chopped

1 large tomato, skinned,
   deseeded and chopped
1 red chilli, diced
1 tbsp lemon juice
6 large flour tortillas
3–4 tbsp sour cream
green salad, to serve

Heat the wok, add the oil, then stir-fry the beef for 3–4 minutes. Add the garlic and spices, and continue to cook for a further 2 minutes. Stir the canned chopped tomatoes into the wok, bring to the boil, cover and simmer gently for 5 minutes.

Meanwhile, blend the kidney beans until slightly broken up (do this in a food processor if you have one), then add to the wok. Continue to cook for a further 5 minutes, adding 2–3 tablespoons water. The mixture should be thick and fairly dry. Stir in the chopped coriander.

Halve and stone the avocado, then peel and chop the flesh into dice. Mix together the chopped avocado, shallot, fresh tomato, chilli and lemon juice. Spoon into a serving dish and reserve.

HELPFUL HINT

Don't make the avocado sauce too far in advance, as avocado has a tendency to discolour. If you do need to make it some time ahead, cover the surface of the sauce with clingfilm.

When ready to serve, warm the tortillas and spread with a little sour cream. Place a spoonful of the beef mixture on top, followed by a spoonful of the avocado sauce, then roll up. Repeat until all the mixture has been used up. Serve immediately with a green salad.

Chilli con Carne with Crispy-skinned Potatoes

SERVES 4

2 tbsp vegetable oil, plus extra for brushing
1 large onion, peeled and finely chopped
1 garlic clove, peeled and finely chopped
1 red chilli, deseeded and finely chopped

450 g/1 lb chuck steak, finely chopped, or lean beef mince
1 tbsp chilli powder
400 g/14 oz can chopped tomatoes
2 tbsp tomato purée
400 g/14 oz can red kidney

beans, drained and rinsed
4 large baking potatoes
coarse salt and freshly ground black pepper

To serve:
ready-made guacamole
sour cream

Preheat the oven to 150°C/300°F/Gas Mark 2. Heat the oil in a large flameproof casserole and add the onion. Cook gently for 10 minutes until soft and lightly browned. Add the garlic and chilli, and cook briefly. Increase the heat. Add the chuck steak or lean mince, and cook for a further 10 minutes, stirring occasionally, until browned.

Sprinkle over the chilli powder and stir well. Cook for about 2 minutes, then add the chopped tomatoes and tomato purée. Bring slowly to the boil. Cover and cook in the preheated oven for 1½ hours. Remove from the oven and stir in the kidney beans. Return to the oven for a further 15 minutes.

Meanwhile, brush a little vegetable oil all over the potatoes and rub on some coarse salt. Put the potatoes in the oven alongside the chilli.

Remove the chilli and potatoes from the oven. Cut a cross in each potato, then squeeze to open slightly and season to taste with salt and pepper. Serve with the chilli, guacamole and sour cream.

TASTY TIP

To make guacamole, mash 1 large peeled, stoned avocado in a bowl with 2 tablespoons each of lemon juice and crème fraîche, ¼ teaspoon Tabasco, 1 crushed garlic clove and salt and pepper.

Spicy Chilli Beef

2 tbsp olive oil
1 onion, peeled and
 finely chopped
1 red pepper, deseeded
 and sliced
450 g/1 lb minced beef
2 garlic cloves, peeled
 and crushed
2 red chillies, deseeded

and finely sliced
salt and freshly ground
 black pepper
400 g/14 oz can chopped
 tomatoes
2 tbsp tomato paste
400 g/14 oz can red kidney
 beans, drained
50 g/2 oz good-quality plain

dark chocolate, grated
350 g/12 oz dried fusilli
knob of butter
2 tbsp freshly chopped
 flat-leaf parsley
paprika, to garnish
sour cream, to serve

Heat the olive oil in a large heavy-based pan. Add the onion and red pepper, and cook for 5 minutes, or until beginning to soften. Add the minced beef and cook over a high heat for 5–8 minutes, or until the meat is browned. Stir with a wooden spoon during cooking to break up any lumps in the meat. Add the garlic and chilli, fry for 1 minute, then season to taste with salt and pepper.

Add the chopped tomatoes, tomato paste and kidney beans to the pan. Bring to the boil, reduce the heat and simmer, covered, for at least 40 minutes, stirring occasionally. Stir in the grated chocolate and cook for 3 minutes, or until melted.

Meanwhile, bring a large pan of lightly salted water to a rolling boil. Add the fusilli and cook according to the packet instructions, or until al dente.

Drain the pasta, return to the pan and toss with the butter and parsley. Tip into a warmed serving dish or spoon onto individual plates. Spoon the sauce over the pasta. Sprinkle with paprika and serve immediately with spoonfuls of sour cream.

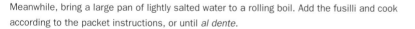

Beef Teriyaki with Green & Black Rice

SERVES 4

3 tbsp sake (Japanese
 rice wine)
3 tbsp dry sherry
3 tbsp dark soy sauce
1½ tbsp soft brown sugar
4 sirloin steaks, each

weighing 175 g/6 oz,
 trimmed
350 g/12 oz long-grain and
 wild rice
2.5 cm/1 inch piece fresh
 root ginger

225 g/8 oz mangetout
salt
6 spring onions, trimmed
 and cut into fine strips

In a small saucepan, gently heat the sake, dry sherry, dark soy sauce and sugar until the sugar has dissolved. Increase the heat and bring to the boil. Remove from the heat and leave until cold. Lightly wipe the steaks, place in a shallow dish and pour the sake mixture over. Cover loosely and leave to marinate in the refrigerator for at least 1 hour, spooning the marinade over the steaks occasionally.

Cook the rice with the piece of root ginger according to the packet instructions. Drain well, then remove and discard the piece of ginger.

Slice the mangetout thinly lengthways into fine shreds. Plunge into a saucepan of boiling salted water, return the water to the boil and drain immediately. Stir the drained mangetout and spring onions into the hot rice.

Meanwhile, heat a griddle pan until almost smoking. Remove the steaks from the marinade and cook on the hot griddle for 3–4 minutes each side, depending on the thickness.

Put the remaining marinade in a saucepan and bring to the boil. Simmer rapidly for 2 minutes and remove from the heat. When the steaks are cooked to personal preference, leave to rest for 2–3 minutes, then slice thinly and serve with the rice and the hot marinade.

Beef with Paprika

SERVES 4

700 g/1½ lb rump steak
3 tbsp plain flour
salt and freshly ground
    black pepper
1 tbsp paprika
350 g/12 oz long-
    grain rice

75 g/3 oz butter
1 tsp vegetable oil
1 onion, peeled and thinly
    sliced into rings
225 g/8 oz button
    mushrooms, wiped
    and sliced

2 tsp dry sherry
150 ml/¼ pint sour cream
2 tbsp freshly
    snipped chives
bundle of fresh chives,
    to garnish

Using a meat mallet or the side of a rolling pin, beat the steak until very thin, then trim off and discard the fat. Cut the steak into thin strips. Season the flour with the salt, pepper and paprika, then toss the steak in the flour until coated.

Meanwhile, put the rice in a saucepan of boiling salted water and simmer for 15 minutes until tender or according to th packet instructions. Drain the rice, then return to the saucepan, add 25 g/1 oz of the butter, cover and keep warm.

Heat the wok, then add the oil and 25 g/1 oz of the butter. When hot, stir-fry the meat for 3–5 minutes until sealed. Remove from the wok with a slotted spoon and reserve. Add the remaining butter to the wok and stir-fry the onion rings and button mushrooms for 3–4 minutes.

Add the sherry while the wok is very hot, then reduce the heat. Return the steak to the wok with the sour cream and seasoning to taste. Heat through until piping hot, then sprinkle with the snipped chives. Garnish with bundles of chives and serve immediately with the cooked rice.

TASTY TIP

The button mushrooms in this recipe could be replaced by exotic or wild mushrooms. Chanterelles go particularly well with beef, as do ceps.

Leek & Ham Risotto

1 tbsp olive oil
25 g/1 oz butter
1 medium onion, peeled
and finely chopped
4 leeks, trimmed and
thinly sliced

1½ tbsp freshly
chopped thyme
350 g/12 oz Arborio rice
1.4 litres/2¼ pints vegetable
or chicken stock, heated
225 g/8 oz cooked ham

175 g/6 oz peas, thawed
if frozen
50 g/2 oz Parmesan cheese,
grated
salt and freshly ground
black pepper

Heat the oil and half the butter together in a large saucepan. Add the onion and leeks, and cook over a medium heat for 6–8 minutes, stirring occasionally, until soft and beginning to colour. Stir in the thyme and cook briefly.

Add the rice and stir well. Continue stirring over a medium heat for about 1 minute until the rice is glossy. Add a ladleful or two of the stock and stir well until the stock is absorbed. Continue adding stock, a ladleful at a time and stirring well between additions, until about two-thirds of the stock has been added.

Meanwhile, either chop or finely shred the ham, then add to the saucepan of rice together with the peas. Continue adding ladlefuls of stock, as described in step 2, until the rice is tender and creamy with just a slight bite, and the ham is heated through thoroughly. You do not have to add all of the stock.

Add the remaining butter, sprinkle over the Parmesan cheese and season to taste with salt and pepper. When the butter has melted and the cheese has softened, stir well to incorporate. Taste and adjust the seasoning, then serve immediately.

Risi e Bisi

SERVES 4

700 g/1½ lb young peas in
    pods or 175 g/6 oz frozen
    petits pois, thawed
25 g/1 oz unsalted butter
1 tsp olive oil
3 rashers pancetta or
    unsmoked back bacon,
    chopped
1 small onion, peeled
    and finely chopped

1 garlic clove, peeled and
    finely chopped
1.3 litres/2¼ pints
    vegetable stock
pinch caster sugar
1 tsp lemon juice
1 bay leaf
200 g/7 oz Arborio rice
3 tbsp freshly
    chopped parsley

50 g/2 oz Parmesan cheese,
    finely grated
salt and freshly ground
    black pepper

To garnish:
fresh parsley sprig
julienne strips of
    orange zest

Shell the peas, if using fresh ones. Melt the butter and olive oil together in a large heavy-based saucepan. Add the chopped pancetta or bacon, chopped onion and garlic, and gently fry for about 10 minutes until the onion is softened and is just beginning to colour.

Add the caster sugar, lemon juice and bay leaf, then pour in the vegetable stock. Add the fresh peas if using. Bring the mixture to a fast boil.

Add the rice, stir and simmer, uncovered, for about 20 minutes until the rice is tender. Occasionally, stir the mixture gently while it cooks. If using frozen petits pois, stir them into the rice about 2 minutes before the end of the cooking time.

When the rice is cooked, remove the bay leaf and discard. Stir in 2½ tablespoons of the chopped parsley and the grated Parmesan cheese. Season to taste with salt and pepper.

Transfer the rice to a large serving dish. Garnish with the remaining chopped parsley, a sprig of fresh parsley and julienne strips of orange zest. Serve immediately while piping hot.

Italian Risotto

1 tbsp olive oil
125 g/4 oz Italian salami or
   speck, chopped
125 g/4 oz fresh asparagus
1 onion, peeled and
   chopped
2 garlic cloves, peeled

and chopped
350 g/12 oz risotto rice
300 ml/½ pt dry white wine
1 litre/1¾ pints chicken
   stock, warmed
125 g/4 oz frozen broad
   beans, defrosted

125g/4 oz Dolcelatte
   cheese, diced
3 tbsp freshly chopped
   mixed herbs, such as
   parsley and basil
salt and freshly ground
   black pepper

Heat the olive oil in a large frying pan and cook the salami for 3–5 minutes until golden. Using a slotted spoon, transfer to a plate and keep warm. Add the asparagus and stir-fry for 2–3 minutes until just wilted. Transfer to the plate with the salami. Add the onion and garlic, and cook for 5 minutes, or until softened.

Add the rice to the pan and cook for about 2 minutes. Add the wine, bring to the boil, then simmer, stirring until the wine has been absorbed. Add half the stock and return to the boil. Simmer, stirring until the liquid has been absorbed.

Add half of the remaining stock and the broad beans to the rice mixture. Bring to the boil, then simmer for a further 5–10 minutes until all of the liquid has been absorbed.

Add the remaining stock, bring to the boil, then simmer until all the liquid is absorbed and the rice is tender. Stir in the remaining ingredients until the cheese has just melted. Serve immediately.

Prosciutto & Gruyère Carbonara

SERVES 4

3 medium egg yolks
50 g/2 oz Gruyère cheese, grated
2 tbsp olive oil
2 garlic cloves, peeled and crushed

2 shallots, peeled and finely chopped
200 g/7 oz prosciutto, cut into strips
4 tbsp dry vermouth
salt and freshly ground

black pepper
450 g/1 lb spaghetti
15 g/½ oz butter
1 tbsp freshly shredded basil leaves
fresh basil sprigs, to garnish

Put the egg yolks in a bowl with 6 tablespoons of the Gruyère cheese and mix lightly until well blended, then reserve.

Heat the olive oil in a large pan and cook the garlic and shallots for 5 minutes, or until golden brown. Add the prosciutto, then cook for a further 1 minute. Pour in the dry vermouth and simmer for 2 minutes, then remove from the heat. Season to taste with salt and pepper, and keep warm.

Meanwhile, bring a large pan of lightly salted water to a rolling boil. Add the pasta and cook according to the packet instructions, or until *al dente*. Drain thoroughly, reserving 4 tablespoons of the cooking water, and return the pasta to the pan.

Remove from the heat, then add the egg and cheese mixture with the butter to the pasta; toss lightly until coated. Add the prosciutto mixture and toss again, adding the reserved pasta water, if needed, to moisten. Season to taste and sprinkle with the remaining Gruyère cheese and the shredded basil leaves. Garnish with basil sprigs and serve immediately.

Special Rosti

SERVES 4

700 g/1½ lb potatoes,
scrubbed but not peeled
75 g/3 oz butter
1 large onion, peeled and
finely chopped
1 garlic clove, peeled
and crushed

2 tbsp freshly chopped
parsley
salt and freshly ground
black pepper
1 tbsp olive oil
75 g/3 oz Parma ham,
thinly sliced

50 g/2 oz sun-dried
tomatoes, chopped
175 g/ 6 oz Emmenthal
cheese, grated
mixed green salad,
to serve

Cook the potatoes in a large saucepan of salted boiling water for about 10 minutes until just tender. Drain in a colander, then rinse in cold water. Drain again. Leave until cool enough to handle, then peel off the skins.

Melt the butter in a large frying pan and gently fry the onion and garlic for about 3 minutes until softened and beginning to colour. Remove from the heat.

Coarsely grate the potatoes into a large bowl, then stir in the onion and garlic mixture. Sprinkle over the parsley and stir well to mix. Season to taste with salt and pepper.

Heat the oil in the frying pan and cover the bottom of the pan with half the potato mixture. Lay the slices of Parma ham on top. Sprinkle with the chopped sun-dried tomatoes, then scatter the grated Emmenthal over the top. Finally, top with the remaining potato mixture.

Cook over a low heat, pressing down with a palette knife from time to time, for 10–15 minutes until the bottom is golden brown. Carefully invert the rosti onto a large plate, then carefully slide back into the pan and cook the other side until golden. Serve cut into wedges with a mixed green salad.

HELPFUL HINT

To make sure the rosti is the right thickness, you will need a heavy-based nonstick frying pan with a diameter of about 23 cm/9 inches.

Gnocchi & Parma Ham Bake

3 tbsp olive oil
1 red onion, peeled
and sliced
2 garlic cloves, peeled
175 g/6 oz plum tomatoes,
skinned and quartered
2 tbsp sun-dried
tomato paste

250 g/9 oz tub mascarpone
cheese
salt and freshly ground
black pepper
1 tbsp freshly
chopped tarragon
300 g/11 oz fresh potato
gnocchi

125 g/4 oz Cheddar or
Parmesan cheese, grated
50 g/2 oz fresh white
breadcrumbs
50 g/2 oz Parma ham, sliced
10 pitted green olives, halved
fresh flat-leaf parsley sprigs,
to garnish

Preheat the oven to 180°C/350°F/Gas Mark 4, 10 minutes before cooking. Heat 2 tablespoons of the olive oil in a large frying pan and cook the onion and garlic for 5 minutes, or until softened. Stir in the tomatoes, sun-dried tomato paste and mascarpone cheese. Season to taste with salt and pepper. Add half the tarragon. Bring to the boil, then reduce the heat immediately and simmer for 5 minutes.

Meanwhile, bring 1.7 litres/3 pints water to the boil in a large pan. Add the remaining olive oil and a good pinch of salt. Add the gnocchi and cook for 1–2 minutes until they rise to the surface.

Drain the gnocchi thoroughly and transfer to a large ovenproof dish. Add the tomato sauce and toss gently to coat the pasta. Combine the Cheddar or Parmesan cheese with the breadcrumbs and remaining tarragon, and scatter over the pasta mixture. Top with the Parma ham and olives and season again.

Cook in the preheated oven for 20–25 minutes until golden and bubbling. Serve immediately, garnished with parsley sprigs.

HELPFUL HINT
Use a large pan of boiling water so that the gnocchi have plenty of room to move around, otherwise they will stick together during cooking. Alternatively, cook the gnocchi in two batches.

Chorizo with Pasta in a Tomato Sauce

SERVES 4

25 g/1 oz butter
2 tbsp olive oil
2 large onions, peeled and
finely sliced
1 tsp soft brown sugar
2 garlic cloves, peeled
and crushed

225 g/8 oz chorizo, sliced
1 chilli, deseeded and
finely sliced
400 g/14 oz can chopped
tomatoes
1 tbsp sun-dried tomato paste
150 ml/¼ pint red wine

salt and freshly ground
black pepper
450 g/1 lb rigatoni
freshly chopped parsley,
to garnish

Melt the butter with the olive oil in a large heavy-based pan. Add the onions and sugar, and cook over a very low heat, stirring occasionally, for 15 minutes, or until soft and starting to caramelise.

Add the garlic and chorizo to the pan and cook for 5 minutes. Stir in the chilli, chopped tomatoes and tomato paste, and pour in the wine. Season well with salt and pepper. Bring to the boil, cover, reduce the heat and simmer for 30 minutes, stirring occasionally. Remove the lid and simmer for a further 10 minutes, or until the sauce starts to thicken.

Meanwhile, bring a large pan of lightly salted water to a rolling boil. Add the pasta and cook according to the packet instructions, or until *al dente*.

Drain the pasta, reserving 2 tablespoons of the cooking water, and return the pasta to the pan. Add the chorizo sauce with the reserved cooking water and toss gently until the pasta is evenly covered. Tip into a warmed serving dish, sprinkle with the parsley and serve immediately.

HELPFUL HINT

Take care when preparing chillies, as the volatile oils in the seeds and the membrane can cause irritation – wash your hands thoroughly afterwards and avoid touching your eyes.

Crispy Baked Potatoes
with Serrano Ham

SERVES 4

4 large baking potatoes
4 tsp crème fraîche
salt and freshly ground
   black pepper
50 g/2 oz lean serrano
   ham or prosciutto, with

fat removed
50 g/2 oz cooked baby
   broad beans
50 g/2 oz cooked
   carrots, diced
50 g/2 oz cooked peas

50 g/2 oz hard cheese
   such as Edam or
   Cheddar, grated
fresh green salad,
   to serve

Preheat the oven to 200°C/400°F/Gas Mark 6. Scrub the potatoes dry. Prick with a fork and place on a baking sheet. Bake in the preheated oven for 1–1½ hours until tender when squeezed. (Use oven gloves or a kitchen towel to pick up the potatoes, as they will be very hot.)

Cut the potatoes in half horizontally and scoop out all the flesh into a bowl, reserving the skins as shells. Spoon the crème fraîche into the bowl and mix thoroughly with the potatoes. Season to taste with a little salt and pepper.

Preheat the grill to high. Cut the ham into strips and carefully stir into the potato mixture with the broad beans, carrots and peas. Pile the mixture back into the reserved potato shells and sprinkle a little grated cheese on the top.

Place under the hot grill and cook until golden and heated through. Serve immediately with a fresh green salad.

Pasta & Pork Ragù

SERVES 4

1 tbsp sunflower oil
1 leek, trimmed and
    thinly sliced
225 g/8 oz pork fillet, diced
1 garlic clove, peeled
    and crushed
2 tsp paprika
¼ tsp cayenne pepper

150 ml/¼ pint white wine
600 ml/1 pint
    vegetable stock
400 g/14 oz can borlotti
    beans, drained and rinsed
2 carrots, peeled and diced
salt and freshly ground
    black pepper

225 g/8 oz fresh
    egg tagliatelle
1 tbsp freshly chopped
    parsley, to garnish
crème fraîche, to serve

Heat the sunflower oil in a large frying pan. Add the sliced leek and cook, stirring frequently, for 5 minutes, or until softened. Add the pork and cook, stirring, for 4 minutes, or until sealed.

Add the crushed garlic, paprika and cayenne pepper to the pan and stir until all the pork is lightly coated in the garlic and pepper mixture.

Pour in the wine and 450 ml/¾ pint of the vegetable stock. Add the borlotti beans and carrots, and season to taste with salt and pepper. Bring the sauce to the boil, then reduce the heat and simmer for 5 minutes.

Meanwhile, put the egg tagliatelle in a large saucepan of lightly salted boiling water, cover and simmer for 5 minutes, or until the pasta is *al dente*.

Drain the pasta, then add to the pork ragù; toss well. Adjust the seasoning, then tip into a warmed serving dish. Sprinkle with chopped parsley and serve with a little crème fraîche.

HELPFUL HINT

Pork fillet, also known as tenderloin, is a very lean and tender cut of pork. It needs little cooking time, and so is perfect for this quick and simple dish.

Pork in Peanut Sauce

450 g/1 lb pork fillet
2 tbsp light soy sauce
1 tbsp vinegar
1 tsp sugar
1 tsp Chinese five-
spice powder
2–4 garlic cloves, peeled
and crushed
2 tbsp groundnut oil

1 large onion, peeled and
finely sliced
125 g/4 oz carrots, peeled
and cut into matchsticks
2 celery stalks, trimmed
and sliced
125 g/4 oz French beans,
trimmed and halved
3 tbsp smooth peanut butter

1 tbsp freshly chopped
flat-leaf parsley

To serve:
freshly cooked basmati
and wild rice
green salad

Remove any fat or sinew from the pork fillet, cut into thin strips and reserve. Blend the soy sauce, vinegar, sugar, Chinese five-spice powder and garlic in a bowl and add the pork. Cover and leave to marinate in the refrigerator for at least 30 minutes.

Drain the pork, reserving any marinade. Heat the wok, then add the oil and, when hot, stir-fry the pork for 3–4 minutes until sealed.

Add the onion, carrots, celery and beans to the wok and stir-fry for 4–5 minutes until the meat is tender and the vegetables are softened.

Blend together the reserved marinade, peanut butter and 2 tablespoons hot water. When smooth, stir into the wok and cook for several minutes more until the sauce is thick and the pork is piping hot. Sprinkle with the chopped parsley and serve immediately with the basmati and wild rice and a green salad.

Pork Goulash & Rice

SERVES 4

700 g/1½ lb boneless
   pork rib chops
1 tbsp olive oil
2 onions, peeled and
   roughly chopped
1 red pepper, deseeded and
   sliced thinly
1 garlic clove, peeled

and crushed
1 tbsp plain flour
1 rounded tbsp paprika
400 g/14 oz can chopped
   tomatoes
salt and freshly ground
   black pepper
250 g/9 oz long-grain

white rice
450 ml/¾ pint chicken stock
fresh flat-leaf parsley sprigs,
   to garnish
150 ml/¼ pint sour cream,
   to serve

Preheat the oven to 140°C/275°F/Gas Mark 1. Cut the pork into large cubes, about 4 cm/1½ inches square. Heat the oil in a large flameproof casserole and brown the pork in batches over a high heat, transferring the cubes to a plate as they brown.

Over a medium heat, add the onions and pepper and cook for about 5 minutes, stirring regularly, until they begin to brown. Add the garlic and return the meat to the casserole, along with any juices on the plate. Sprinkle in the flour and paprika, and stir well to soak up the oil and juices.

Add the tomatoes and season to taste with salt and pepper. Bring slowly to the boil, cover with a tight-fitting lid and cook in the preheated oven for 1½ hours.

Meanwhile, rinse the rice in several changes of water until the water remains relatively clear. Drain well and put in a saucepan with the chicken stock or water, and a little salt. Cover tightly and bring to the boil. Reduce the heat to as low as possible and cook for 10 minutes, without removing the lid. After 10 minutes, remove from the heat and leave to stand for a further 10 minutes, without removing the lid. Fluff up the grains with a fork.

When the meat is tender, lightly stir in the sour cream to create a marbled effect, or serve separately. Garnish with parsley and serve immediately with the rice.

Pork Cabbage Parcels

SERVES 4

8 large green cabbage
leaves, such as Savoy
1 tbsp vegetable oil
2 celery stalks, trimmed
and chopped
1 carrot, peeled and cut
into matchsticks
125 g/4 oz pork mince
50 g/2 oz button

mushrooms, wiped
and sliced
1 tsp Chinese five-spice
powder
50 g/2 oz cooked
long-grain rice
juice of 1 lemon
1 tbsp soy sauce
150 ml/¼ pint chicken stock

For the tomato sauce:
1 tbsp vegetable oil
1 bunch spring onions,
trimmed and chopped
400 g/14 oz can chopped
tomatoes
1 tbsp light soy sauce
1 tbsp freshly chopped mint
freshly ground black pepper

Preheat the oven to 180°C/350°F/Gas Mark 4, 10 minutes before cooking. To make the sauce, heat the oil in a heavy-based saucepan, add the spring onions and cook for 2 minutes or until softened.

Add the tomatoes, soy sauce and mint to the saucepan, bring to the boil, cover, then simmer for 10 minutes. Season to taste with pepper. Reheat when required.

Meanwhile, blanch the whole cabbage leaves in a large saucepan of lightly salted water for 3 minutes. Drain and refresh under cold running water. Pat dry with absorbent kitchen paper, being careful not to tear them, and reserve.

Heat the oil in a small saucepan, add the celery, carrot and pork mince, and cook for 3 minutes. Add the mushrooms and cook for 3 minutes. Stir in the Chinese five-spice powder, rice, lemon juice and soy sauce and heat through.

Put some of the filling in the centre of each cabbage leaf and fold to enclose the filling. Place in a shallow ovenproof dish seam-side down. Pour over the stock and cook in the preheated oven for 30 minutes. Serve immediately with the reheated tomato sauce.

Sweet & Sour Pork

SERVES 4

450 g/1 lb pork fillet
1 medium egg white
4 tsp cornflour
salt and freshly ground
    black pepper
300 ml/½ pint groundnut oil
1 small onion, peeled and
    finely sliced

125 g/4 oz carrots, peeled
    and cut into matchsticks
2.5 cm/1 inch piece fresh
    root ginger, peeled and
    cut into thin strips
150 ml/¼ pint orange juice
150 ml/¼ pint chicken stock
1 tbsp light soy sauce

220 g/8 oz can pineapple
    pieces, drained with juice
    reserved
1 tbsp white wine vinegar
1 tbsp freshly
    chopped parsley
freshly cooked rice, to serve

Trim, then cut the pork fillet into small cubes. In a bowl, whisk together the egg white and cornflour with a little seasoning, then add the pork to the egg white mixture and stir until the cubes are well coated.

Heat the wok, then add the oil and heat until very hot before adding the pork and stir-frying for 30 seconds. Turn off the heat and continue to stir for 3 minutes. The meat should be white and sealed. Drain off the oil, reserving the oil and pork separately and wipe the wok clean.

Pour 2 teaspoons of the drained groundnut oil back into the wok and cook the onion, carrots and ginger for 2–3 minutes. Blend the orange juice with the chicken stock and soy sauce, and make up to 300 ml/½ pint with the reserved pineapple juice.

Return the pork to the wok with the juice mixture and simmer for 3–4 minutes. Stir in the pineapple pieces and vinegar. Heat through, then sprinkle with the chopped parsley and serve immediately with freshly cooked rice.

Pork with Spring Vegetables & Sweet Chilli Sauce

SERVES 4

450 g/16 oz pork fillet
2 tbsp sunflower oil
2 garlic cloves, peeled
   and crushed
2.5 cm/1 inch piece fresh
   root ginger, peeled
   and grated

125 g/4 oz carrots, peeled
   and cut into matchsticks
4 spring onions, trimmed
125 g/4 oz sugar snap peas
125 g/4 oz baby sweetcorn
2 tbsp sweet chilli sauce
2 tbsp light soy sauce

1 tbsp vinegar
½ tsp sugar, or to taste
125 g/4 oz beansprouts
grated zest of 1 orange
freshly cooked rice,
   to serve

Trim, then cut the pork fillet into thin strips and reserve. Heat a wok and pour in the oil. When hot, add the garlic and ginger, and stir-fry for 30 seconds. Add the carrots to the wok and continue to stir-fry for 1–2 minute until they start to soften.

Slice the spring onions lengthways, then cut into three lengths. Trim the sugar snap peas and the sweetcorn. Add the spring onions, sugar snap peas and sweetcorn to the wok and stir-fry for 30 seconds.

Add the pork to the wok and continue to stir-fry for 2–3 minutes until the meat is sealed and browned all over. Blend together the sweet chilli sauce, soy sauce, vinegar and sugar, then stir into the wok with the beansprouts.

Continue to stir-fry until the meat is cooked and the vegetables are tender but still crisp. Sprinkle with the orange zest and serve immediately with the freshly cooked rice.

TASTY TIP

Sweet chilli sauce can still have a good hot kick. It is wise to taste a little before adding it to the sauce and adjust the quantity according to preference.

Pork Sausages with Onion Gravy & Best–ever Mash

SERVES 4

50 g/2 oz butter
1 tbsp olive oil
2 large onions, peeled
   and thinly sliced
pinch sugar
1 tbsp freshly
   chopped thyme

1 tbsp plain flour
100 ml/3½ fl oz Madeira
200 ml/7 fl oz vegetable
   stock
8–12 good-quality butcher's
   pork sausages, depending
   on size

For the mash:
900 g/2 lb floury
   potatoes, peeled
75 g/3 oz butter
4 tbsp crème fraîche or
   sour cream
salt and freshly ground
   black pepper

Melt the butter with the oil and add the onions. Cover and cook gently for about 20 minutes until the onions have collapsed. Add the sugar and stir well. Uncover and continue to cook, stirring often, until the onions are very soft and golden. Add the thyme, stir well, then add the flour, stirring. Gradually add the Madeira and the stock. Bring to the boil and simmer gently for 10 minutes.

Meanwhile, put the sausages in a large frying pan and cook over a medium heat for 15–20 minutes, turning often, until golden brown and slightly sticky all over.

For the mash, boil the potatoes in plenty of lightly salted water for 15–18 minutes until tender. Drain well and return to the saucepan. Put the saucepan over a low heat to allow the potatoes to dry thoroughly. Remove from the heat and add the butter and crème fraîche or sour cream. Season to taste with salt and pepper. Mash thoroughly. Serve the potato mash topped with the sausages and onion gravy.

HELPFUL HINT
Sausages should always be cooked slowly over a gentle heat to ensure that they are cooked through.

Sausage & Redcurrant Pasta Bake

SERVES 4

450 g/1 lb good-quality thick pork sausages
2 tsp sunflower oil
25 g/1 oz butter
1 onion, peeled and sliced
2 tbsp plain white flour
450 ml/¾ pint chicken stock

150 ml/¼ pint port or good-quality red wine
1 tbsp freshly chopped thyme leaves, plus extra sprigs to garnish
1 bay leaf
4 tbsp redcurrant jelly

salt and freshly ground black pepper
350 g/12 oz penne
75 g/3 oz Gruyère cheese, grated

Preheat the oven to 220°C/425°F/Gas Mark 7, 15 minutes before cooking. Prick the sausages, place in a shallow ovenproof dish and toss in the sunflower oil. Cook in the oven for 25–30 minutes until golden brown.

Meanwhile, melt the butter in a frying pan, add the sliced onion and fry for 5 minutes, or until golden brown. Stir in the flour and cook for 2 minutes. Remove the pan from the heat and gradually stir in the chicken stock with the port or red wine.

Return the pan to the heat and bring to the boil, stirring continuously until the sauce starts to thicken. Add the thyme, bay leaf and redcurrant jelly, and season well with salt and pepper. Simmer the sauce for 5 minutes.

Bring a large pan of salted water to a rolling boil, add the pasta and cook for about 4 minutes, or until *al dente*. Drain thoroughly and reserve.

Reduce the oven temperature to 200°C/400°F/Gas Mark 6. Remove the sausages from the oven, drain off any excess fat and return the sausages to the dish. Add the pasta. Pour over the sauce, removing the bay leaf, and toss together. Sprinkle with the Gruyère cheese and return to the oven for 15–20 minutes until bubbling and golden brown. Serve immediately, garnished with the extra thyme sprigs.

Oven–baked Pork Balls with Peppers

SERVES 4

For the garlic bread:
2–4 garlic cloves, peeled
50 g/2 oz butter, softened
1 tbsp freshly
   chopped parsley
2–3 tsp lemon juice
1 focaccia loaf

For the pork balls:
450 g/1 lb fresh pork mince

4 tbsp freshly chopped basil
2 garlic cloves, peeled
   and chopped
3 sun-dried tomatoes,
   chopped
salt and freshly ground
   black pepper
3 tbsp olive oil
1 medium red pepper,
   deseeded and cut

into chunks
1 medium green pepper,
   deseeded and cut
   into chunks
1 medium yellow pepper,
   deseeded and cut
   into chunks
225 g/8 oz cherry tomatoes
2 tbsp balsamic vinegar

Crush the garlic, then blend with the softened butter, parsley and enough lemon juice to give a soft consistency. Shape into a roll, wrap in baking paper and chill in the refrigerator for at least 30 minutes.

Preheat oven to 200°C/400°F/Gas Mark 6, 15 minutes before cooking. Mix together the pork, basil, 1 chopped garlic clove, sun-dried tomatoes and seasoning until well combined. With damp hands, divide the mixture into 16, roll into balls and reserve.

Spoon the olive oil in a large roasting tin and place in the preheated oven for about 3 minutes until very hot. Remove from the heat and stir in the pork balls, the remaining chopped garlic and the peppers. Bake for about 15 minutes. Remove from the oven and stir in the cherry tomatoes and season to taste with plenty of salt and pepper. Bake for about a further 20 minutes.

Just before the pork balls are ready, slice the focaccia, toast lightly and spread with the prepared garlic butter. Remove the pork balls from the oven, stir in the vinegar and serve immediately with the garlic bread.

HELPFUL HINT
You can prepare the garlic butter ahead: make to the end of step 1. Refrigerate for up to 1 week or freeze for up to 2 months.

Italian Meatballs in Tomato Sauce

SERVES 4

For the tomato sauce:
4 tbsp olive oil
1 large onion, peeled and finely chopped
2 garlic cloves, peeled and chopped
400 g/14 oz can chopped tomatoes
1 tbsp sun-dried tomato paste
1 tbsp dried mixed herbs
150 ml/¼ pint red wine
salt and freshly ground black pepper

For the meatballs:
450 g/1 lb pork mince
50 g/2 oz fresh breadcrumbs
1 medium egg yolk
75 g/3 oz Parmesan cheese, grated
20 small stuffed green olives, such as pimento-, almond- or anchovy-stuffed
freshly snipped chives, to garnish
freshly cooked pasta, to serve

To make the tomato sauce, heat half the olive oil in a saucepan and cook half the chopped onion for 5 minutes until softened. Add the garlic, chopped tomatoes, tomato paste, mixed herbs and red wine to the pan and season to taste with salt and pepper. Stir well until blended. Bring to the boil, then cover and simmer for 15 minutes.

To make the meatballs, put the pork, breadcrumbs, remaining chopped onion, egg yolk and half the Parmesan cheese in a large bowl. Season well and mix together with your hands. Divide the mixture into 20 balls.

Flatten out one ball in the palm of your hands, place an olive in the centre, then squeeze the meat around the olive to enclose completely. Repeat with the remaining mixture and olives. Place the meatballs on a baking sheet, cover with clingfilm and chill in the refrigerator for 30 minutes.

Heat the remaining oil in a large frying pan and cook the meatballs for 8–10 minutes, turning occasionally, until golden brown. Pour in the sauce and heat through. Sprinkle with chives and the remaining Parmesan. Serve immediately with the freshly cooked pasta.

Shepherd's Pie

SERVES 4

2 tbsp vegetable or olive oil
1 onion, peeled and finely chopped
1 carrot, peeled and finely chopped
1 celery stalk, trimmed and finely chopped
1 tbsp fresh thyme sprigs

450 g/1 lb leftover roast lamb, finely chopped
150 ml/¼ pint red wine
150 ml/¼ pint lamb or vegetable stock or leftover gravy
2 tbsp tomato purée
salt and freshly ground

black pepper
700 g/1½ lb potatoes, peeled and cut into chunks
25 g/1 oz butter
6 tbsp milk
1 tbsp freshly chopped parsley
fresh herbs, to garnish

Preheat the oven to 200°C/400°F/Gas Mark 6, about 15 minutes before cooking. Heat the oil in a large saucepan and add the onion, carrot and celery. Cook over a medium heat for 8–10 minutes until softened and starting to brown.

Add the thyme and cook briefly, then add the cooked lamb, wine, stock or gravy and tomato purée. Season to taste with salt and pepper, and simmer gently for 25–30 minutes until reduced and thickened. Remove from the heat to cool slightly, and season again.

Meanwhile, boil the potatoes in plenty of salted water for 12–15 minutes until tender. Drain and return to the saucepan over a low heat to dry out. Remove from the heat and add the butter, milk and parsley. Mash until creamy, adding a little more milk, if necessary. Adjust the seasoning.

Transfer the lamb mixture to a shallow ovenproof dish. Spoon the mash over the filling and spread evenly to cover completely. Fork the surface, place the dish on a baking sheet, then cook in the preheated oven for 25–30 minutes until the potato topping is browned and the filling is piping hot. Garnish with fresh herbs and serve.

TASTY TIP

You can make this with minced lamb if preferred. Simply dry-fry 450 g/1 lb lean mince over a high heat until well browned, then follow the recipe as before.

Lamb Arrabbiata

SERVES 4

4 tbsp olive oil
450 g/1 lb lamb fillets, fat
    trimmed, cubed
1 large onion, peeled
    and sliced
4 garlic cloves, peeled and
    finely chopped

1 red chilli, deseeded and
    finely chopped
400 g/14 oz can chopped
    tomatoes
175 g/6 oz pitted black
    olives, halved
150 ml/¼ pint white wine

salt and freshly ground
    black pepper
275 g/10 oz farfalle
1 tsp butter
4 tbsp freshly chopped
    parsley, plus 1 tbsp extra
    to garnish

Heat 2 tablespoons of the olive oil in a large frying pan and cook the lamb for 5–7 minutes until sealed. Remove the meat from the pan using a slotted spoon and reserve.

Heat the remaining oil in the same pan, add the onion, garlic and chilli, and cook until softened. Add the tomatoes, bring to the boil, then simmer for 10 minutes.

Return the browned lamb to the pan with the olives and pour in the wine. Bring the sauce back to the boil, reduce the heat, then simmer, uncovered, for 15 minutes, until the lamb is tender. Season to taste with salt and pepper.

Meanwhile, bring a large pan of lightly salted water to a rolling boil. Add the pasta and cook according to the packet instructions, or until *al dente*.

Drain the pasta, toss in the butter, then add to the sauce and mix lightly. Stir in the 4 tablespoons chopped parsley, then tip into a warmed serving dish. Sprinkle with the extra 1 tablespoon parsley and serve immediately.

FOOD FACT

When cooking pasta, remember to use a very large saucepan so that the pasta has plenty of room to move around freely.

Lamb with Stir–fried Vegetables

SERVES 4

550 g/1¼ lb lamb fillet, cut into strips
2.5 cm/1 inch piece fresh root ginger, peeled and cut into matchsticks
2 garlic cloves, peeled and chopped
4 tbsp soy sauce
2 tbsp dry sherry

2 tsp cornflour
4 tbsp groundnut oil
75 g/3 oz French beans, trimmed and cut in half
2 medium carrots, peeled and cut into matchsticks
1 red pepper, deseeded and cut into chunks
1 yellow pepper, deseeded

and cut into chunks
225 g/8 oz can water chestnuts, drained and halved
3 tomatoes, chopped
freshly cooked sticky rice in banana leaves, to serve (optional)

Put the lamb strips in a shallow dish. Mix together the ginger and half the garlic in a small bowl. Pour over the soy sauce and sherry, and stir well. Pour over the lamb and stir until coated lightly. Cover with clingfilm and leave to marinate in the refrigerator for at least 30 minutes, occasionally spooning the marinade over the lamb.

Using a slotted spoon, lift the lamb from the marinade and place on a plate. Blend together the cornflour and marinade until smooth and reserve.

Heat a wok or large frying pan, add 2 tablespoons of the oil and, when hot, add the remaining garlic, French beans, carrots and red and yellow peppers, and stir-fry for 5 minutes. Using a slotted spoon, transfer the vegetables to a plate and keep warm.

Heat the remaining oil in the wok, add the lamb and stir-fry for 2 minutes or until tender. Return the vegetables to the wok with the water chestnuts, tomatoes and reserved marinade mixture. Bring to the boil, then simmer for 1 minute. Serve immediately with freshly cooked sticky rice in banana leaves, if liked.

Poultry

Chicken & Baby Vegetable Stir-fry

SERVES 4

2 tbsp groundnut oil
1 small red chilli, deseeded
    and finely chopped
150 g/5 oz chicken breast
    or thigh meat, skinned
    and cut into cubes
2 baby leeks, trimmed
    and sliced
12 fresh asparagus
spears, halved
125 g/4 oz mangetout,
    trimmed
125 g/4 oz baby carrots,
    trimmed and halved
    lengthways
125 g/4 oz fine green
    beans, trimmed and
    diagonally sliced
125 g/4 oz baby sweetcorn,
    diagonally halved
50 ml/2 fl oz chicken stock
2 tsp light soy sauce
1 tbsp dry sherry
1 tsp sesame oil
toasted sesame seeds,
    to garnish

Heat the wok until very hot and add the oil. Add the chopped chilli and chicken, and stir-fry for 4–5 minutes until the chicken is cooked and golden.

Increase the heat, add the leeks and stir-fry for 2 minutes. Add the asparagus spears, mangetout, baby carrots, green beans and baby sweetcorn. Stir-fry for 3–4 minutes until the vegetables soften slightly but still retain a slight crispness.

In a small bowl, mix together the chicken stock, soy sauce, sherry and sesame oil. Pour into the wok, stir and cook until heated through. Sprinkle with the toasted sesame seeds and serve immediately.

HELPFUL HINT

Look for packets of mixed baby vegetables in the supermarket. They are often available ready-trimmed and will save a lot of time.

Braised Chicken with Aubergine

SERVES 4

3 tbsp vegetable oil
12 chicken thighs
2 large aubergines,
   trimmed and cubed
4 garlic cloves, peeled
   and crushed
2 tsp freshly grated
   root ginger

900 ml/1½ pints
   vegetable stock
2 tbsp light soy sauce
2 tbsp Chinese preserved
   black beans
6 spring onions, trimmed
   and thinly sliced
   diagonally

1 tbsp cornflour
1 tbsp sesame oil
spring onion tassels,
   to garnish
freshly cooked noodles
   or rice, to serve

Heat a wok or large frying pan, add the oil and, when hot, add the chicken thighs and cook over a medium high heat for 5 minutes, or until browned all over. Transfer to a large plate and keep warm.

Add the aubergine to the wok and cook over a high heat for 5 minutes or until browned, turning occasionally. Add the garlic and ginger, and stir-fry for 1 minute.

Return the chicken to the wok, pour in the stock and add the soy sauce and black beans. Bring to the boil, then simmer for 20 minutes, or until the chicken is tender. Add the spring onions after 10 minutes.

Blend the cornflour with 2 tablespoons water. Stir into the wok and simmer until the sauce has thickened. Stir in the sesame oil, heat for 30 seconds, then remove from the heat. Garnish with spring onion tassels and serve immediately with noodles or rice.

Pan-cooked Chicken with Thai Spices

SERVES 4

4 kaffir lime leaves
5 cm/2 inch piece fresh
    root ginger, peeled
    and chopped
300 ml/½ pint chicken
    stock, boiling
4 skinless chicken breast fillets,
    each about 175 g/6 oz

2 tsp groundnut oil
5 tbsp coconut milk
1 tbsp fish sauce
2 red chillies, deseeded
    and finely chopped
225 g/8 oz Thai jasmine rice
1 tbsp lime juice
3 tbsp freshly

chopped coriander
salt and freshly ground
    black pepper

To garnish:
lime wedges
freshly chopped coriander

Lightly bruise the kaffir lime leaves and put in a bowl with the chopped ginger. Pour over the chicken stock, cover and leave to infuse for 30 minutes.

Meanwhile, cut each chicken breast into two pieces. Heat the oil in a large nonstick frying pan or flameproof casserole and brown the chicken pieces for 2–3 minutes on each side.

Strain the infused chicken stock into the pan. Half-cover the pan with a lid and gently simmer for 10 minutes.

Stir in the coconut milk, fish sauce and chopped chillies. Simmer, uncovered, for 5–6 minutes until the chicken is tender and cooked through and the sauce has reduced slightly.

Meanwhile, cook the rice in boiling salted water according to the packet instructions. Drain the rice thoroughly.

Stir the lime juice and chopped coriander into the sauce. Season to taste with salt and pepper. Serve the chicken and sauce on a bed of rice. Garnish with wedges of lime and freshly chopped coriander and serve immediately.

FOOD FACT

Kaffir lime leaves can be found, usually frozen, in Asian food stores. Most supermarkets now stock dried kaffir lime leaves. If using dried, crumble lightly and use as above.

Stir-fried Chicken with Basil

SERVES 4

3 tbsp sunflower oil
3 tbsp Thai green
  curry paste
450 g/1 lb skinless chicken
  breast fillets, trimmed and
  cut into cubes
8 cherry tomatoes

100 ml/3½ fl oz coconut
  cream
2 tbsp soft brown sugar
2 tbsp Thai fish sauce
1 red chilli, deseeded and
  thinly sliced
1 green chilli, deseeded

and thinly sliced
75 g/3 oz fresh torn
  basil leaves
fresh coriander sprigs,
  to garnish
freshly steamed white rice,
  to serve

Heat the wok, then add the oil and heat for 1 minute. Add the green curry paste and cook, stirring, for 1 minute to release the flavour and cook the paste. Add the chicken and stir-fry over a high heat for 2 minutes, making sure that the chicken is coated thoroughly with the green curry paste.

Reduce the heat under the wok, then add the cherry tomatoes and cook, stirring gently, for 2–3 minutes until the tomatoes burst and begin to disintegrate into the green curry paste.

Add half the coconut cream to the wok with the brown sugar, Thai fish sauce and red and green chillies. Stir-fry gently for 5 minutes, or until the sauce is amalgamated and the chicken is cooked thoroughly.

Just before serving, sprinkle the chicken with the torn basil leaves and add the remaining coconut cream, then serve immediately with freshly steamed white rice, garnished with fresh coriander sprigs.

Spicy Chicken Skewers with Mango Tabbouleh

SERVES 4

400 g/14 oz skinless chicken breast fillets
200 ml/7 fl oz plain yogurt
1 garlic clove, peeled and crushed
1 small red chilli, deseeded and finely chopped
½ tsp ground turmeric
finely grated zest and juice of ½ lemon

fresh mint sprigs, to garnish

For the mango tabbouleh:
175 g/6 oz bulgur wheat
1 tsp olive oil
juice of ½ lemon
½ red onion, finely chopped
1 ripe mango, halved, stoned, peeled

and chopped
¼ cucumber, finely diced
2 tbsp freshly chopped parsley
2 tbsp freshly shredded mint
salt and freshly ground black pepper

If using wooden skewers, soak them in cold water for at least 30 minutes before using. (This stops them from burning during grilling.)

Cut the chicken into 5 x 1 cm/2 x ½ inch strips and place in a shallow dish. Mix together the yogurt, garlic, chilli, turmeric, lemon zest and juice. Pour over the chicken and toss to coat. Cover and leave to marinate in the refrigerator for up to 8 hours.

To make the tabbouleh, put the bulgur wheat in a bowl. Pour over enough boiling water to cover. Put a plate over the bowl and leave to soak for 20 minutes. Whisk together the oil and lemon juice in a bowl. Add the red onion and leave to marinade for 10 minutes. Drain the bulgur wheat and squeeze out any excess moisture in a clean tea towel. Add to the red onion with the mango, cucumber and herbs, and season to taste with salt and pepper. Toss together.

Thread the chicken strips on to eight wooden or metal skewers. Cook under a hot grill for 8 minutes. Turn and brush with the marinade, until the chicken is lightly browned and cooked through. Spoon the tabbouleh onto individual plates. Arrange the chicken skewers on top and garnish with the mint sprigs. Serve warm or cold.

Aromatic Chicken Curry

SERVES 4

125 g/4 oz red lentils
2 tsp ground coriander
½ tsp cumin seeds
2 tsp mild curry paste
1 bay leaf
small strip of lemon zest
600 ml/1 pint chicken or

vegetable stock
8 chicken thighs, skinned
175 g/6 oz spinach leaves,
    rinsed and shredded
1 tbsp freshly
    chopped coriander
2 tsp lemon juice

salt and freshly ground
    black pepper

To serve:
freshly cooked rice
plain yogurt

Put the lentils in a sieve and rinse thoroughly under cold running water.

Dry-fry the ground coriander and cumin seeds in a large saucepan over a low heat for about 30 seconds. Stir in the curry paste and cook, stirring, for a minute or so until fragrant.

Add the lentils to the saucepan with the bay leaf and lemon zest, then pour in the stock. Stir, then slowly bring to the boil. Reduce the heat, half-cover the pan with a lid and simmer gently for 5 minutes, stirring occasionally.

Secure the chicken thighs with cocktail sticks to keep their shape. Place in the pan and half-cover. Simmer for 15 minutes. Stir in the shredded spinach and cook for a further 25 minutes or until the chicken is very tender and the sauce is thick.

Remove the bay leaf and lemon zest. Stir in the coriander and lemon juice, then season to taste with salt and pepper. Serve immediately with the rice and a little yogurt.

Red Chicken Curry

SERVES 4

225 ml/8 fl oz coconut cream
2 tbsp vegetable oil
2 garlic cloves, peeled
    and finely chopped
2 tbsp Thai red curry paste
2 tbsp Thai fish sauce

2 tsp sugar
350 g/12 oz skinless chicken
    breast fillets, finely sliced
450 ml/¾ pint chicken stock
2 kaffir lime leaves,
    shredded

chopped red chilli,
    to garnish
freshly boiled rice or
    steamed Thai fragrant
    rice, to serve

Pour the coconut cream into a small saucepan and heat gently. Meanwhile, heat a wok or large frying pan and add the oil. When the oil is very hot, swirl the oil around the wok until the wok is lightly coated, then add the garlic and stir-fry for 10–20 seconds until the garlic begins to brown. Add the curry paste and stir-fry for a few more seconds, then pour in the warmed coconut cream.

Cook the coconut cream mixture for 5 minutes, or until the cream has curdled and thickened. Stir in the fish sauce and sugar. Add the finely sliced chicken breast and cook for 3–4 minutes until the chicken has turned white.

Pour the stock into the wok, bring to the boil, then simmer for 1–2 minutes until the chicken is cooked through. Stir in the shredded lime leaves. Turn into a warmed serving dish, garnish with chopped red chilli and serve immediately with rice.

Persian Chicken Pilaf

SERVES 4-6

2–3 tbsp vegetable oil
700 g/1½ lb skinless
    chicken fillets (breast and
    thighs), cut into 2.5 cm/
    1 inch pieces
2 medium onions, peeled
    and coarsely chopped
1 tsp ground cumin

200 g/7 oz long-grain
    white rice
1 tbsp tomato purée
1 tsp saffron strands
salt and freshly ground
    black pepper
100 ml/3½ fl oz
    pomegranate juice

900 ml/1½ pints chicken stock
125 g/4 oz ready-to-eat dried
    apricots or prunes, halved
2 tbsp raisins
2 tbsp freshly chopped mint
    or parsley
pomegranate seeds, to
    garnish (optional)

Heat the oil in a large heavy-based saucepan over a medium-high heat. Cook the chicken pieces, in batches, until lightly browned. Return all the browned chicken to the saucepan.

Add the onions to the saucepan, reduce the heat to medium and cook for 3–5 minutes, stirring frequently, until the onions begin to soften. Add the cumin and rice, and stir to coat the rice. Cook for about 2 minutes until the rice is golden and translucent. Stir in the tomato purée and saffron strands, then season to taste with salt and pepper.

Add the pomegranate juice and stock, and bring to the boil, stirring once or twice. Add the apricots or prunes and the raisins, and stir gently. Reduce the heat to low and cook for 30 minutes until the chicken and rice are tender and the liquid is absorbed.

Turn into a shallow serving dish and sprinkle with the chopped mint or parsley. Serve immediately, garnished with pomegranate seeds, if using.

HELPFUL HINT
Pomegranate juice
is available from Middle
Eastern groceries and some
speciality shops. Substitute
unsweetened grape or apple
juice if you cannot find
pomegranate juice.

Pad Thai

SERVES 4

225 g/8 oz flat dried
   rice noodles
2 tbsp vegetable oil
225 g/8 oz skinless chicken
   breast fillets, thinly sliced
4 shallots, peeled and
   thinly sliced
2 garlic cloves, peeled
   and finely chopped
4 spring onions, trimmed

and cut diagonally into
   5 cm/2 inch pieces
350 g/12 oz fresh white crab
   meat or tiny prawns
75 g/3 oz fresh beansprouts,
   rinsed and drained
2 tbsp preserved or fresh
   radish, chopped
2–3 tbsp roasted peanuts,
   chopped (optional)

For the sauce:
3 tbsp Thai fish sauce
2–3 tbsp rice vinegar or
   cider vinegar
1 tbsp chilli bean or
   oyster sauce
1 tbsp toasted sesame oil
1 tbsp light brown sugar
1 red chilli, deseeded and
   thinly sliced

To make the sauce, whisk together all the sauce ingredients in a bowl and reserve. Put the rice noodles in a large bowl and pour over enough hot water to cover. Leave to stand for about 15 minutes until softened. Drain and rinse, then drain again.

Heat the oil in a wok over a high heat until hot but not smoking. Add the chicken strips and stir-fry constantly until they begin to colour. Using a slotted spoon, transfer to a plate. Reduce the heat to medium-high.

Add the shallots, garlic and spring onions, and stir-fry for 1 minute. Stir in the rice noodles, then the reserved sauce; mix well. Add the reserved chicken strips, with the crab meat or prawns, beansprouts and radish, and stir well. Cook for about 5 minutes, stirring frequently, until heated through. If the noodles begin to stick, add a little water.

Turn into a large shallow serving dish and sprinkle with the chopped peanuts, if liked. Serve immediately.

Chicken with Porcini Mushrooms & Cream

SERVES 4

2 tbsp olive oil
4 boneless chicken breasts,
    preferably free-range
2 garlic cloves, peeled
    and crushed
150 ml/¼ pint dry vermouth

or dry white wine
salt and freshly ground
    black pepper
25 g/1 oz butter
450 g/1 lb porcini or wild
    mushrooms, thickly sliced

120 ml/4 fl oz double cream
1 tbsp freshly chopped
    oregano
fresh basil sprigs, to garnish
    (optional)
freshly cooked rice, to serve

Heat the olive oil in a large heavy-based frying pan, then add the chicken breasts, skin-side down, and cook for about 10 minutes until they are well browned. Remove the chicken breasts and reserve. Add the garlic, stir into the juices and cook for 1 minute.

Pour the vermouth or white wine into the pan and season to taste with salt and pepper. Return the chicken to the pan. Bring to the boil, reduce the heat to low and simmer for about 20 minutes until tender.

In another large frying pan, melt the butter and add the sliced porcini or wild mushrooms. Stir-fry for about 5 minutes until the mushrooms are golden and tender.

Add the porcini or wild mushrooms and any juices to the chicken. Stir in the cream, season to taste, then add the chopped oregano. Stir together gently and cook for 2–3 minutes longer. Transfer to a large serving plate and garnish with sprigs of fresh basil, if using. Serve immediately with rice.

Chicken Parcels with Courgettes & Pasta

2 tbsp olive oil
125 g/4 oz farfalle
1 onion, peeled and
   thinly sliced
1 garlic clove, peeled and
   finely chopped

2 medium courgettes,
   trimmed and thinly sliced
salt and freshly ground
   black pepper
2 tbsp freshly
   chopped oregano

4 plum tomatoes, deseeded
   and coarsely chopped
4 skinless chicken breast
   fillets, each about 175 g/6 oz
150 ml/¼ pint Italian
   white wine

Preheat oven to 200°C/400°F/Gas Mark 6, 15 minutes before cooking. Lightly brush four large sheets of nonstick baking paper with half the oil. Bring a saucepan of lightly salted water to the boil and cook the pasta for 10 minutes, or until *al dente*. Drain and reserve.

Heat the remaining oil in a frying pan and cook the onion for 2–3 minutes. Add the garlic and cook for 1 minute. Add the courgettes and cook for 1 minute, then remove from the heat, season to taste with salt and pepper, and add half the oregano.

Divide the cooked pasta equally among the four sheets of baking paper, positioning the pasta in the centre. Top the pasta with equal amounts of the vegetable mixture, and sprinkle a quarter of the chopped tomatoes over each.

Score the surface of each chicken breast about 1 cm/½ inch deep. Place a chicken breast on top of the pasta and sprinkle each with the remaining oregano and the white wine. Fold the edges of the paper along the top, then along each side, creating a sealed envelope.

Bake in the preheated oven for 30–35 minutes until cooked. Serve immediately.

Lemon Chicken with Potatoes, Rosemary & Olives

SERVES 6

12 skinless chicken
thigh fillets
1 large lemon
125 ml/4 fl oz extra virgin
olive oil
6 garlic cloves, peeled
and sliced

2 onions, peeled and thinly
sliced
1 bunch fresh rosemary
1.1 kg/2½ lb potatoes,
peeled and cut into
4 cm/1½ inch pieces
salt and freshly ground

black pepper
18–24 black olives, pitted

To serve:
steamed carrots
steamed courgettes

Trim the chicken thighs and place in a shallow baking dish large enough to hold them in a single layer. Remove the zest from the lemon with a zester or if using a peeler cut into thin julienne strips. Reserve half and add the remainder to the chicken. Squeeze the lemon juice over the chicken, toss to coat well and leave to stand for 10 minutes.

Add the remaining lemon zest or julienne strips, olive oil, garlic, onions and half the rosemary sprigs. Toss gently and leave for about 20 minutes. Preheat the oven to 200°C/400°F/ Gas Mark 6, 15 minutes before cooking.

Cover the potatoes with lightly salted water and bring to the boil. Cook for 2 minutes, then drain well and add to the chicken. Season to taste with salt and pepper.

Roast the chicken in the preheated oven for 50 minutes, turning frequently and basting, or until the chicken is cooked. Just before the end of cooking time, discard the rosemary, and add the remaining fresh rosemary sprigs. Add the olives and stir. Serve immediately with steamed carrots and courgettes.

HELPFUL HINT

It is worth seeking out unwaxed lemons for any recipe in which the zest is to be eaten. If unwaxed fruit are not available, pour hot water over them and scrub well before removing the zest.

Chicken Pie with Sweet Potato Topping

SERVES 4

700 g/1½ lb sweet potatoes, peeled and cut into chunks
salt and freshly ground black pepper
250 g/9 oz potatoes, peeled and cut into chunks
150 ml/¼ pint milk
25 g/1 oz butter
2 tsp brown sugar

grated zest of 1 orange
4 skinless chicken breast fillets, diced
1 medium onion, peeled and coarsely chopped
125 g/4 oz baby mushrooms, stems trimmed
2 leeks, trimmed and thickly sliced

150 ml/¼ pint dry white wine
1 chicken stock cube
1 tbsp freshly chopped parsley
50 ml/2 fl oz crème fraîche or thick double cream
green vegetables, to serve

Cook the potatoes in lightly salted boiling water until tender. Drain well, then return to the saucepan and mash until smooth and creamy, gradually adding the milk, then the butter, sugar and orange zest. Season to taste with salt and pepper, and reserve.

Put the chicken in a saucepan with the onion, mushrooms, leeks, wine and stock cube, and season to taste. Simmer, covered, until the chicken and vegetables are tender. Using a slotted spoon, transfer the chicken and vegetables to a 1.1 litre/2 pint pie dish. Add the parsley and crème fraîche or cream to the liquid in the pan and bring to the boil. Simmer until thickened and smooth, stirring constantly. Pour over the chicken in the pie dish, mix and cool. Preheat the oven to 190°C/375°F/Gas Mark 5, 10 minutes before required.

Spread the mashed potato over the chicken filling, and swirl the surface into decorative peaks. Bake in the preheated oven for 35 minutes, or until the top is golden and the chicken filling is heated through. Serve immediately with fresh green vegetables.

HELPFUL HINT

There are two types of sweet potato: one has a creamy-coloured flesh, the other orange. The former has a drier texture, so, if using, you may need a little more milk.

Chicken & Asparagus with Tagliatelle

SERVES 4

275 g/10 oz fresh asparagus
50 g/2 oz butter
4 spring onions, trimmed
and coarsely chopped
350 g/12 oz skinless chicken
breast fillets, thinly sliced

2 tbsp white vermouth
300 ml/½ pint double cream
2 tbsp freshly
chopped chives
400 g/14 oz fresh tagliatelle
50 g/2 oz Parmesan or

pecorino cheese, grated
snipped chives, to garnish
extra Parmesan cheese
(optional), to serve

Using a swivel-bladed vegetable peeler, lightly peel the asparagus stalks and then cook in lightly salted boiling water for 2–3 minutes until just tender. Drain and refresh in cold water, then cut into 4 cm/1½ inch pieces and reserve.

Melt the butter in a large frying pan, then add the spring onions and chicken, and fry for 4 minutes. Add the vermouth and allow to reduce until the liquid has evaporated. Pour in the cream and half the chives. Cook gently for 5–7 minutes until the sauce has thickened and slightly reduced and the chicken is tender.

Bring a large saucepan of lightly salted water to the boil and cook the tagliatelle for 4–5 minutes, or until *al dente*. Drain and immediately add to the chicken and cream sauce.

Using a pair of spaghetti tongs or kitchen forks, lightly toss the sauce and pasta until it is mixed thoroughly. Add the remaining chives and the Parmesan or pecorino cheese, and toss gently. Garnish with snipped chives and serve immediately, with extra Parmesan cheese, if liked.

HELPFUL HINT
Freshly made pasta will cook in 30–60 seconds. It is cooked when it rises to the surface. Bought fresh pasta will take 2–3 minutes. Dried pasta takes 4–10 minutes, depending on the variety.

Chicken Marengo

SERVES 4

2 tbsp plain flour
salt and freshly ground
    black pepper
4 skinless chicken
    breast fillets, cut into
    bite-size pieces
4 tbsp olive oil
1 Spanish onion, peeled

and chopped
1 garlic clove, peeled
    and chopped
400 g/14 oz can chopped
    tomatoes
2 tbsp sun-dried
    tomato paste
3 tbsp freshly chopped basil

3 tbsp freshly
    chopped thyme
125 ml/4 fl oz dry white
    wine or chicken stock
350 g/12 oz rigatoni
3 tbsp freshly chopped
    flat-leaf parsley

Season the flour with salt and pepper, and toss the chicken in the flour to coat. Heat 2 tablespoons of the olive oil in a large frying pan and cook the chicken for 7 minutes, or until browned all over, turning occasionally. Remove from the pan using a slotted spoon and keep warm.

Add the remaining oil to the pan, add the onion and cook, stirring occasionally, for 5 minutes, or until softened and starting to brown. Add the garlic, tomatoes, tomato paste, basil and thyme. Pour in the wine or chicken stock and season well. Bring to the boil. Stir in the chicken pieces and simmer for 15 minutes, or until the chicken is tender and the sauce has thickened.

Meanwhile, bring a large pan of lightly salted water to a rolling boil. Add the rigatoni and cook according to the packet instructions, or until *al dente*.

Drain the rigatoni thoroughly, return to the pan and stir in the chopped parsley. Tip the pasta into a warmed large serving dish or spoon onto individual plates. Spoon over the chicken sauce and serve immediately.

Warm Chicken & Potato Salad with Peas & Mint

SERVES 4-6

450 g/1 lb new potatoes,
peeled or scrubbed, and
cut into bite-size pieces
salt and freshly ground
black pepper
2 tbsp cider vinegar
175 g/6 oz frozen garden
peas, thawed

1 small ripe avocado
4 cooked skinless chicken
breast fillets, each about
450 g/1 lb, diced
2 tbsp freshly chopped mint
2 heads little gem lettuce
fresh mint sprigs,
to garnish

For the dressing:
2 tbsp raspberry or sherry
vinegar
2 tsp Dijon mustard
1 tsp clear honey
50 ml/2 fl oz sunflower oil
50 ml/2 fl oz extra virgin
olive oil

Cook the potatoes in lightly salted boiling water for 15 minutes, or until just tender when pierced with the tip of a sharp knife; do not overcook. Rinse under cold running water to cool slightly, then drain and turn into a large bowl. Sprinkle with the cider vinegar and toss gently.

Run the peas under hot water to ensure that they are thawed, pat dry with absorbent kitchen paper and add to the potatoes.

Cut the avocado in half lengthways and remove the stone. Peel and cut the avocado into cubes and add to the potatoes and peas. Add the chicken and stir together lightly.

To make the dressing, put all the ingredients in a screw-top jar, with a little salt and pepper, and shake well to mix; add a little more oil if the flavour is too sharp. Pour over the salad and toss gently to coat. Sprinkle in half the mint and stir lightly.

Separate the lettuce leaves and spread onto a large shallow serving plate. Spoon the salad on top and sprinkle with the remaining mint. Garnish with mint sprigs and serve.

Spicy Chicken & Pasta Salad

SERVES 6

450 g/1 lb pasta shells
25 g/1 oz butter
1 onion, peeled
 and chopped
2 tbsp mild curry paste
125 g/4 oz ready-to-eat dried
 apricots, chopped

2 tbsp tomato paste
3 tbsp mango chutney
300 ml/½ pint mayonnaise
425 g/15 oz can pineapple
 slices in fruit juice
salt and freshly ground
 black pepper

450 g/1 lb cooked skinless
 chicken fillets, cut into
 bite-size pieces
25 g/1 oz flaked toasted
 almond slivers
fresh coriander sprigs,
 to garnish

Bring a large pan of lightly salted water to a rolling boil. Add the pasta shells and cook according to the packet instructions, or until *al dente*. Drain and refresh under cold running water, then drain thoroughly and put in a large serving bowl.

Meanwhile, melt the butter in a heavy-based pan, add the onion and cook for 5 minutes, or until softened. Add the curry paste and cook, stirring, for 2 minutes. Stir in the apricots and tomato paste, then cook for 1 minute. Remove from the heat and allow to cool.

Blend together the mango chutney and mayonnaise in a small bowl. Drain the pineapple slices, adding 2 tablespoons of the pineapple juice to the mayonnaise mixture; reserve the pineapple slices. Season the mayonnaise to taste with salt and pepper.

Cut the pineapple slices into chunks and stir into the pasta together with the mayonnaise mixture, curry paste and cooked chicken pieces. Toss together lightly to coat the pasta. Sprinkle with the almond slivers, garnish with coriander sprigs and serve.

Pasta & Pepper Salad

SERVES 4

4 tbsp olive oil
1 each red, orange and
  yellow pepper, deseeded
  and cut into chunks
1 large courgette, trimmed
  and cut into chunks
1 medium aubergine,
  trimmed and diced

275 g/10 oz fusilli
4 plum tomatoes, quartered
1 bunch fresh basil leaves,
  roughly chopped
2 tbsp pesto
2 garlic cloves, peeled
  and roughly chopped
1 tbsp lemon juice

225 g/8 oz roasted skinless
  chicken breast fillets
salt and freshly ground
  black pepper
125 g/4 oz feta cheese,
  crumbled
crusty bread, to serve

Preheat the oven to 200°C/400°F/Gas Mark 6. Spoon the olive oil into a roasting tin and heat in the oven for 2 minutes, or until almost smoking. Remove from the oven, add the peppers, courgette and aubergine, and stir until coated. Bake for 30 minutes, or until charred, stirring occasionally.

Bring a large pan of lightly salted water to a rolling boil. Add the pasta and cook according to the packet instructions, or until *al dente*. Drain and refresh under cold running water. Drain thoroughly, transfer to a large salad bowl and reserve.

Remove the cooked vegetables from the oven and allow to cool. Add to the cooled pasta, together with the quartered tomatoes, chopped basil leaves, pesto, garlic and lemon juice. Toss lightly to mix.

Shred the chicken roughly into small pieces and stir into the pasta and vegetable mixture. Season to taste with salt and pepper, then sprinkle the crumbled feta cheese over the pasta and stir gently. Cover the dish and leave to marinate for 30 minutes, stirring occasionally. Serve the salad with fresh crusty bread.

Mixed Vegetable & Chicken Pasta

3 skinless chicken
breast fillets
2 leeks
1 red onion
350 g/12 oz pasta shells
25 g/1 oz butter
2 tbsp olive oil

1 garlic clove, peeled
and chopped
175 g/6 oz cherry
tomatoes, halved
200 ml/7 fl oz double cream
425 g/15 oz can asparagus
tips, drained

salt and freshly ground
black pepper
125 g/4 oz double Gloucester
cheese with chives,
crumbled
green salad, to serve

Preheat the grill just before using. Cut the chicken into thin strips. Trim the leeks, leaving some of the dark green tops, then shred and wash thoroughly in plenty of cold water. Peel the onion and cut into thin wedges.

Bring a large pan of lightly salted water to a rolling boil. Add the pasta and cook according to the packet instructions, or until *al dente*.

Meanwhile, melt butter with the olive oil in a large heavy-based pan, add the chicken and cook, stirring occasionally, for 8 minutes, or until browned all over. Add the leeks and onion, and cook for 5 minutes, or until softened. Add the garlic and cherry tomatoes, and cook for a further 2 minutes.

Stir the cream and asparagus tips into the chicken and vegetable mixture, bring to the boil slowly, then remove from the heat. Drain the pasta thoroughly and return to the pan. Pour the sauce over the pasta, season to taste with salt and pepper, then toss lightly.

Tip the pasta mixture into a gratin dish and sprinkle with the cheese. Cook under the preheated grill for 5 minutes, or until bubbling and golden, turning the dish occasionally. Serve immediately with a green salad.

TASTY TIP

Fresh asparagus is in season during late spring, and can be used in place of canned. Tie in small bundles and cook in lightly salted, boiling water for 5–8 minutes.

Chicken & White Wine Risotto

SERVES 4-6

2 tbsp oil
125 g/4 oz unsalted butter
2 shallots, peeled and
finely chopped
300 g/11 oz Arborio rice
600 ml/1 pint dry white wine

750 ml/1¼ pints chicken
stock, heated
350 g/12 oz skinless chicken
breast fillets, thinly sliced
50 g/2 oz Parmesan
cheese, grated

2 tbsp freshly chopped
dill or parsley
salt and freshly ground
black pepper

Heat the oil and half the butter in a large heavy-based saucepan over a medium-high heat. Add the shallots and cook for 2 minutes, or until softened, stirring frequently. Add the rice and cook for 2–3 minutes, stirring frequently, until the rice is translucent and well coated.

Pour in half the wine; it will bubble and steam rapidly. Cook, stirring constantly, until the liquid is absorbed. Add a ladleful of the hot stock and cook until the liquid is absorbed. Carefully stir in the chicken.

Continue adding the stock, about half a ladleful at a time, allowing each addition to be absorbed before adding the next; never allow the rice to cook dry. This process should take about 20 minutes. The risotto should have a creamy consistency and the rice should be tender but firm to the bite.

HELPFUL HINT
Keep the stock to be added to the risotto at a low simmer in a separate saucepan, so that it is piping hot when added to the rice. This will help to achieve a perfect creamy texture.

Stir in the remaining wine and cook for 2–3 minutes. Remove from the heat and stir in the remaining butter with the Parmesan cheese and half the chopped herbs. Season to taste with salt and pepper. Spoon into warmed shallow bowls and sprinkle each with the remaining chopped herbs. Serve immediately.

Cheesy Chicken Burgers

SERVES 6

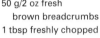

1 tbsp sunflower oil
1 small onion, peeled
and finely chopped
1 garlic clove, peeled
and crushed
½ red pepper, deseeded
and finely chopped
450 g/1 lb fresh chicken mince
2 tbsp Greek-style yogurt
50 g/2 oz fresh
brown breadcrumbs
1 tbsp freshly chopped

herbs, such as parsley
or tarragon
50 g/2 oz Cheshire
cheese, crumbled
salt and freshly ground
black pepper

**For the sweetcorn and
carrot relish:**
200 g/7 oz can
sweetcorn, drained
1 carrot, peeled and grated

½ green chilli, deseeded
and finely chopped
2 tsp cider vinegar
2 tsp light soft brown sugar

To serve:
wholemeal or granary rolls
lettuce
sliced tomatoes
mixed salad leaves

Heat the oil in a frying pan and gently cook the onion and garlic for 5 minutes. Add the red pepper and cook for 5 minutes. Transfer to a mixing bowl.

Add the chicken, yogurt, breadcrumbs, herbs and cheese, and season to taste with salt and pepper. Mix well. Divide the mixture equally into six and shape into burgers. Cover and chill in the refrigerator for at least 20 minutes.

To make the relish, put all the ingredients in a small saucepan with 1 tablespoon water. Heat gently, stirring occasionally until all the sugar has dissolved. Cover and cook over a low heat for 2 minutes, then uncover and cook for a further minute, or until the relish is thick.

Preheat the grill to medium. Place the burgers on a lightly oiled grill pan and cook under the grill for 8–10 minutes on each side until browned and completely cooked through. Warm the rolls, if liked, then split in half and fill with the burgers, lettuce, sliced tomatoes and the prepared relish. Serve immediately with the salad leaves.

Cheesy Baked Chicken Macaroni

SERVES 4

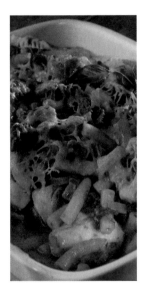

1 tbsp olive oil
350 g/12 oz skinless chicken
   breast fillets, diced
75 g/3 oz pancetta, diced
1 onion, peeled
   and chopped
1 garlic clove, peeled
   and chopped

350 g/12 oz packet fresh
   tomato sauce
400 g/14 oz can chopped
   tomatoes
2 tbsp freshly chopped basil,
   plus leaves to garnish
salt and freshly ground
   black pepper

350 g/12 oz macaroni or
   other small pasta shapes
150 g/5oz mozzarella cheese,
   drained and chopped
50 g/2 oz Gruyère
   cheese, grated
50 g/2 oz Parmesan cheese,
   freshly grated

Preheat the grill just before cooking. Heat the oil in large frying pan and cook the chicken for 8 minutes, or until browned, stirring occasionally. Drain on absorbent kitchen paper and reserve. Add the pancetta slices to the pan and fry on both sides until crispy. Remove from the pan and reserve.

Add the onion and garlic to the frying pan and cook for 5 minutes, or until softened. Stir in the tomato sauce, chopped tomatoes and chopped basil, and season to taste with salt and pepper. Bring to the boil, reduce the heat and simmer the sauce for 5 minutes.

Meanwhile, bring a large pan of lightly salted water to a rolling boil. Add the macaroni and cook according to the packet instructions, or until *al dente*.

Drain the macaroni thoroughly, return to the pan and stir in the sauce, chicken and mozzarella cheese. Spoon into a shallow ovenproof dish.

Sprinkle the pancetta over the macaroni. Sprinkle over the Gruyère and Parmesan cheeses. Place under the preheated grill and cook for 5–10 minutes until golden brown; turn the dish occasionally. Garnish and serve immediately.

FOOD FACT

Pancetta (cured dried belly of pork) imparts a wonderful flavour to a dish; it is available from Italian delicatessens.

Sweet & Sour Turkey

2 tbsp groundnut oil
2 garlic cloves, peeled
   and chopped
1 tbsp freshly grated
   root ginger
4 spring onions, trimmed
   and cut into 4 cm/
   1½ inch lengths
450 g/1 lb turkey breast,

skinned and cut into strips
1 red pepper, deseeded and
   cut into 2.5 cm/1 inch
   squares
225 g/8 oz canned water
   chestnuts, drained
150 ml/¼ pint chicken stock
2 tbsp Chinese rice wine
3 tbsp light soy sauce

2 tsp dark soy sauce
2 tbsp tomato paste
2 tbsp white wine vinegar
1 tbsp sugar
1 tbsp cornflour
boiled rice or egg-fried rice,
   to serve

Heat the wok over a high heat, add the oil and, when hot, add the garlic, ginger and spring onions. Stir-fry for 20 seconds.

Add the turkey to the wok and stir-fry for 2 minutes, or until beginning to colour. Add the red pepper and water chestnuts, and stir-fry for a further 2 minutes.

Mix together the chicken stock, Chinese rice wine, light and dark soy sauce, tomato paste, white wine vinegar and sugar in a small jug or bowl. Add the mixture to the wok, stir and bring the sauce to the boil.

Mix together the cornflour and 2 tablespoons water and add to the wok. Reduce the heat and simmer for 3 minutes, or until the turkey is cooked thoroughly and the sauce is slightly thickened and glossy. Serve immediately with plain or egg-fried rice.

Green Turkey Curry

SERVES 4

4 baby aubergines, trimmed
    and quartered
1 tsp salt
2 tbsp sunflower oil
4 shallots, peeled and
    halved or quartered
    if large
2 garlic cloves, peeled
    and sliced

2 tbsp Thai green curry
    paste
150 ml/¼ pint chicken stock
1 tbsp Thai fish sauce
1 tbsp lemon juice
350 g/12 oz skinless turkey
    breast fillets, cubed
1 red pepper, deseeded
    and sliced

125 g/4 oz French beans,
    trimmed and halved
25 g/1 oz creamed coconut
freshly boiled rice or
    steamed Thai fragrant
    rice, to serve

Put the aubergines into a colander and sprinkle with the salt. Set over a plate or in the sink to drain and leave for 30 minutes. Rinse under cold running water and pat dry on absorbent kitchen paper. Reserve.

Heat a wok or large frying pan, add the sunflower oil and, when hot, add the shallots and garlic, and stir-fry for 3 minutes, or until beginning to brown. Add the curry paste and stir-fry for 1–2 minutes. Pour in the stock, fish sauce and lemon juice, and simmer for 10 minutes.

Add the turkey, red pepper and French beans to the wok with the aubergines. Return to the boil, then simmer for 10–15 minutes until the turkey and vegetables are tender. Add the creamed coconut and stir until melted and the sauce has thickened. Turn into a warmed serving dish and serve immediately with rice.

Creamy Turkey & Tomato Pasta

4 tbsp olive oil
450 g/1 lb skinturkey breasts,
   cut into bite-size pieces
550 g/1¼ lb cherry tomatoes,
   on the vine

2 garlic cloves, peeled
   and chopped
4 tbsp balsamic vinegar
salt and freshly ground
   black pepper

4 tbsp freshly chopped basil
200 ml/7 floz tub crème fraîche
350 g/12 oz tagliatelle
shaved Parmesan cheese,
   to garnish

Preheat the oven to 200°C/400°F/Gas Mark 6. Heat 2 tablespoons of the olive oil in a large frying pan. Add the turkey and cook for 5 minutes, or until sealed, turning occasionally. Transfer to a roasting tin and add the remaining olive oil, cherry tomatoes, garlic and balsamic vinegar. Stir well and season to taste with salt and pepper. Cook in the preheated oven for 30 minutes, or until the turkey is tender, turning the tomatoes and turkey once.

Meanwhile, bring a large pan of lightly salted water to a rolling boil. Add the pasta and cook according to the packet instructions, or until *al dente*. Drain, return to the pan and keep warm. Stir the basil and seasoning into the crème fraîche.

Remove the roasting tin from the oven and discard the vines from the tomatoes. Stir the crème fraîche and basil mixture into the turkey and tomato mixture, and return to the oven for 1–2 minutes until thoroughly heated through.

Stir the turkey and tomato mixture into the pasta and toss together lightly. Tip into a warmed serving dish. Garnish with Parmesan cheese shavings and serve immediately.

Turkey & Tomato Tagine

SERVES 4

For the meatballs:
450 g/1 lb fresh turkey mince
1 small onion, peeled and
    very finely chopped
1 garlic clove, peeled
    and crushed
1 tbsp freshly
    chopped coriander
1 tsp ground cumin
1 tbsp olive oil

salt and freshly ground
    black pepper

For the sauce:
1 onion, peeled and
    finely chopped
1 garlic clove, peeled
    and crushed
150 ml/¼ pint turkey stock
400 g/14 oz can chopped

    tomatoes
½ tsp ground cumin
½ tsp ground cinnamon
pinch of cayenne pepper
freshly chopped parsley
freshly chopped herbs,
    to garnish
freshly cooked couscous
    or plain boiled rice,
    to serve

Preheat the oven to 190°C/375°F/Gas Mark 5. Put all the ingredients for the meatballs in a bowl, except the oil, and mix well. Season to taste with salt and pepper. Shape into 20 balls about the size of walnuts. Put on a tray, cover lightly and chill in the refrigerator while making the sauce.

Put the onion and garlic in a pan with 125 ml/4 fl oz of the stock. Cook over a low heat until all the stock has evaporated. Continue cooking for 1 minute, or until the onions begin to colour. Add the remaining stock to the pan with the tomatoes, cumin, cinnamon and cayenne pepper. Simmer for 10 minutes until slightly thickened and reduced. Stir in the parsley and season to taste.

Heat the oil in a large nonstick frying pan and cook the meatballs in two batches until lightly browned all over. Lift out the meatballs with a slotted spoon and drain on absorbent kitchen paper.

Pour the sauce into a tagine or an ovenproof casserole. Top with the meatballs, cover and cook in the preheated oven for 25–30 minutes until the meatballs are cooked through and the sauce is bubbling. Garnish with freshly chopped herbs and serve immediately on a bed of couscous or rice.

Turkey Escalopes with Apricot Chutney

SERVES 4

4 turkey steaks, each
175–225 g/6–8 oz
1 tbsp plain flour
salt and freshly ground
black pepper
1 tbsp olive oil
fresh flat-leaf parsley
sprigs, to garnish
orange wedges,
to serve

For the apricot chutney:
125 g/4 oz ready-to-eat dried
apricots, chopped
1 red onion, peeled and
finely chopped
1 tsp grated fresh
root ginger
2 tbsp caster sugar
finely grated zest of
½ orange

125 ml/4 fl oz fresh
orange juice
125 ml/4 fl oz ruby port
1 whole clove
1 tbsp freshly chopped
coriander

Put a turkey steak on a sheet of clingfilm or nonstick baking paper. Cover with a second sheet. Using a rolling pin, gently pound the turkey until the meat is flattened to about 5 mm/¼ inch thick. Repeat to make 4 escalopes.

Mix the flour with the salt and pepper, and use to lightly dust the turkey escalopes. Put the turkey escalopes on a board or baking tray, and cover with a piece of clingfilm or nonstick baking paper. Chill in the refrigerator until ready to cook.

To make the apricot chutney, put the apricots, onion, ginger, sugar, orange zest, orange juice, port and clove into a saucepan. Slowly bring to the boil and simmer, uncovered, for 10 minutes, stirring occasionally, until thick and syrupy. Remove the clove and stir in the chopped coriander.

Heat the oil in a pan and chargrill the turkey escalopes, in two batches if necessary, for 3–4 minutes on each side until golden brown and tender. Spoon the chutney onto four individual serving plates. Place a turkey escalope on top of each spoonful of chutney. Garnish with sprigs of parsley and serve immediately with orange wedges.

Turkey & Pesto Rice Roulades

SERVES 4

125 g/4 oz cooked white rice, at room temperature
1 garlic clove, peeled and crushed
1–2 tbsp Parmesan cheese, grated
2 tbsp prepared pesto sauce
2 tbsp pine nuts, lightly toasted and chopped
4 turkey steaks, each weighing about 150 g/5 oz
salt and freshly ground black pepper
4 slices Parma ham
2 tbsp olive oil
50 ml/2 fl oz white wine
25 g/1 oz unsalted butter, chilled

To serve:
freshly cooked spinach
freshly cooked pasta

Put the rice in a bowl and add the garlic, Parmesan cheese, pesto and pine nuts. Stir to combine the ingredients, then reserve.

Place the turkey steaks on a chopping board and, using a sharp knife, cut horizontally through each steak, without cutting right through. Open up the steaks and cover with baking parchment. Flatten slightly by pounding with a meat mallet or rolling pin.

Season each steak with salt and pepper. Divide the stuffing equally among the steaks, spreading evenly over one half. Fold the steaks in half to enclose the filling, then roll each steak in a slice of Parma ham and secure with cocktail sticks.

Heat the oil in a large frying pan over medium heat. Cook the steaks for 5 minutes, or until golden on one side. Turn and cook for a further 2 minutes. Push the steaks to the side and pour in the wine. Allow the wine to bubble and evaporate. Add the butter, a little at a time, whisking constantly until the sauce is smooth. Discard the cocktail sticks, then serve the steaks drizzled with the sauce and accompanied by spinach and pasta.

Turkey Tetrazzini

SERVES 4

275 g/10 oz green and white tagliatelle
50 g/2 oz butter
4 slices streaky bacon, diced
1 onion, peeled and finely chopped
175 g/6 oz mushrooms, thinly sliced
40 g/1½ oz plain flour

450 ml/¾ pint chicken stock
150 ml/¼ pint double cream
2 tbsp sherry
450 g/1 lb cooked turkey meat, cut into bite-size pieces
1 tbsp freshly chopped parsley
freshly grated nutmeg

salt and freshly ground black pepper
25 g/1 oz Parmesan cheese, grated

To garnish:
freshly chopped parsley
Parmesan cheese, grated

Preheat the oven to 180°C/350°F/Gas Mark 4. Lightly oil a large ovenproof dish. Bring a large saucepan of lightly salted water to the boil. Add the tagliatelle and cook for 7–9 minutes until *al dente*. Drain well and reserve.

In a heavy-based saucepan, melt the butter and add the bacon. Cook for 2–3 minutes until crisp and golden. Add the onion and mushrooms, and cook for 3–4 minutes until the vegetables are tender.

Stir in the flour and cook for 2 minutes. Remove from the heat and slowly stir in the stock. Return to the heat and cook, stirring, until a smooth, thick sauce has formed. Add the tagliatelle, then pour in the cream and sherry. Add the turkey and parsley. Season to taste with the nutmeg and salt and pepper. Toss well to coat.

Turn the mixture into the prepared dish, spreading evenly. Sprinkle the top with the Parmesan cheese and bake in the preheated oven for 30–35 minutes until crisp, golden and bubbling. Garnish with chopped parsley and Parmesan cheese. Serve straight from the dish.

Turkey Hash with Potato & Beetroot

SERVES 4-6

2 tbsp vegetable oil
50 g/2 oz butter
4 slices streaky bacon,
   diced or sliced
1 medium onion, peeled
   and finely chopped

450 g/1 lb cooked
   turkey, diced
450 g/1 lb finely chopped
   cooked potatoes
2–3 tbsp freshly
   chopped parsley

2 tbsp plain flour
250 g/9 oz cooked medium
   beetroot, diced
green salad, to serve

In a large heavy-based frying pan, heat the oil and half the butter over a medium heat until sizzling. Add the bacon and cook for 4 minutes, or until crisp and golden, stirring occasionally. Using a slotted spoon, transfer to a large bowl. Add the onion to the pan and cook for 3–4 minutes until soft and golden, stirring frequently.

Meanwhile, add the turkey, potatoes, parsley and flour to the cooked bacon in the bowl. Stir and toss gently, then fold in the diced beetroot.

Add half the remaining butter to the frying pan, then the turkey vegetable mixture. Stir, then spread the mixture to evenly cover the bottom of the frying pan. Cook for 15 minutes, or until the underside is crisp and brown, pressing the hash firmly into a cake with a spatula. Remove from the heat.

Invert a large plate over the frying pan and, holding the plate and frying pan together with an oven glove, turn the hash out onto the plate. Heat the remaining butter in the pan, carefully slide the hash back into the pan and cook for 4 minutes, or until crisp and brown on the other side. Invert onto the plate again and serve immediately with a green salad.

TASTY TIP

Make sure that you buy plainly cooked beetroot, rather than the type preserved in vinegar.

Stir–fried Duck with Cashews

SERVES 4

450 g/1 lb duck breast, skinned
3 tbsp groundnut oil
1 garlic clove, peeled and finely chopped
1 tsp freshly grated ginger root

1 carrot, peeled and sliced
125 g/4 oz mangetout, trimmed
2 tsp Chinese rice wine or dry sherry
1 tbsp light soy sauce
1 tsp cornflour

50 g/2 oz unsalted cashew nuts, roasted
1 spring onion, trimmed and finely chopped
1 spring onion, shredded
boiled or steamed rice, to serve

Trim the duck breasts, discarding any fat, and slice thickly. Heat the wok, add 2 tablespoons of the oil and, when hot, add the sliced duck breast. Cook for 3–4 minutes until sealed. Using a slotted spoon, remove from the wok and leave to drain on absorbent kitchen paper.

Wipe the wok clean and return to the heat. Add the remaining oil and, when hot, add the garlic and ginger. Stir-fry for 30 seconds, then add the carrot and mangetout. Stir-fry for a further 2 minutes, then pour in the Chinese rice wine or sherry and the soy sauce.

Blend the cornflour with 1 teaspoon water and stir into the wok. Mix well and bring to the boil. Return the duck slices to the wok and simmer for 5 minutes, or until the meat and vegetables are tender. Add the cashews, then remove the wok from the heat.

Sprinkle over the chopped and shredded spring onion and serve immediately with plain boiled or steamed rice.

HELPFUL HINT

To prepare the mangetout, simply top and tail, pulling away as much string from the edges as you can. Dry-fry the cashew nuts in the wok before starting to seal the duck breasts. Take care that the nuts do not burn.

Vegetables & Vegetarian

Spring Vegetable & Herb Risotto

SERVES 2-3

1 litre/1¾ pints
   vegetable stock
125 g/4 oz fresh asparagus
   tips, trimmed
125 g/4 oz baby
   carrots, scrubbed
50 g/2 oz peas, fresh
   or frozen
50 g/2 oz fine French

beans, trimmed
1 tbsp olive oil
1 onion, peeled and
   finely chopped
1 garlic clove, peeled and
   finely chopped
2 tsp freshly chopped thyme
225 g/8 oz risotto rice,
   such as Arborio

150 ml/¼ pint white wine
1 tbsp freshly chopped basil
1 tbsp freshly chopped chives
1 tbsp freshly chopped
   parsley
zest of ½ lemon
3 tbsp crème fraîche
salt and freshly ground
   black pepper

Bring the vegetable stock to the boil in a large saucepan and add the asparagus, baby carrots, peas and beans. Bring the stock back to the boil and remove the vegetables at once using a slotted spoon. Rinse under cold running water. Drain again and reserve. Keep the stock hot.

Heat the oil in a large deep frying pan and add the onion. Cook over a medium heat for 4–5 minutes until starting to brown. Add the garlic and thyme, and cook for a further few seconds. Add the rice and stir well for a minute until the rice is hot and coated in oil.

Add the white wine and stir constantly until the wine is almost completely absorbed by the rice. Begin adding the stock a ladleful at a time, stirring well and waiting until the last ladleful has been absorbed before stirring in the next. Add the vegetables after using about half of the stock. Continue until all the stock has been used. This will take 20–25 minutes. The rice and vegetables should both be tender.

Remove the pan from the heat. Stir in the herbs, lemon zest and crème fraîche. Season to taste with salt and pepper, and serve immediately.

Roast Butternut Squash Risotto

SERVES 4

1 medium butternut squash
2 tbsp olive oil
1 garlic bulb, cloves
    separated, but unpeeled
15 g/½ oz unsalted butter
275 g/10 oz Arborio rice
large pinch saffron strands

150 ml/¼ pint dry white wine
1 litre/1¾ pints
    vegetable stock
1 tbsp freshly
    chopped parsley
1 tbsp freshly
    chopped oregano

50 g/2 oz Parmesan cheese,
    finely grated, plus extra,
    to serve
salt and freshly ground
    black pepper
fresh oregano sprigs,
    to garnish

Preheat oven to 190°C/375°F/Gas Mark 5. Cut the butternut squash in half, thickly peel, then scoop out the seeds and discard. Cut the flesh into 2 cm/¾ inch cubes.

Pour the oil into a large roasting tin and heat in the preheated oven for 5 minutes. Add the butternut squash and garlic cloves. Turn in the oil to coat, then roast in the oven for 25–30 minutes until golden brown and very tender, turning the vegetables halfway through cooking time.

Meanwhile, melt the butter in a large saucepan. Add the rice and stir over a high heat for a few seconds. Add the saffron and the wine, and bubble fiercely until almost totally reduced, stirring frequently. At the same time, heat the stock in a separate saucepan and keep at a steady simmer.

Reduce the heat under the rice to low. Add a ladleful of stock to the saucepan and simmer, stirring, until absorbed. Continue adding the stock in this way until the rice is tender. This will take about 20 minutes and it may not be necessary to add all the stock.

Turn off the heat and stir in the herbs and the 50 g/2 oz Parmesan cheese. Season to taste with salt and pepper. Cover and leave to stand for 2–3 minutes. Quickly remove the skins from the roasted garlic. Add to the risotto with the butternut squash and mix gently. Garnish with sprigs of oregano and serve immediately with extra Parmesan cheese.

Aduki Bean & Rice Burgers

SERVES 4

2½ tbsp sunflower oil
1 medium onion, peeled
   and very finely chopped
1 garlic clove, peeled
   and crushed
1 tsp curry paste
225 g/8 oz basmati rice
400 g/14 oz can aduki beans,
   drained and rinsed
225 ml/8 fl oz
   vegetable stock

125 g/4 oz firm tofu,
   crumbled
1 tsp garam masala
2 tbsp freshly chopped
   coriander
salt and freshly ground
   black pepper

For the carrot raita:
2 large carrots, peeled

   and grated
½ cucumber, cut into tiny dice
150 ml/¼ pint Greek-style
   yogurt

To serve:
wholemeal baps
tomato slices
lettuce leaves

Heat 1 tablespoon of the oil in a saucepan and gently cook the onion for 10 minutes until soft. Add the garlic and curry paste, and cook for a few more seconds. Stir in the rice and beans.

Pour in the stock, bring to the boil and simmer for 12 minutes, or until all the stock has been absorbed – do not lift the lid for the first 10 minutes of cooking. Reserve.

Lightly mash the tofu. Add to the rice mixture with the garam masala, coriander, salt and pepper. Mix. Divide the mixture into eight and shape into burgers. Chill in the refrigerator for 30 minutes.

Meanwhile, make the raita. Mix together the carrots, cucumber and yogurt. Spoon into a small bowl and chill in the refrigerator until ready to serve.

Heat the remaining oil in a large frying pan. Fry the burgers, in batches if necessary, for 4–5 minutes on each side until lightly browned. Serve in the baps with tomato slices and lettuce. Accompany with the raita.

Mediterranean Feast

SERVES 4

1 small iceberg lettuce
225 g/8 oz French beans
225 g/8 oz baby new
   potatoes, scrubbed
4 medium eggs
1 green pepper, deseeded
   and cut into think strips
1 medium onion, peeled and
   finely chopped
200 g/7 oz can tuna in brine,

drained and flaked
50 g/2 oz hard cheese,
   such as Edam, cut into
   small cubes
8 ripe but firm cherry
   tomatoes, quartered
50 g/2 oz black pitted
   olives, halved
freshly chopped basil,
   to garnish

For the lime vinaigrette:
3 tbsp light olive oil
2 tbsp white wine vinegar
4 tbsp lime juice
grated zest of 1 lime
1 tsp Dijon mustard
1–2 tsp caster sugar
salt and freshly ground
   black pepper

Cut the lettuce into four and remove the hard core. Tear into bite-size pieces and arrange on a large serving platter or four individual plates.

Cook the French beans in boiling salted water for 8 minutes and the potatoes for 10 minutes or until tender. Drain and rinse in cold water until cool, then cut both the beans and potatoes in half with a sharp knife.

Boil the eggs for 10 minutes, then rinse thoroughly under a cold running tap until cool. Remove the shells under water and cut each egg into four.

Arrange the beans, potatoes, eggs, peppers and onion on top of the lettuce. Add the tuna, cheese and tomatoes. Sprinkle over the olives and garnish with the basil.

To make the vinaigrette, put all the ingredients in a screw-top jar and shake vigorously until everything is mixed thoroughly. Spoon 4 tablespoons over the top of the prepared salad and serve the remainder separately.

Carrot, Celeriac & Sesame Seed Salad

SERVES 6

225 g/8 oz celeriac
225 g/8 oz carrots, peeled
and finely grated
50 g/2 oz seedless raisins
2 tbsp sesame seeds
freshly chopped parsley,

to garnish
**For the lemon and
chilli dressing:**
grated zest of 1 lemon
4 tbsp lemon juice
2 tbsp sunflower oil

2 tbsp clear honey
1 red bird's-eye
chilli, deseeded and
finely chopped
salt and freshly ground
black pepper

Slice the celeriac into thin matchsticks. Put in a small saucepan of boiling salted water and boil for 2 minutes.

Drain and rinse the celeriac in cold water and transfer to a mixing bowl.

Add the carrot and the raisins to the celeriac in the bowl.

Toast the sesame seeds under a hot grill or dry-fry in a frying pan for 1–2 minutes until golden brown, then leave to cool. Watch carefully as they can quickly scorch.

Make the dressing by whisking together the lemon zest, lemon juice, oil, honey, chilli and seasoning in a small bowl or by shaking thoroughly in a screw-topd jar.

Pour 2 tablespoons of the dressing over the salad and toss well. Turn into a serving dish and sprinkle over the toasted sesame seeds and chopped parsley. Serve the remaining dressing separately.

FOOD FACT

Celeriac is a root vegetable that is similar in taste to fennel, but with a texture closer to parsnip. This versatile vegetable has a creamy taste and is also delicious in soups and gratins.

Indonesian Salad with Peanut Dressing

SERVES 4

225 g/8 oz new potatoes, scrubbed
1 large carrot, peeled and cut into matchsticks
125 g/4 oz French beans, trimmed
225 g/8 oz tiny cauliflower florets
125 g/4 oz cucumber, cut into matchsticks
75 g/3 oz fresh beansprouts
3 medium eggs, hard-boiled and quartered

For the peanut dressing:
2 tbsp sesame oil
1 garlic clove, peeled and crushed
1 red chilli, deseeded and finely chopped
150 g/5 oz crunchy peanut butter
6 tbsp hot vegetable stock
2 tsp soft light brown sugar
2 tsp dark soy sauce
1 tbsp lime juice

Cook the potatoes in a saucepan of boiling salted water for 15–20 minutes until tender. Remove with a slotted spoon and thickly slice into a large bowl. Keep the saucepan of water boiling.

Add the carrot, French beans and cauliflower to the water, return to the boil and cook for 2 minutes, or until just tender. Drain and refresh under cold running water, then drain well. Add to the potatoes with the cucumber and beansprouts.

To make the dressing, gently heat the sesame oil in a small saucepan. Add the garlic and chilli, and cook for a few seconds, then remove from the heat. Stir in the peanut butter.

Stir in the stock, a little at a time. Add the remaining ingredients and mix together to make a thick, creamy dressing.

Divide the vegetables evenly among four plates and arrange the eggs on top. Drizzle the dressing over the salad and serve immediately.

Chinese Salad with Soy & Ginger Dressing

SERVES 4

1 head Chinese cabbage
200 g/7 oz can water
  chestnuts, drained
6 spring onions, trimmed
4 ripe but firm
  cherry tomatoes
125 g/4 oz mangetout

125 g/4 oz beansprouts
2 tbsp freshly
  chopped coriander

For the soy and ginger dressing:
2 tbsp sunflower oil

4 tbsp light soy sauce
2.5 cm/1 inch piece root ginger,
  peeled and finely grated
zest and juice of 1 lemon
salt and freshly ground
  black pepper
crusty white bread, to serve

Rinse and finely shred the Chinese cabbage and place in a serving dish.

Slice the water chestnuts into small slivers and cut the spring onions diagonally into 2.5 cm/ 1 inch lengths, then split lengthways into thin strips.

Cut the tomatoes in half, then slice each half into three wedges and reserve.

Simmer the mangetout in boiling water for 2 minutes until beginning to soften, drain and cut in half diagonally.

Arrange the water chestnuts, spring onions, mangetout, tomatoes and beansprouts on top of the shredded Chinese cabbage. Garnish with the freshly chopped coriander.

Make the dressing by whisking all the ingredients together in a small bowl until mixed thoroughly. Serve with the bread and the salad.

Vegetables in Coconut Milk with Rice Noodles

SERVES 4

75 g/3 oz creamed coconut
1 tsp salt
2 tbsp sunflower oil
2 garlic cloves, peeled and finely chopped
2 red peppers, deseeded and cut into thin strips
2.5 cm/1 inch piece fresh root ginger, peeled and cut into thin strips
125 g/4 oz baby sweetcorn
2 tsp cornflour
2 medium ripe but still firm avocados
1 small Cos lettuce, cut into thick strips
freshly cooked rice noodles, to serve

Roughly chop the creamed coconut, put in a bowl with the salt, then pour over 600 ml/1 pint boiling water. Stir until the coconut has dissolved completely and reserve.

Heat a wok or large frying pan, add the oil and, when hot, add the chopped garlic, sliced peppers and ginger. Cook for 30 seconds, then cover and cook very gently for 10 minutes or until the peppers are soft.

Pour in the reserved coconut milk and bring to the boil. Stir in the baby sweetcorn, cover and simmer for 5 minutes. Blend the cornflour with 2 teaspoons water, pour into the wok and cook, stirring, for 2 minutes or until thickened slightly.

Cut the avocados in half, peel, remove the stone and slice. Add to the wok with the lettuce strips and stir until well mixed and heated through. Serve immediately on a bed of rice noodles.

FOOD FACT
Dried flat rice noodles, rice sticks and stir-fry rice noodles are all made from rice flour and come in varying thicknesses. Check the packet for cooking instructions.

Mixed Vegetables Stir-fry

SERVES 4

2 tbsp groundnut oil
4 garlic cloves, peeled and
    finely sliced
2.5 cm/1 inch piece fresh
    root ginger, peeled and
    finely sliced
75 g/3 oz broccoli florets
50 g/2 oz mangetout,

trimmed
75 g/3 oz carrots, peeled and
    cut into matchsticks
1 green pepper, deseeded
    and cut into strips
1 red pepper, deseeded and
    cut into strips
1 tbsp soy sauce

1 tbsp hoisin sauce
1 tsp sugar
salt and freshly ground
    black pepper
4 spring onions, trimmed
    and shredded,
    to garnish

Heat a wok, add the oil and, when hot, add the garlic and ginger slices, and stir-fry for 1 minute.

Add the broccoli florets to the wok, stir-fry for 1 minute, then add the mangetout, carrots and the green and red peppers, and stir-fry for a further 3–4 minutes until tender but still crisp.

Blend together the soy sauce, hoisin sauce and sugar in a small bowl. Stir well, season to taste with salt and pepper, and pour into the wok. Transfer the vegetables to a warmed serving dish. Garnish with shredded spring onions and serve immediately with a selection of other Thai dishes.

HELPFUL HINT

Vary the combination of vegetables – try asparagus spears cut into short lengths, sliced mushroons, French beans, red onion wedges and cauliflower florets.

Bean & Cashew Stir-fry

SERVES 4

3 tbsp sunflower oil
1 onion, peeled and
   finely chopped
1 celery stalk, trimmed
   and chopped
2.5 cm/1 inch piece fresh
   root ginger, peeled
   and grated
2 garlic cloves, peeled
   and crushed

1 red chilli, deseeded and
   finely chopped
175 g/6 oz fine French beans,
   trimmed and halved
175 g/6 oz mangetout, sliced
   diagonally into three
75 g/3 oz unsalted
   cashew nuts
1 tsp brown sugar
125 ml/4 fl oz

vegetable stock
2 tbsp dry sherry
1 tbsp light soy sauce
1 tsp red wine vinegar
salt and freshly ground
   black pepper
freshly chopped coriander,
   to garnish

Heat a wok or large frying pan, add the oil and, when hot, add the onion and celery, and stir-fry gently for 3–4 minutes until softened.

Add the ginger, garlic and chilli to the wok and stir-fry for 30 seconds. Stir in the French beans and mangetout, together with the cashew nuts, and continue to stir-fry for 1–2 minutes until the nuts are golden brown.

Dissolve the sugar in the stock, then blend with the sherry, soy sauce and vinegar. Stir into the bean mixture and bring to the boil. Simmer gently, stirring occasionally, for 3–4 minutes until the beans and mangetout are tender but still crisp and the sauce has thickened slightly. Season to taste with salt and pepper. Transfer to a warmed serving bowl or spoon onto individual plates. Sprinkle with freshly chopped coriander and serve immediately.

Thai Fried Noodles

SERVES 4

450 g/1 lb tofu
2 tbsp dry sherry
125 g/4 oz medium
egg noodles
125 g/4 oz mangetout,
halved
3 tbsp groundnut oil
1 onion, peeled and
finely sliced

1 garlic clove, peeled and
finely sliced
2.5 cm/1 inch piece fresh
root ginger, peeled
and finely sliced
125 g/4 oz beansprouts
1 tbsp Thai fish sauce
2 tbsp light soy sauce
½ tsp sugar

salt and freshly ground
black pepper
½ courgette, cut into
matchsticks

To garnish:
2 tbsp roasted peanuts,
roughly chopped
fresh basil sprigs

Cut the tofu into cubes and place in a bowl. Sprinkle over the sherry and toss to coat. Cover loosely and leave to marinate in the refrigerator for 30 minutes.

Bring a large saucepan of lightly salted water to the boil and add the noodles and mangetout. Simmer for 3 minutes, or according to the packet instructions, then drain and rinse under cold running water. Leave to drain again.

Heat a wok or large frying pan, add the oil and, when hot, add the onion and stir-fry for 2–3 minutes. Add the garlic and ginger, and stir-fry for 30 seconds. Add the beansprouts and tofu, stir in the Thai fish sauce, soy sauce and sugar, and season to taste with salt and pepper.

Stir-fry the tofu mixture over a medium heat for 2–3 minutes, then add the courgette, noodles and mangetout, and stir-fry for a further 1–2 minutes. Tip into a warmed serving dish or spoon onto individual plates. Sprinkle with the peanuts, add a sprig of basil and serve immediately.

Thai Noodles & Vegetables with Tofu

SERVES 4

225 g/8 oz firm tofu
2 tbsp soy sauce
grated zest of 1 lime
2 lemon grass stalks
1 red chilli
1 litre/1¾ pints
   vegetable stock
2 slices fresh root
   ginger, peeled

2 garlic cloves, peeled
2 fresh coriander sprigs
175 g/6 oz dried thread
   egg noodles
125 g/4 oz shiitake or
   button mushrooms,
   sliced if large
2 carrots, peeled and
   cut into matchsticks

125 g/4 oz mangetout
125 g/4 oz bok choy or
   other Chinese leaf
1 tbsp freshly
   chopped coriander
salt and freshly ground
   black pepper
coriander sprigs,
   to garnish

Drain the tofu well and cut into cubes. Put in a shallow dish with the soy sauce and lime zest. Stir well to coat and leave to marinate for 30 minutes.

Meanwhile, put the lemon grass and chilli on a chopping board and bruise with the side of a large knife, ensuring that the blade is pointing away from you. Put the vegetable stock in a large saucepan and add the lemon grass, chilli, ginger, garlic and coriander. Bring to the boil, cover and simmer gently for 20 minutes.

Strain the stock into a clean pan. Return to the boil and add the noodles, tofu and its marinade and the mushrooms. Simmer gently for 4 minutes.

Add the carrots, mangetout, bok choy and chopped coriander and simmer for a further 3–4 minutes until the vegetables are just tender. Season to taste with salt and pepper. Garnish with coriander sprigs and serve immediately.

Pad Thai Noodles with Mushrooms

SERVES 4

125 g/4 oz flat rice noodles or rice vermicelli
1 tbsp vegetable oil
2 garlic cloves, peeled and finely chopped
1 medium egg, lightly beaten
225 g/8 oz mixed

mushrooms, including shiitake, oyster, field, brown and wild mushrooms
2 tbsp lemon juice
1½ tbsp Thai fish sauce
½ tsp sugar
½ tsp cayenne pepper

2 spring onions, trimmed and cut into 2.5 cm/ 1 inch pieces
50 g/2 oz fresh beansprouts

To garnish:
chopped roasted peanuts
freshly chopped coriander

Cook the noodles according to the packet instructions. Drain well and reserve.

Heat a wok or large frying pan. Add the oil and garlic. Fry until just golden. Add the egg and stir quickly to break it up.

Cook for a few seconds before adding the noodles and mushrooms. Scrape down the sides of the pan to ensure that they mix with the egg and garlic.

Add the lemon juice, fish sauce, sugar, cayenne pepper, spring onions and half the beansprouts, stirring quickly all the time.

Cook over a high heat for a further 2–3 minutes until everything is heated through.

Turn out onto a serving plate. Top with the remaining beansprouts. Garnish with the chopped peanuts and coriander, and serve immediately.

TASTY TIP

An aromatic alternative for this dish is to use lemon grass. Discard the outer leaves, finely chop and add instead of the lemon juice.

Coconut–baked Courgettes

SERVES 4

3 tbsp groundnut oil
1 onion, peeled and
    finely sliced
4 garlic cloves, peeled
    and crushed

½ tsp chilli powder
1 tsp ground coriander
6–8 tbsp desiccated coconut
1 tbsp tomato purée
700 g/1½ lb courgettes,

thinly sliced
freshly chopped parsley,
    to garnish

Preheat the oven to 180°C/350°F/Gas Mark 4, 10 minutes before cooking. Lightly oil a 1.4 litre/2½ pint ovenproof gratin dish. Heat a wok, add the oil and when hot, add the onion and stir-fry for 2–3 minutes until softened. Add the garlic, chilli powder and coriander, and stir-fry for 1–2 minutes.

Pour 300 ml/½ pint cold water into the wok and bring to the boil. Add the coconut and tomato purée, and simmer for 3–4 minutes; most of the water will evaporate at this stage. Spoon 4 tablespoons of the spice and coconut mixture into a small bowl and reserve.

Stir the courgettes into the remaining spice and coconut mixture, coating well. Spoon the courgettes into the oiled gratin dish and sprinkle the reserved spice and coconut mixture evenly over the top. Bake, uncovered, in the preheated oven for 15–20 minutes until golden. Garnish with chopped parsley and serve immediately.

HELPFUL HINT

Desiccated coconut has a relatively short shelflife. Unless you use it in large quantities, buy it in small packets, checking the sell-by date. Once opened, it should be used within 2 months.

Courgette Lasagne

SERVES 8

2 tbsp olive oil
1 medium onion, peeled and finely chopped
225 g/8 oz mushrooms, wiped and thinly sliced
3–4 courgettes, trimmed and thinly sliced
2 garlic cloves, peeled and finely chopped
½ tsp dried thyme
1–2 tbsp freshly chopped basil or flat-leaf parsley
salt and freshly ground black pepper
1 quantity prepared white sauce (*see* page 187)

350 g/12 oz lasagne sheets, cooked
225 g/8 oz mozzarella cheese, grated
50 g/2 oz Parmesan cheese, grated
400 g/14 oz can chopped tomatoes, drained

Preheat the oven to 200°C/400°F/Gas Mark 6, 15 minutes before cooking. Heat the oil in a large frying pan, add the onion and cook for 3–5 minutes. Add the mushrooms, cook for 2 minutes, then add the courgettes and cook for a further 3–4 minutes until tender. Stir in the garlic, thyme and basil or parsley, and season to taste with salt and pepper. Remove from the heat and reserve.

Spoon one-third of the white sauce over the bottom of a lightly oiled large baking dish. Arrange a layer of lasagne over the sauce. Spread half the courgette mixture over the pasta, then sprinkle with some of the mozzarella and some of the Parmesan cheese. Repeat with more white sauce and another layer of lasagne, then cover with half the drained tomatoes.

Cover the tomatoes with lasagne, the remaining courgette mixture and some mozzarella and Parmesan cheese. Repeat the layers, ending with a layer of lasagne sheets, white sauce and the remaining Parmesan cheese. Bake in the preheated oven for 35 minutes, or until golden. Serve immediately.

Fusilli with Courgettes & Sun-dried Tomatoes

SERVES 6

5 tbsp olive oil
1 large onion, peeled and
    thinly sliced
2 garlic cloves, peeled and
    finely chopped
700 g/1½ lb courgettes,
    trimmed and sliced

400 g/14 oz can chopped
    plum tomatoes
12 sun-dried tomatoes,
    cut into thin strips
salt and freshly ground
    black pepper
450 g/1 lb fusilli

25 g/1 oz butter, diced
2 tbsp freshly chopped basil
    or flat-leaf parsley
grated Parmesan or
    pecorino cheese,
    to serve

Heat 2 tablespoons of the olive oil in a large frying pan, add the onion and cook for 5–7 minutes until softened. Add the chopped garlic and courgette slices and cook for a further 5 minutes, stirring occasionally.

Stir the chopped tomatoes and sun-dried tomatoes into the frying pan and season to taste with salt and pepper. Cook until the courgettes are just tender and the sauce is slightly thickened.

Bring a large pan of lightly salted water to a rolling boil. Add the fusilli and cook according to the packet instructions, or until *al dente*.

Drain the fusilli thoroughly and return to the pan. Add the butter and remaining oil, and toss to coat. Stir the chopped basil or parsley into the courgette mixture and pour over the fusilli. Toss and tip into a warmed serving dish. Serve with grated Parmesan or pecorino cheese.

Pasta with Courgettes, Rosemary & Lemon

SERVES 4

350 g/12 oz dried pasta shapes, such as rigatoni
1½ tbsp good-quality extra virgin olive oil
2 garlic cloves, peeled and finely chopped
4 medium courgettes, thinly sliced
1 tbsp freshly chopped rosemary
1 tbsp freshly chopped parsley
zest and juice of 2 lemons
25 g/1 oz pitted black olives, roughly chopped
25 g/1 oz pitted green olives, roughly chopped
salt and freshly ground black pepper

To garnish:
lemon slices
fresh rosemary sprigs

Bring a large saucepan of salted water to the boil and add the pasta. Return to the boil and cook according to the packet instructions, or until *al dente*.

Meanwhile, when the pasta is almost done, heat the oil in a large frying pan and add the garlic. Cook over a medium heat until the garlic just begins to brown. Be careful not to overcook at this stage or the garlic will become bitter.

Add the courgettes, rosemary, parsley and lemon zest and juice. Cook for 3–4 minutes until the courgettes are just tender.

Add the olives to the frying pan and stir well. Season to taste with salt and pepper and remove from the heat.

Drain the pasta well and add to the frying pan. Stir until thoroughly combined. Garnish with lemon slices and sprigs of fresh rosemary and serve immediately.

Vegetarian Spaghetti Bolognese

SERVES 4

2 tbsp olive oil
1 onion, peeled and
    finely chopped
1 carrot, peeled and
    finely chopped
1 celery stalk, trimmed and
    finely chopped

225 g/8 oz Quorn mince
150 ml/¼ pint red wine
300 ml/½ pint
    vegetable stock
1 tsp mushroom ketchup
4 tbsp tomato purée
350 g/12 oz dried spaghetti

4 tbsp crème fraîche
salt and freshly ground
    black pepper
1 tbsp freshly
    chopped parsley

Heat the oil in a large saucepan and add the onion, carrot and celery. Cook gently for 10 minutes, adding a little water if necessary, until softened and starting to brown.

Add the Quorn mince and cook a further 2–3 minutes before adding the red wine. Increase the heat and simmer gently until nearly all the wine has evaporated.

Mix together the vegetable stock and mushroom ketchup and add about half to the Quorn mixture along with the tomato purée. Cover and simmer gently for about 45 minutes, adding the remaining stock as necessary.

Meanwhile, bring a large pan of salted water to the boil and add the spaghetti. Cook according to the packet instructions, or until *al dente*. Drain well. Remove the sauce from the heat, add the crème fraîche and season to taste with salt and pepper. Stir in the parsley and serve immediately with the pasta.

HELPFUL HINT

Quorn is a mycroprotein derived from the mushroom family and readily takes on any flavour it is put with. An equivalent amount of soya mince can be used in this recipe.

Creamy Vegetable Korma

SERVES 4-6

2 tbsp ghee or vegetable oil
1 large onion, peeled
   and chopped
2 garlic cloves, peeled
   and crushed
2.5 cm/1 inch piece root
   ginger, peeled and grated
4 cardamom pods
2 tsp ground coriander
1 tsp ground cumin

1 tsp ground turmeric
finely grated zest and juice
   of ½ lemon
50 g/2 oz ground almonds
400 ml/14 fl oz
   vegetable stock
450 g/1 lb potatoes, peeled
   and diced
450 g/1 lb mixed vegetables,
   such as cauliflower,

carrots and turnip,
   cut into chunks
150 ml/¼ pint double cream
3 tbsp freshly chopped
   coriander
salt and freshly ground
   black pepper
naan bread, to serve

Heat the ghee or oil in a large saucepan. Add the onion and cook for 5 minutes. Stir in the garlic and ginger, and cook for a further 5 minutes, or until soft and just beginning to colour.

Stir in the cardamom, ground coriander, cumin and turmeric. Continue cooking over a low heat for 1 minute, stirring.

Stir in the lemon zest and juice and the almonds. Blend in the vegetable stock. Slowly bring to the boil, stirring occasionally.

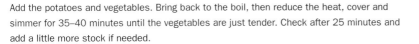

Add the potatoes and vegetables. Bring back to the boil, then reduce the heat, cover and simmer for 35–40 minutes until the vegetables are just tender. Check after 25 minutes and add a little more stock if needed.

Slowly stir in the cream and chopped coriander. Season to taste with salt and pepper. Cook very gently until heated through, but do not boil. Serve immediately with naan bread.

Pumpkin & Chickpea Curry

SERVES 4

1 tbsp vegetable oil
1 small onion, peeled and sliced
2 garlic cloves, peeled and finely chopped
2.5 cm/1 inch piece root ginger, peeled and grated
1 tsp ground coriander
½ tsp ground cumin
½ tsp ground turmeric

¼ tsp ground cinnamon
2 tomatoes, chopped
2 red bird's-eye chillies, deseeded and finely chopped
450 g/1 lb pumpkin or butternut squash flesh, cubed
1 tbsp hot curry paste
300 ml/½ pint

vegetable stock
1 large firm banana
400 g/14 oz can chickpeas, drained and rinsed
salt and freshly ground black pepper
1 tbsp freshly chopped coriander
coriander sprigs, to garnish
rice or naan bread, to serve

Heat the oil in a saucepan and add the onion. Fry gently for 5 minutes until softened.

Add the garlic, ginger and spices, and fry for a further minute. Add the chopped tomatoes and chillies, and cook for another minute.

Add the pumpkin and curry paste, and fry gently for 3–4 minutes before adding the stock. Stir well, bring to the boil and simmer for 20 minutes until the pumpkin is tender.

Thickly slice the banana and add to the pumpkin mixture along with the chickpeas. Simmer for a further 5 minutes.

Season to taste with salt and pepper, and add the chopped coriander. Serve immediately, garnished with coriander sprigs, and with some rice or naan bread.

HELPFUL HINT

Curry pastes come in mild, medium and hot varieties. Although hot curry paste is recommended in this recipe use whichever one you prefer.

Mushroom Stew

SERVES 4

15 g/½ oz dried
  porcini mushrooms
900 g/2 lb assorted fresh
  mushrooms, wiped
2 tbsp good-quality
  virgin olive oil
1 onion, peeled and
  finely chopped

2 garlic cloves, peeled and
  finely chopped
1 tbsp fresh thyme leaves
pinch ground cloves
salt and freshly ground
  black pepper
700 g/1½ lb tomatoes,
  peeled, deseeded

and chopped
225 g/8 oz instant polenta
600ml/1 pint vegetable stock
3 tbsp freshly chopped
  mixed herbs
fresh parsley sprigs,
  to garnish

Soak the porcini mushrooms in a small bowl of hot water for 20 minutes. Drain, reserving the porcini mushrooms and their soaking liquor. Cut the fresh mushrooms in half and reserve.

In a saucepan, heat the oil and add the onion. Cook gently for 5–7 minutes until softened. Add the garlic, thyme and cloves, and continue cooking for 2 minutes.

Add all the mushrooms and cook for 8–10 minutes until the mushrooms have softened, stirring often. Season to taste with salt and pepper, and add the tomatoes and the reserved soaking liquor.

Simmer, partly covered, over a low heat for about 20 minutes until thickened. Adjust the seasoning to taste.

Meanwhile, cook the polenta according to the packet instructions using the vegetable stock. Stir in the herbs and divide among four dishes. Ladle the mushrooms over the polenta, garnish with the parsley and serve immediately.

Pasta Shells with Broccoli & Capers

SERVES 4

400 g/14 oz conchiglie (shells)
450 g/1 lb broccoli florets, cut into small pieces
5 tbsp olive oil
1 large onion, peeled and finely chopped

4 tbsp capers in brine, rinsed and drained
½ tsp dried chilli flakes (optional)
75 g/3 oz freshly grated Parmesan cheese, plus extra to serve

25 g/1 oz pecorino cheese, grated
salt and freshly ground black pepper
2 tbsp freshly chopped flat-leaf parsley, to garnish

Bring a large pan of lightly salted water to a rolling boil. Add the conchiglie, return to the boil and cook for 2 minutes. Add the broccoli to the pan. Return to the boil and continue cooking for 8–10 minutes until the conchiglie is *al dente*.

Meanwhile, heat the olive oil in a large frying pan, add the onion and cook for 5 minutes, or until softened, stirring frequently. Stir in the capers and chilli flakes, if using, and cook for a further 2 minutes.

Drain the pasta and broccoli, and add to the frying pan. Toss the ingredients to mix thoroughly. Sprinkle over the 75 g/3 oz grated Parmesan and the pecorino cheese, then stir until the cheeses have just melted. Season to taste with salt and pepper, then tip into a warmed serving dish. Garnish with the chopped parsley and serve immediately with extra Parmesan cheese.

Fusilli Pasta with Spicy Tomato Salsa

SERVES 4

6 large ripe tomatoes
2 tbsp lemon juice
2 tbsp lime juice
grated zest of 1 lime
2 shallots, peeled and

finely chopped
2 garlic cloves, peeled
  and finely chopped
1–2 red chillies
1–2 green chillies

450 g/1 lb fusilli pasta
4 tbsp crème fraîche
2 tbsp freshly chopped basil
fresh oregano sprig,
  to garnish

Put the tomatoes in a bowl and cover with boiling water. Allow to stand until the skins start to peel away.

Remove the skins from the tomatoes, divide each tomato into four and remove all the seeds. Chop the flesh into small dice and put in a small pan. Add the lemon and lime juices and the grated lime zest and stir well.

Add the chopped shallots and garlic. Remove the seeds carefully from the chillies, chop finely and add to the pan. Bring to the boil and simmer gently for 5–10 minutes until the salsa has thickened slightly. Reserve the salsa to allow the flavours to develop while the pasta is cooking.

Bring a large pan of water to the boil and add the pasta. Simmer gently according to packet instructions, or until *al dente*.

Drain the pasta and rinse in boiling water. Top with a large spoonful of salsa and a small spoonful of crème fraîche. Garnish with the chopped basil and oregano, and serve immediately.

Tortellini, Cherry Tomato & Mozzarella Skewers

SERVES 6

250 g/9 oz mixed green and plain cheese- or vegetable-filled fresh tortellini
150 ml/¼ pint extra virgin olive oil

2 garlic cloves, peeled and crushed
pinch dried thyme or basil
salt and freshly ground black pepper
225 g/8 oz cherry tomatoes

450 g/1 lb mozzarella cheese, cut into 2.5 cm/ 1 inch cubes
basil leaves, to garnish
dressed salad leaves, to serve

Preheat the grill and line a grill pan with kitchen foil, just before cooking. Bring a large pan of lightly salted water to a rolling boil. Add the tortellini and cook according to the packet instructions, or until *al dente*. Drain, rinse under cold running water, drain again and toss with 2 tablespoons of the olive oil and reserve.

Pour the remaining olive oil into a small bowl. Add the crushed garlic and thyme or basil, then blend well. Season to taste with salt and black pepper, and reserve.

To assemble the skewers, thread the tortellini alternately with the cherry tomatoes and cubes of mozzarella. Arrange the skewers on the grill pan and brush generously on all sides with the olive oil mixture.

Cook the skewers under the preheated grill for about 5 minutes, or until they begin to turn golden, turning them halfway through cooking. Arrange two skewers on each plate and garnish with a few basil leaves. Serve immediately with dressed salad leaves.

HELPFUL HINT

If using wooden skewers for this recipe, soak them in cold water for at least 30 minutes before cooking to prevent them scorching. The tips skewers may be protected with small pieces of foil.

Marinated Vegetable Kebabs

SERVES 4

2 small courgettes, cut into
　2 cm/¾ inch pieces
½ green pepper, deseeded
　and cut into 2.5 cm/
　1 inch pieces
½ red pepper, deseeded
　and cut into 2.5 cm /
　1 inch pieces
½ yellow pepper, deseeded
　and cut into 2.5 cm/
　1 inch pieces

8 baby onions, peeled
8 button mushrooms
8 cherry tomatoes
freshly chopped parsley,
　to garnish
freshly cooked couscous,
　to serve

For the marinade:
1 tbsp light olive oil
4 tbsp dry sherry

2 tbsp light soy sauce
1 red chilli, deseeded and
　finely chopped
2 garlic cloves, peeled
　and crushed
2.5 cm/1 inch piece root
　ginger, peeled and
　finely grated

Put the courgettes, green, red and yellow peppers and baby onions in a pan of just boiled water. Bring back to the boil and simmer for about 30 seconds. Drain and rinse the cooked vegetables in cold water and dry on absorbent kitchen paper.

Thread the cooked vegetables and the mushrooms and tomatoes alternately onto skewers and place in a large shallow dish.

Make the marinade by whisking together all the ingredients until thoroughly blended. Pour the marinade evenly over the kebabs, then leave to marinate in the refrigerator for at least 1 hour. Spoon the marinade over the kebabs occasionally during this time.

Arrange the kebabs side by side in a hot griddle pan or on a hot barbecue and cook gently for 10–12 minutes. Turn the kebabs frequently and brush with the marinade when needed. When the vegetables are tender, sprinkle over the chopped parsley and serve immediately with couscous.

TASTY TIP

Although these kebabs use only vegetables, large chunks of fish, such as cod, or indeed tiger prawns could be added alternately between the vegetables and cooked in the same way.

Spanish Baked Tomatoes

175 g/6 oz whole-grain rice
600 ml/1 pint
    vegetable stock
2 tsp sunflower oil
2 shallots, peeled and
    finely chopped
1 garlic clove, peeled
    and crushed

1 green pepper, deseeded
    and cut into small dice
1 red chilli, deseeded and
    finely chopped
50 g/2 oz button mushrooms
    finely chopped
1 tbsp freshly
    chopped oregano

salt and freshly ground
    black pepper
4 large ripe beef tomatoes
1 large egg, beaten
1 tsp caster sugar
fresh basil leaves, to garnish
crusty bread, to serve

Preheat the oven to 180°C/350°F/Gas Mark 4. Put the rice in a saucepan, pour over
the vegetable stock and bring to the boil. Simmer for 30 minutes or until the rice is tender.
Drain and turn into a mixing bowl.

Add 1 teaspoon of the sunflower oil to a small nonstick pan and gently fry the shallots, garlic,
pepper, chilli and mushrooms for 2 minutes. Add to the rice with the chopped oregano.
Season with plenty of salt and pepper.

Slice the top off each tomato and reserve. Cut and scoop out the flesh, removing the hard
core. Pass the tomato flesh through a sieve. Add 1 tablespoon of the resulting juice to the rice
mixture. Stir in the beaten egg and mix. Sprinkle a little sugar in the bottom of each tomato.
Pile the rice mixture into the shells.

Place the tomatoes in a baking dish and pour a little cold water around them. Replace their
lids and drizzle a few drops of sunflower oil over the tops.

Bake in the preheated oven for about 25 minutes. Garnish with the basil leaves, season with
black pepper and serve immediately with crusty bread.

Stuffed Onions with Pine Nuts

SERVES 4

4 medium onions, peeled
2 garlic cloves, peeled
    and crushed
2 tbsp fresh brown
    breadcrumbs
2 tbsp white breadcrumbs

25 g/1 oz sultanas
25 g/1 oz pine nuts
50 g/2 oz hard cheese such
    as Edam, grated
2 tbsp freshly
    chopped parsley

1 medium egg, beaten
salt and freshly ground
    black pepper
salad leaves, to serve

Preheat the oven to 200°C/400°F/Gas Mark 6. Bring a pan of water to the boil, add the onions and cook gently for about 15 minutes. Drain well.

Allow the onions to cool, then slice each one in half horizontally. Scoop out most of the onion flesh, but leave a reasonably firm shell.

Chop up 4 tablespoons of the onion flesh and place in a bowl with the crushed garlic, breadcrumbs, sultanas, pine nuts, grated cheese and parsley. Mix together thoroughly, then bind together with as much of the beaten egg as necessary to make a firm filling. Season to taste with salt and pepper.

Pile the mixture back into the onion shells and top with the grated cheese. Place on a oiled baking tray and cook in the preheated oven for 20–30 minutes until golden brown. Serve immediately with the salad leaves.

TASTY TIP

While this dish is delicious on its own, it also complements barbecued meat and fish. The onion takes on a mellow, nutty flavour when baked.

Melanzane Parmigiana

SERVES 4

900 g/2 lb aubergines
salt and freshly ground
    black pepper
5 tbsp olive oil
1 red onion, peeled
    and chopped
½ tsp mild paprika

150 ml/¼ pint dry red wine
150 ml/¼ pint
    vegetable stock
400 g/14 oz can chopped
    tomatoes
1 tsp tomato purée
1 tbsp freshly

chopped oregano
175 g/6 oz mozzarella
    cheese, thinly sliced
40 g/1½ oz Parmesan cheese,
    coarsely grated
fresh basil sprig,
    to garnish

Cut the aubergines lengthways into thin slices. Sprinkle with salt and leave to drain in a colander over a bowl for 30 minutes.

Meanwhile, heat 1 tablespoon of the olive oil in a saucepan and fry the onion for 10 minutes until softened. Add the paprika and cook for 1 minute. Stir in the wine, stock, chopped tomatoes and tomato purée. Simmer, uncovered, for 25 minutes, or until fairly thick. Stir in the oregano and season to taste with salt and pepper. Remove from the heat. Preheat oven to 200°C/400°F/Gas Mark 6.

Rinse the aubergine slices thoroughly under cold water and pat dry on absorbent kitchen paper. Heat 2 tablespoons of the oil in a griddle pan and cook the aubergines in batches, for 3 minutes on each side, until golden. Drain well on absorbent kitchen paper.

Pour half the tomato sauce into the bottom of a large ovenproof dish. Cover with half the aubergine slices, then top with the mozzarella. Cover with the remaining aubergine slices and pour over the remaining tomato sauce. Sprinkle with the grated Parmesan cheese.

Bake in the preheated oven for 30 minutes, or until the aubergines are tender and the sauce is bubbling. Garnish with a sprig of fresh basil and cool for a few minutes before serving.

HELPFUL HINT

Salting the aubergine draws out some of the moisture, so you'll need less oil when frying.

Light Ratatouille

SERVES 4

1 red pepper
2 courgettes, trimmed
1 small aubergine, trimmed
1 onion, peeled

2 ripe tomatoes
50 g/2 oz button
    mushrooms, wiped
    and halved or quartered

200 ml/7 fl oz tomato juice
1 tbsp freshly chopped basil
salt and freshly ground
    black pepper

Deseed the peppers, remove the membrane with a small sharp knife and cut into small dice. Thickly slice the courgettes and cut the aubergine into small dice. Slice the onion into rings.

Put the tomatoes in a bowl of boiling water until their skins begin to peel away. Remove the skins from the tomatoes, cut into quarters and remove the seeds.

Put all the vegetables in a saucepan with the tomato juice and basil. Season to taste with salt and pepper. Bring to the boil, cover and simmer for 15 minutes, or until the vegetables are tender.

Remove the vegetables with a slotted spoon and arrange in a serving dish. Bring the liquid in the pan to the boil and boil for 20 seconds until it is slightly thickened. Season the sauce to taste with salt and pepper.

Pass the sauce through a sieve to remove some of the seeds and pour over the vegetables. Serve the ratatouille hot or cold.

TASTY TIP

This dish would be perfect, served as an accompaniment to any baked fish dish. It is also delicious in an omelette or as a jacket potato filling.

Rigatoni with Oven–dried Cherry Tomatoes & Mascarpone

SERVES 4

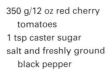

350 g/12 oz red cherry
  tomatoes
1 tsp caster sugar
salt and freshly ground
  black pepper

2 tbsp olive oil
400 g/14 oz dried rigatoni
125 g/4 oz petits pois
2 tbsp mascarpone cheese
1 tbsp freshly chopped mint

1 tbsp freshly chopped
  parsley
fresh mint sprigs,
  to garnish

Preheat oven to 140°C/275°F/Gas Mark 1. Halve the cherry tomatoes and place close together on a nonstick baking tray, cut-side up. Sprinkle lightly with the sugar, then with a little salt and pepper. Bake in the preheated oven for 1¼ hours, or until dry but not beginning to colour. Leave to cool on the baking tray. Put in a bowl, drizzle over the olive oil and toss to coat.

Bring a large saucepan of lightly salted water to the boil and cook the pasta according to packet instructions, or until *al dente*. Add the petits pois 2–3 minutes before the end of the cooking time. Drain thoroughly and return the pasta and the petits pois to the saucepan.

Add the mascarpone to the saucepan. When melted, add the tomatoes, mint, parsley and a little black pepper. Toss together gently, then transfer to a warmed serving dish or individual plates, and garnish with sprigs of fresh mint. Serve immediately.

Spaghetti alla Puttanesca

SERVES 4

4 tbsp olive oil
50 g/2 oz anchovy fillets in
    olive oil, drained and
    coarsely chopped
2 garlic cloves, peeled
    and finely chopped
½ tsp crushed dried chillies

400 g/14 oz can chopped
    plum tomatoes
125 g/4 oz pitted black
    olives, cut in half
2 tbsp capers, rinsed
    and drained
1 tsp freshly

chopped oregano
1 tbsp tomato purée
salt and freshly ground
    black pepper
400 g/14 oz spaghetti
2 tbsp freshly
    chopped parsley

Heat the olive oil in a large frying pan, add the anchovies and cook, stirring with a wooden spoon and crushing the anchovies until they disintegrate. Add the garlic and dried chillies, and cook for 1 minute, stirring frequently.

Add the tomatoes, olives, capers, oregano and tomato purée and cook, stirring occasionally, for 15 minutes, or until the liquid has evaporated and the sauce is thickened. Season the tomato sauce to taste with salt and pepper.

Meanwhile, bring a large pan of lightly salted water to a rolling boil. Add the spaghetti and cook according to the packet instructions, or until *al dente*.

Drain the spaghetti thoroughly, reserving 1–2 tablespoons of the the cooking water. Return the spaghetti with the reserved water to the pan. Pour the tomato sauce over the spaghetti, add the chopped parsley and toss to coat. Tip into a warmed serving dish or spoon onto individual plates, and serve immediately.

HELPFUL HINT

For a less salty dish, drain the anchovies and soak in a little milk for about 20 minutes before using. You can, of course, omit the anchovies to make a vegetarian dish.

Baked Macaroni Cheese

SERVES 8

450 g/1 lb macaroni
75 g/3 oz butter
1 onion, peeled and
 finely chopped
40 g/1½ oz plain flour
1 litre/1¾ pints milk
1–2 dried bay leaves
½ tsp dried thyme

salt and freshly ground
 black pepper
cayenne pepper
freshly grated nutmeg
2 small leeks, trimmed,
 finely chopped, cooked
 and drained
1 tbsp Dijon mustard

400 g/14 oz mature
 Cheddar cheese, grated
2 tbsp dried breadcrumbs
2 tbsp freshly grated
 Parmesan cheese
fresh basil sprig, to garnish

Preheat the oven to 190°C/375°F/Gas Mark 5, 10 minutes before cooking. Bring a large pan of lightly salted water to a rolling boil. Add the macaroni and cook according to the packet instructions, or until *al dente*. Drain thoroughly and reserve.

Meanwhile, melt 50 g/2 oz of the butter in a large heavy-based saucepan, add the onion and cook, stirring frequently, for 5–7 minutes until softened. Sprinkle in the flour and cook, stirring constantly, for 2 minutes. Remove the pan from the heat, stir in the milk, return to the heat and cook, stirring, until a smooth sauce has formed.

Add the bay leaf and thyme to the sauce and season to taste with salt, pepper, cayenne and freshly grated nutmeg. Simmer for about 15 minutes, stirring frequently, until thickened and smooth.

HELPFUL HINT

Make sure that you simmer the macaroni only until just *al dente* and drain straight away, as it will be further cooked in the oven, where it needs to soak up the flavoursome sauce.

Remove the sauce from the heat. Add the cooked leeks, mustard and Cheddar cheese, and stir until the cheese has melted. Stir in the macaroni, then tip into a lightly oiled baking dish.

Sprinkle the breadcrumbs and Parmesan cheese over the macaroni. Dot with the remaining butter, then bake in the preheated oven for 1 hour, or until golden. Garnish with a basil sprig and serve immediately.

Four-cheese Tagliatelle

SERVES 4

300 ml/½ pint whipping
cream
4 garlic cloves, peeled and
lightly bruised
75 g/3 oz fontina
cheese, diced
75 g/3 oz Gruyère

cheese, grated
75 g/3 oz mozzarella
cheese, diced
50 g/2 oz Parmesan cheese,
grated, plus extra to serve
salt and freshly ground
black pepper

275 g/10 oz fresh green
tagliatelle
1–2 tbsp freshly
snipped chives
fresh basil leaves,
to garnish

Put the whipping cream and garlic cloves in a medium pan and heat gently until small bubbles begin to form around the edge of the pan. Using a slotted spoon, remove and discard the garlic cloves.

Add all the cheeses to the pan and stir until melted. Season with a little salt and a lot of black pepper. Keep the sauce warm over a low heat, but do not allow to boil.

Meanwhile, bring a large pan of lightly salted water to the boil. Add the taglietelle, return to the boil and cook for 2–3 minutes until *al dente*.

Drain the pasta thoroughly and return to the pan. Pour the sauce over the pasta, add the chives, then toss lightly until well coated. Tip into a warmed serving dish or spoon onto individual plates. Garnish with a few basil leaves and serve immediately with extra Parmesan cheese.

Rigatoni with Gorgonzola & Walnuts

SERVES 4

400 g/14 oz rigatoni
50 g/2 oz butter
125 g/4 oz crumbled
    Gorgonzola cheese
2 tbsp brandy (optional)
200 ml/7 fl oz whipping or
    double cream
75 g/3 oz walnut pieces,
lightly toasted and
    coarsely chopped
1 tbsp freshly chopped basil
50 g/2 oz freshly grated
    Parmesan cheese
salt and freshly ground
    black pepper

To serve:
cherry tomatoes
fresh green salad leaves

Bring a large pan of lightly salted water to a rolling boil. Add the rigatoni and cook according to the packet instructions, or until al dente. Drain the pasta thoroughly, reserve and keep warm.

Melt the butter in a large saucepan or wok over a medium heat. Add the Gorgonzola cheese and stir until just melted. Add the brandy if using and cook for 30 seconds, then pour in the cream and cook for 1–2 minutes, stirring until the sauce is smooth.

Stir in the walnut pieces, basil and half the Parmesan cheese, then add the rigatoni. Season to taste with salt and pepper. Return to the heat,stirring frequently, until heated through. Divide the pasta among 4 warmed pasta bowls, sprinkle with the remaining Parmesan cheese and serve immediately with cherry tomatoes and fresh green salad leaves.

TASTY TIP

Either whipping or double cream may be used here; double cream is higher in fat, so will give a richer, creamier finish. If preferred, you could use sour cream, but heat it gently to avoid curdling.

Spinach Dumplings with Rich Tomato Sauce

SERVES 4

For the sauce:
2 tbsp olive oil
1 onion, peeled and
  chopped
1 garlic clove, peeled
  and crushed
1 red chilli, deseeded
  and chopped
150 ml/¼ pint dry
  white wine

400 g/14 oz can chopped
  tomatoes
pared strip of lemon zest

For the dumplings:
450 g/1 lb fresh spinach
50 g/2 oz ricotta cheese
25 g/1 oz fresh white
  breadcrumbs
25 g/1 oz Parmesan

cheese, grated
1 medium egg yolk
¼ tsp freshly grated nutmeg
salt and freshly ground
  black pepper
5 tbsp plain flour
2 tbsp olive oil, for frying
fresh basil leaves, to garnish
freshly cooked tagliatelle,
  to serve

To make the tomato sauce, heat the olive oil in a large saucepan and fry the onion gently for 5 minutes. Add the garlic and chilli, and cook for a further 5 minutes until softened.

Stir in the wine, chopped tomatoes and lemon zest. Bring to the boil, cover and simmer for 20 minutes, then uncover and simmer for 15 minutes, or until the sauce has thickened. Remove the lemon zest and season to taste with salt and pepper.

To make the spinach dumplings, wash the spinach thoroughly and remove any tough stalks. Cover and cook in a large saucepan over a low heat with just the water clinging to the leaves. Drain, then squeeze out all the excess water. Finely chop and put in a large bowl.

Add the ricotta, breadcrumbs, Parmesan cheese and egg yolk to the spinach. Season with the nutmeg and salt and pepper. Mix together and shape into 20 walnut-sized balls.

Toss the spinach balls in the flour. Heat the olive oil in a large nonstick frying pan and fry the balls gently for 5–6 minutes, carefully turning occasionally. Garnish with fresh basil leaves and serve immediately with the tomato sauce and tagliatelle.

HELPFUL HINT

It is very important to squeeze out all the excess water from the cooked spinach, otherwise the dumplings will fall apart when they are fried.

Vegetable Frittata

SERVES 2

6 medium eggs
2 tbsp freshly
   chopped parsley
1 tbsp freshly
   chopped tarragon
25 g/1 oz pecorino or
   Parmesan cheese,
   finely grated

freshly ground black pepper
175 g/6 oz tiny new potatoes
2 small carrots, peeled
   and sliced
125 g/4 oz broccoli, cut into
   small florets
1 courgette, about 125 g/
   4 oz, sliced

2 tbsp olive oil
4 spring onions, trimmed
   and thinly sliced

To serve:
mixed green salad
crusty Italian bread

Preheat the grill just before cooking. Lightly beat the eggs with the parsley, tarragon and half the cheese. Season to taste with pepper and reserve. (Salt is not needed because the pecorino is very salty.)

Bring a large saucepan of lightly salted water to the boil. Add the new potatoes and cook for 8 minutes. Add the carrots and cook for 4 minutes, then add the broccoli florets and courgette. Cook for a further 3–4 minutes until all the vegetables are barely tender. Drain well.

Heat the oil in a 20 cm/8 inch heavy-based frying pan. Add the spring onions and cook for 3–4 minutes until softened. Add all the vegetables and cook for a few seconds, then pour in the beaten egg mixture. Stir gently for about a minute, then cook for a further 1–2 minutes until the bottom of the frittata is set and golden brown.

Place the pan under a hot grill for 1 minute, or until almost set and just beginning to brown. Sprinkle with the remaining cheese and grill for a further 1 minute, or until lightly browned. Loosen the edges and slide out of the pan. Cut into wedges and serve hot or warm with a mixed green salad and crusty Italian bread.

Crispy Pancake Rolls

MAKES 8

250 g/9 oz plain flour
pinch salt
1 medium egg
4 tsp sunflower oil
2 tbsp light olive oil
2 cm/¾ inch piece fresh root
    ginger, peeled and grated
1 garlic clove, peeled
and crushed
225 g/8 oz tofu, drained
    and cut into small dice
2 tbsp soy sauce
1 tbsp dry sherry
175 g/6 oz button
    mushrooms, wiped
    and chopped
1 celery stalk, trimmed
    and finely chopped
2 spring onions, trimmed
    and finely chopped
2 tbsp groundnut oil
fresh coriander sprig,
    to garnish

Sift 225 g/8 oz of the flour with the salt into a large bowl, make a well in the centre and drop in the egg. Beat to form a smooth, thin batter, gradually adding 300 ml/½ pint water and drawing in the flour from the sides of the bowl. Mix the remaining flour with 1–2 tablespoons water to make a thick paste. Reserve.

Heat a little sunflower oil in a 20 cm/8 inch omelette or frying pan and pour in 2 tablespoons of the batter. Cook for 1–2 minutes, flip over and cook for a further 1–2 minutes until firm. Slide from the pan and keep warm. Make more pancakes with the remaining batter.

Heat a wok or large frying pan, add the olive oil and, when hot, add the ginger, garlic and tofu, stir-fry for 30 seconds, then pour in the soy sauce and sherry. Add the mushrooms, celery and spring onions. Stir-fry for 1–2 minutes, then remove from the wok and leave to cool.

Place a little filling in the centre of each pancake. Brush the edges with the flour paste, fold in the edges, then roll up into parcels. Heat the groundnut oil to 180°C/350°F in the wok (a small cube of bread dropped into the oil should sizzle and brown in about 40 seconds). Fry the pancake rolls for 2–3 minutes until golden on both sides. Serve immediately, garnished with a coriander sprig.

Desserts & Cakes

Creamy Puddings with Mixed Berry Compote

SERVES 6

300 ml/½ pint double cream
250 g/9 oz carton
   ricotta cheese
50 g/2 oz caster sugar

125 g/4 oz white chocolate,
   broken into pieces
350 g/12 oz mixed summer
   fruits such as

strawberries, blueberries
   and raspberries
2 tbsp Cointreau

Set the freezer to rapid freeze. Whip the cream until soft peaks form. Fold in the ricotta cheese and half the sugar.

Put the chocolate in a bowl set over a saucepan of simmering water. Stir until melted. Remove from the heat and leave to cool, stirring occasionally. Stir into the cheese mixture until well blended.

Spoon the mixture into 6 individual pudding moulds and level the surface of each pudding with the back of a spoon. Place in the freezer and freeze for 4 hours.

Put the fruits and the remaining sugar in a pan and heat gently, stirring occasionally until the sugar has dissolved and the juices are just beginning to run. Stir in the Cointreau to taste.

Dip the pudding moulds in hot water for 30 seconds and invert onto six serving plates. Spoon the fruit compote over the puddings and serve immediately. Remember to return the freezer to its usual setting.

Rice Pudding

SERVES 4

60 g/2½ oz pudding rice
50 g/2 oz granulated sugar
410 g/14 oz can
   evaporated milk

300 ml/½ pint semi-
   skimmed milk
pinch of freshly
   grated nutmeg

25 g/1 oz butter or
   margarine
jam, to decorate

Preheat the oven to 150°C/300°F/Gas Mark 2. Lightly oil a large ovenproof dish.

Sprinkle the rice and sugar into the dish and mix.

Bring the evaporated milk and milk to the boil in a small pan, stirring occasionally.

Stir the milks into the rice and mix well until the rice is coated thoroughly. Sprinkle over the nutmeg, cover with kitchen foil and bake in the preheated oven for 30 minutes.

Remove the pudding from the oven and stir well, breaking up any lumps. Cover again with the same foil. Return to the oven for a further 30 minutes. Remove from the oven and stir well again.

Dot the pudding with butter and bake for a further 45–60 minutes until the rice is tender and the skin is browned.

Divide the pudding among four individual serving bowls. Top with a large spoonful of the jam and serve immediately.

TASTY TIP

The main trick to achieving traditional creamy rice pudding is not using cream and full-fat milk, but rather long, slow cooking at a low temperature.

Crunchy Rhubarb Crumble

SERVES 6

125 g/4 oz plain flour
50 g/2 oz softened butter
50 g/2 oz rolled oats
50 g/2 oz demerara sugar

1 tbsp sesame seeds
½ tsp ground cinnamon
450 g/1 lb fresh rhubarb
50 g/2 oz caster sugar,

plus extra as needed
custard or cream, to serve

Preheat the oven to 180°C/350°F/Gas Mark 4. Put the flour in a large bowl and cut the butter into cubes. Add to the flour and rub in with the fingertips until the mixture looks like fine breadcrumbs, or blend for a few seconds in a food processor.

Stir in the rolled oats, demerara sugar, sesame seeds and cinnamon. Mix well and reserve.

Prepare the rhubarb by removing the thick ends of the stalks and cut diagonally into 2.5 cm/ 1 inch chunks. Wash thoroughly and pat dry with a clean tea towel. Put the rhubarb in a 1.1 litre/2 pint pie dish.

Sprinkle the caster sugar over the rhubarb and top with the reserved crumble mixture. Level the top of the crumble so that all the fruit is well covered and press down firmly. If liked, sprinkle the top with a little extra caster sugar.

Place on a baking sheet and bake in the preheated oven for 40–50 minutes until the fruit is soft and the topping is golden brown. Sprinkle the pudding with some more caster sugar and serve hot with custard or cream.

Osborne Pudding

SERVES 4

8 slices white bread
50 g/2 oz butter
2 tbsp marmalade
50 g/2 oz luxury mixed
    dried fruit
2 tbsp fresh orange juice

40 g/1½ oz caster sugar
2 large eggs
450 ml/¾ pint milk
150 ml/¼ pint
    whipping cream

For the marmalade sauce:
zest and juice of 1 orange
2 tbsp thick-cut
    orange marmalade
1 tbsp brandy (optional)
2 tsp cornflour

Preheat the oven to 170°C/325°F/Gas Mark 3. Lightly oil a 1.1 litre/2 pint baking dish.

Remove and discard the crusts from the bread and spread the bread slices thickly with butter and marmalade. Cut the bread into small triangles. Place half the bread in the bottom of the dish and sprinkle over the dried mixed fruit, 1 tablespoon of the orange juice and half the caster sugar. Top with the remaining bread and marmalade, buttered-side up, and pour over the remaining orange juice. Sprinkle over the remaining caster sugar.

Whisk the eggs with the milk and cream, and pour over the pudding. Leave to stand for about 30 minutes to allow the bread to absorb the liquid.

Place the baking dish in a roasting tin and pour in enough boiling water to come halfway up the sides of the dish. Bake in the preheated oven for 50–60 minutes until the pudding is set and the top is crisp and golden.

TASTY TIP

To make an 'orange sauce', replace the marmalade with the juice of 3 more oranges and a squeeze of lemon juice to make 250 ml/9 fl oz, and increase the cornflour to 1½ tablespoons.

Meanwhile, make the marmalade sauce. Heat the orange zest and juice with the marmalade and brandy, if using. Mix 1 tablespoon water with the cornflour and mix together well. Add to the saucepan and cook over a low heat, stirring, until warmed through and thickened. Serve the pudding hot with the marmalade sauce.

Tipsy Tropical Fruit

SERVES 4

225 g/8 oz can pineapple
   chunks in natural juice
2 guavas
1 papaya
2 passion fruit
25 g/1 oz unsalted butter

1 tbsp orange juice
50 g/2 oz creamed
   coconut, chopped
50 g/2 oz soft light
   brown sugar
2 tbsp Malibu liqueur or

white rum
fresh mint sprigs,
   to decorate
vanilla ice cream,
   to serve

Drain the pineapple chunks, reserving the juice. Pat the pineapple dry on absorbent kitchen paper. Peel the guavas and cut into wedges. Halve the papaya and scoop out the black seeds. Peel and cut into 2.5 cm/1 inch chunks. Halve the passion fruit and scoop out the seeds into a small bowl.

Heat the butter in a wok, add the pineapple and stir-fry over a high heat for 30 seconds. Reduce the heat and add the guavas and papaya. Drizzle over the orange juice and cook for 2 minutes, stirring occasionally, taking care not to break up the fruit.

Using a slotted spoon, remove the fruit from the wok, leaving any juices behind, and transfer to a warmed serving dish. Add the creamed coconut to the wok with the sugar and pineapple juice. Simmer for 2–3 minutes, stirring until the coconut has melted.

Add the Malibu or white rum to the wok and heat through, then pour over the fruit. Spoon the passion fruit pulp on top and serve hot with spoonfuls of ice cream decorated with a sprig of mint.

Stir–fried Bananas & Peaches with Rum Butterscotch Sauce

SERVES 4

2 medium-firm bananas
1 tbsp caster sugar
2 tsp lime juice
4 firm, ripe peaches or
   nectarines
1 tbsp sunflower oil

**For the rum butterscotch
   sauce:**
50 g/2 oz unsalted butter
50 g/2 oz soft light
   brown sugar
125 g/4 oz demerara sugar

300 ml/½ pint double cream
2 tbsp dark rum

Peel the bananas and cut into 2.5 cm/1 inch diagonal slices. Place in a bowl and sprinkle with the caster sugar and lime juice and stir until lightly coated. Reserve.

Put the peaches or nectarines in a large bowl and pour over boiling water to cover. Leave for 30 seconds, then plunge them into cold water and peel off their skins. Cut each one into 8 thick slices, discarding the stones.

Heat a wok, add the oil and swirl it around the wok to coat the sides. Add the fruit and cook for 3–4 minutes, shaking the wok and gently turning the fruit until lightly browned. Spoon the fruit into a warmed serving bowl and clean the wok with absorbent kitchen paper.

To make the sauce, add the butter and sugars to the wok and stir continuously over a very low heat until the sugar has dissolved. Remove from the heat and leave to cool for 2–3 minutes.

Stir the cream and rum into the sugar syrup and return to the heat. Bring to the boil and simmer for 2 minutes, stirring continuously until smooth. Leave for 2–3 minutes to cool slightly, then serve warm with the stir-fried peaches and bananas.

Sweet–stewed Dried Fruits

500 g/1 lb 2 oz packet mixed
   dried fruit salad
450 ml/¾ pint apple juice
2 tbsp clear honey

2 tbsp brandy
1 lemon
1 orange

To decorate:
crème fraîche
fine strips of pared
   orange zest

Put the dried fruits, apple juice, clear honey and brandy in a small saucepan.

Using a small, sharp knife or a zester, carefully remove the zest from the lemon and orange, and add to the pan.

Squeeze the juice from the lemon and oranges, and add to the pan.

Bring the fruit mixture to the boil and simmer for about 1 minute. Remove the pan from the heat and allow the mixture to cool completely.

Transfer the mixture to a large bowl, cover with clingfilm and chill in the refrigerator overnight to allow the flavours to blend.

Spoon the stewed fruit into four shallow dessert dishes. Decorate with a large spoonful of crème fraîche and a few strips of the pared orange zest and serve.

Poached Pears

SERVES 4

2 small cinnamon sticks	thinly pared zest and juice	orange slices, to decorate
125 g/4 oz caster sugar	of 1 small orange	frozen vanilla yogurt,
300 ml/½ pint red wine	4 firm pears	or ice cream, to serve

Place the cinnamon sticks on the work surface and, with a rolling pin, slowly roll down the side of the cinnamon stick to bruise. Place in a large heavy-based saucepan.

Add the sugar, wine, 150 ml/¼ pint water and pared orange zest and juice to the pan and bring slowly to the boil, stirring occasionally, until the sugar is dissolved.

Meanwhile, peel the pears, leaving the stalks on. Cut out the cores from the bottom of the pears and level them so that they stand upright. Stand the pears in the syrup, cover the pan and simmer for 20 minutes or until tender. Remove the pan from the heat and leave the pears to cool in the syrup, turning occasionally.

Arrange the pears on serving plates and spoon over the syrup. Decorate with the orange slices and serve with the yogurt or ice cream and any remaining juices.

Coconut Rice Served with Stewed Ginger Fruits

SERVES 6-8

1 vanilla pod
450 ml/¾ pint coconut milk
1.1 litres/2 pints semi-
 skimmed milk
600 ml/1 pint double cream
100 g/3½ oz caster sugar
2 star anise

8 tbsp toasted desiccated
 coconut
250 g/9 oz short-grain
 pudding rice
1 tsp melted butter
2 mandarin oranges, peeled
 and pith removed

1 star fruit, sliced
50 g/2 oz preserved stem
 ginger, finely diced
300 ml/½ pint sweet
 white wine
caster sugar,
 to taste

Preheat the oven to 160°C/325°F/Gas Mark 3. Using a sharp knife, split the vanilla pod in half lengthways, scrape out the seeds from the pods and place both the pod and seeds in a large heavy-based casserole dish. Pour in the coconut milk, the semi-skimmed milk and the double cream and stir in the sugar, star anise and 4 tablespoons of the toasted coconut. Bring to the boil, then simmer for 10 minutes, stirring occasionally. Remove the vanilla pod and star anise.

Wash the rice and add to the milk. Simmer gently for 25–30 minutes until the rice is tender, stirring frequently. Stir in the melted butter.

Divide the mandarins into segments and place in a saucepan with the sliced star fruit and stem ginger. Pour in the white wine and 300 ml/½ pint water, bring to the boil, then reduce the heat and simmer for 20 minutes or until the liquid has reduced and the fruits softened. Add caster sugar to taste.

Serve the rice topped with the stewed fruits and the remaining toasted coconut.

Chocolate Pear Pudding

SERVES 6

140 g/4½ oz butter, softened
2 tbsp soft brown sugar
400 g/14 oz can pear
   halves, drained and
   juice reserved

25 g/1 oz walnut halves
125 g/4 oz golden caster
   sugar
2 medium eggs, beaten
75 g/3 oz self-raising

flour, sifted
50 g/2 oz cocoa powder
1 tsp baking powder
prepared chocolate custard,
   to serve

Preheat the oven to 190°C/375°F/Gas Mark 5, 10 minutes before baking. Butter a 20.5 cm/ 8 inch sandwich tin with 15 g/½ oz of the butter and sprinkle the base with the soft brown sugar. Arrange the drained pear halves on top of the sugar, cut-side down. Fill the spaces between the pears with the walnut halves, flat-side upwards.

Cream the remaining butter with the caster sugar, then gradually beat in the beaten eggs, adding 1 tablespoon of the flour after each addition. When all the eggs have been added, stir in the remaining flour.

Sift together the cocoa powder and baking powder, then stir into the creamed mixture with 1–2 tablespoons of the reserved pear juice to give a smooth dropping consistency.

Spoon the mixture over the pear halves, smoothing the surface. Bake in the preheated oven for 20–25 minutes until well risen and the surface springs back when lightly pressed. Remove from the oven and leave to cool for 5 minutes.

Using a palette knife, loosen the sides and invert onto a serving plate. Serve with custard.

HELPFUL HINT

To soften butter, cut into small pieces and leave in a warmed bowl at room temperature for a short time. Do not use the microwave, as this makes the fat oily and affects the cake's texture.

Maple Pears with Pistachios & Simple Chocolate Sauce

SERVES 4

25 g/1 oz unsalted butter
50 g/2 oz unsalted pistachios
4 medium-ripe firm pears,
    peeled, quartered
    and cored
2 tsp lemon juice

pinch of ground ginger
    (optional)
6 tbsp maple syrup

For the chocolate sauce:
150 ml/¼ pint double cream

2 tbsp milk
½ tsp vanilla essence
150 g/5 oz plain dark
    chocolate, broken into
    squares and roughly
    chopped

Melt the butter in a wok over a medium heat until sizzling. Reduce the heat a little, add the pistachios and stir-fry for 30 seconds.

Add the pears to the wok and continue cooking for about 2 minutes, turning frequently and carefully, until the nuts are beginning to brown and the pears are tender.

Add the lemon juice, ground ginger, if using, and maple syrup. Cook for 3–4 minutes until the syrup has reduced slightly. Spoon the pears and the syrup into a serving dish and leave to cool for 1–2 minutes while making the chocolate sauce.

Pour the cream and milk into the wok. Add the vanilla essence and heat just to boiling point. Remove the wok from the heat.

Add the chocolate to the wok and leave for 1 minute to melt, then stir until the chocolate is evenly mixed with the cream. Pour into a jug and serve while still warm, with the pears.

Coffee & Peach Creams

SERVES 4

4 peaches
50 g/2 oz caster sugar
2 tbsp coffee essence
200 g/7 oz carton

Greek-style yogurt
300 g carton ready-
made custard

To decorate:
peach slices
fresh mint sprigs
crème fraîche

Using a sharp knife, cut the peaches in half and remove the stones. Put the peaches in a large bowl, cover with boiling water and leave for 2–3 minutes.

Drain the peaches, then carefully remove the skin.

Put the caster sugar in a saucepan and add 50 ml/2 fl oz water. Bring the sugar mixture to the boil, stirring occasionally, until the sugar has dissolved. Boil rapidly for about 2 minutes.

Add the peaches and coffee essence to the pan, mixing to coat the peaches. Remove from the heat and allow the peach mixture to cool.

Meanwhile, mix together the Greek yogurt and custard until well combined.

Divide the peaches among the four glass dishes. Spoon over the custard mixture, then top with remaining peach mixture.

Chill for 30 minutes and then serve, decorated with peach slices, mint sprigs and a little crème fraîche.

Fudgy Mocha Pie with Espresso Custard Sauce

CUTS INTO 10 SLICES

125 g/4 oz plain dark
  chocolate, chopped
125 g/4 oz butter, diced
1 tbsp instant
  espresso powder
4 large eggs
1 tbsp golden syrup

125 g/4 oz sugar
1 tsp ground cinnamon
3 tbsp milk
icing sugar, for dusting
a few fresh strawberries,
  to serve

Espresso custard sauce:
2–3 tbsp instant espresso
  powder, or to taste
225 ml/8 fl oz prepared
  custard
225 ml/8 fl oz single cream
2 tbsp coffee-flavoured
  liqueur (optional)

Preheat the oven to 180°C/350°F/Gas Mark 4, 10 minutes before serving. Line with kitchen foil or lightly oil a deep 23 cm/9 inch pie plate. Melt the chocolate and butter in a small saucepan over a low heat and stir until smooth, then reserve. Dissolve the instant espresso powder in 1–2 tablespoons hot water and reserve.

Beat the eggs with the golden syrup, sugar, dissolved espresso powder, cinnamon and milk until blended. Add the melted chocolate mixture and whisk until blended. Pour into the pie plate.

Bake the pie in the preheated oven for 20–25 minutes until the edge has set but the centre is still very soft. Leave to cool, remove from the plate, then dust lightly with icing sugar.

To make the custard sauce, dissolve the instant espresso powder with 2–3 tablespoons hot water, then whisk into the prepared custard sauce. Slowly add the single cream, whisking constantly, then stir in the coffee-flavoured liqueur, if using. Serve slices of the pie in a pool of espresso custard with strawberries.

HELPFUL HINT

Many brands of ready-made custard are available, including brands in tins, but supermarkets now also sell fresh custard in tubs that is usually found with the dairy products.

Chocolate Mousse

SERVES 6

175 g/6 oz milk or plain chocolate orange
535 g/1¼ lb carton ready-made custard
450 ml/¾ pint double cream
12 Cape gooseberries, to decorate
sweet biscuits, to serve

Break the chocolate into segments and place in a bowl set over a saucepan of simmering water. Leave until melted, stirring occasionally. Remove the bowl in the pan from the heat and allow the melted chocolate to cool slightly.

Put the custard in a bowl and fold the melted chocolate into it using a metal spoon or rubber spatula. Stir well until completely combined.

Pour the cream into a small bowl and whip until the cream forms soft peaks.

Using a metal spoon or rubber spatula, fold most of the whipped cream into the chocolate mixture.

Spoon into six tall glasses and carefully top with the remaining cream.

Leave the desserts to chill in the refrigerator for at least 1 hour or preferably overnight.

Peel back the skins from the gooseberries to form petal shapes and use to decorate the chocolate desserts. Serve with sweet biscuits.

FOOD FACT

Cape gooseberries are also known as Physallis and can be found in most major supermarkets. They have a sweet flavour with a slight acidity, and taste similar to yogurt.

Chocolate Fudge Sundae

SERVES 2

**For the chocolate
  fudge sauce:**
75 g/3 oz plain dark
  chocolate, broken
  into pieces
450ml/¾ pint double cream
175g/6 oz golden
  caster sugar

25 g/1 oz plain flour
pinch salt
15 g/½ oz unsalted butter
1 tsp vanilla essence

For the sundae:
125 g/4 oz raspberries, fresh
  or thawed if frozen

3 scoops vanilla ice cream
3 scoops chocolate
  ice cream
2 tbsp toasted
  flaked almonds
a few wafers, to serve

To make the chocolate fudge sauce, put the chocolate and cream in a heavy-based saucepan and heat gently until the chocolate has melted into the cream. Stir until smooth. Mix the sugar with the flour and salt, then stir in sufficient chocolate mixture to make a smooth paste.

Gradually blend the remaining melted chocolate mixture into the paste, then pour into a clean saucepan. Cook over a low heat, stirring frequently until smooth and thick. Remove from the heat and add the butter and vanilla essence. Stir until smooth, then cool slightly.

To make the sundae, crush the raspberries lightly with a fork and reserve. Spoon a little of the chocolate sauce into the bottom of two sundae glasses. Add a layer of crushed raspberries, then a scoop each of vanilla and chocolate ice cream. Top each one with a scoop of the vanilla ice cream. Pour over the sauce, sprinkle over the almonds and serve with a wafer.

HELPFUL HINT
Store any remaining
fudge sauce in the
refrigerator for 1–2 weeks,
warming it just
before serving.

Chocolate Mallow Pie

SERVES 6

200 g/7 oz digestive biscuits
75 g/3 oz butter, melted
175 g/6 oz plain
   dark chocolate

20 marshmallows
1 medium egg, separated
300 ml/½ pint double cream

Put the biscuits in a polythene bag and finely crush with a rolling pin. Alternatively, put in a food processor and blend until fine crumbs are formed.

Melt the butter in a medium-sized saucepan, add the crushed biscuits and mix together. Press into the bottom of the prepared tin and leave to cool in the refrigerator.

Melt 125 g/4 oz of the chocolate with the marshmallows and 2 tablespoons water in a saucepan over a gentle heat, stirring constantly. Leave to cool slightly, then stir in the egg yolk, beat well, then leave in the refrigerator until cool.

Whisk the egg white until stiff and standing in peaks, then fold into the chocolate mixture.

Lightly whip the cream and fold three-quarters of the cream into the chocolate mixture. Reserve the remainder. Spoon the chocolate cream into the flan case and chill in the refrigerator until set.

When ready to serve, spoon the remaining cream over the chocolate pie, swirling in a decorative pattern. Grate the remaining dark chocolate and sprinkle over the cream, then serve.

TASTY TIP

Replace the digestive biscuits with an equal weight of chocolate-covered digestive biscuits to make a quick change to this recipe.

Fruit & Nut
Refrigerator Fingers

14 pink and white
  marshmallows
75 g/3 oz luxury dried
  mixed fruit
25 g/1 oz candied orange
  peel, chopped

75 g/3 oz glacé cherries,
  quartered
75 g/3 oz walnuts, chopped
1 tbsp brandy
175 g/6 oz digestive
  biscuits, crushed

225 g/8 oz plain
  dark chocolate
125 g/4 oz unsalted butter
1 tbsp icing sugar,
  for dusting (optional)

Lightly oil and line the bottom of a 18 cm/7 inch square cake tin with nonstick baking parchment. Using oiled kitchen scissors, snip each marshmallow into 4 or 5 pieces over a bowl. Add the dried mixed fruit, orange peel, cherries and walnuts to the bowl. Sprinkle with the brandy and stir together. Add the crushed biscuits and stir until mixed.

Break the chocolate into squares and put in a heatproof bowl with the butter set over a saucepan of almost boiling water. Stir occasionally until melted, then remove from the heat. Pour the melted chocolate mixture over the dry ingredients and mix together well. Spoon into the prepared tin, pressing down firmly.

Chill in the refrigerator for 15 minutes, then mark into 12 fingers using a sharp knife. Chill in the refrigerator for a further 1 hour or until set. Turn out of the tin, remove the lining paper and cut into fingers. Dust with icing sugar before serving.

Almond Cake

CUTS INTO 8 SLICES

225 g/8 oz butter
or margarine
225 g/8 oz caster sugar
3 large eggs

1 tsp vanilla essence
1 tsp almond essence
125 g/4 oz self-raising flour
175 g/6 oz ground almonds

50 g/2 oz whole
almonds, blanched
25 g/1 oz plain dark
chocolate

Preheat the oven to 150°C/300°F/Gas Mark 2. Lightly oil and line the bottom of a 20.5 cm/8 inch deep round cake tin with greaseproof or baking paper.

Cream together the butter or margarine and sugar with a wooden spoon until light and fluffy.

Beat together the eggs and essences. Gradually add to the sugar and butter mixture and mix well between each addition.

Sift the flour and mix with the ground almonds. Beat into the egg mixture until mixed well and smooth. Pour into the prepared cake tin.

Roughly chop the whole almonds and scatter over the cake before baking in the preheated oven. Bake for 45 minutes, or until golden and risen, and a skewer inserted into the centre of the cake comes out clean. Remove from the tin and leave to cool on a wire rack.

Melt the chocolate in a small bowl placed over a saucepan of gently simmering water, stirring until smooth and free of lumps. Drizzle the melted chocolate over the cooled cake and serve once the chocolate has set.

Honey Cake

50 g/2 oz butter
25 g/1 oz caster sugar
125 g/4 oz clear honey
175 g/6 oz plain flour

½ tsp bicarbonate of soda
½ tsp mixed spice
1 medium egg
2 tbsp milk

25 g/1 oz flaked almonds
1 tbsp clear honey, to drizzle

Preheat the oven to 180°C/350°F/Gas Mark 4, 10 minutes before baking. Lightly oil and line the bottom of an 18 cm/7 inch deep round cake tin with lightly oiled greaseproof or baking paper.

In a saucepan, gently heat the butter, sugar and honey together until the butter has just melted.

Sift together the flour, bicarbonate of soda and mixed spice into a bowl.

Beat the egg and the milk until mixed thoroughly.

Make a well in the centre of the sifted flour and pour in the melted butter and honey. Using a wooden spoon, beat well, gradually drawing in the flour from the sides of the bowl. When all the flour has been beaten in, add the egg mixture and mix thoroughly. Pour into the prepared tin and sprinkle with the flaked almonds.

Bake in the preheated oven for 30–35 minutes until well risen and golden brown and a skewer inserted into the centre of the cake comes out clean. Remove from the oven and cool for a few minutes in the tin before turning out and leaving to cool on a wire rack. Drizzle with the remaining tablespoon of honey and serve.

Fruit Cake

CUTS INTO 10 SLICES

225 g/8 oz butter
   or margarine
200 g/7 oz soft brown sugar
finely grated zest of
   1 orange
1 tbsp black treacle
3 large eggs, beaten

275 g/10 oz plain flour
¼ tsp ground cinnamon
½ tsp mixed spice
pinch of freshly
   grated nutmeg
¼ tsp bicarbonate of soda
75 g/3 oz mixed peel

50 g/2 oz glacé cherries
125 g/4 oz raisins
125 g/4 oz sultanas
125 g/4 oz ready-to-eat dried
   apricots, chopped

Preheat the oven to 150°C/300°C/Gas Mark 2, 10 minutes before baking. Lightly oil and line a 23 cm/9 inch deep round cake tin with a double thickness of greaseproof paper.

In a large bowl, cream together the butter or margarine, sugar and orange zest until light and fluffy, then beat in the treacle.

Beat in the eggs a little at a time, beating well between each addition.

Reserve 1 tablespoon of the flour. Sift the remaining flour, the spices and bicarbonate of soda into the mixture.

Mix all the fruits and the reserved flour together, then stir into the cake mixture. Turn into the prepared tin and smooth the top, making a small hollow in the centre of the cake mixture.

Bake in the preheated oven for 1 hour, then reduce the heat to 140°C/275°F/Gas Mark 1. Bake for a further 1½ hours, or until cooked and a skewer inserted into the centre comes out clean. Leave to cool in the tin, then turn out the cake and serve. Otherwise, when cold, store in an airtight tin.

Carrot Cake

CUTS INTO 8 SLICES

200 g/7 oz plain flour
½ tsp ground cinnamon
½ tsp freshly grated nutmeg
1 tsp baking powder
1 tsp bicarbonate of soda
150 g/5 oz dark
   muscovado sugar

200 ml/7 fl oz vegetable oil
3 medium eggs
225 g/8 oz carrots, peeled
   and roughly grated
50 g/2 oz chopped walnuts

For the icing:
175 g/6 oz cream cheese
finely grated zest of
   1 orange
1 tbsp orange juice
1 tsp vanilla essence
125 g/4 oz icing sugar

Preheat the oven to 150°C/300°F/Gas Mark 2, 10 minutes before baking. Lightly oil and line the bottom of a 15 cm/6 inch deep square cake tin with greaseproof or baking paper.

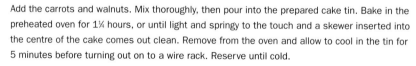

Sift together the flour, spices, baking powder and bicarbonate of soda into a large bowl. Stir in the dark muscovado sugar and mix together.

Lightly whisk together the oil and eggs, then gradually stir into the flour and sugar mixture. Stir well.

Add the carrots and walnuts. Mix thoroughly, then pour into the prepared cake tin. Bake in the preheated oven for 1¼ hours, or until light and springy to the touch and a skewer inserted into the centre of the cake comes out clean. Remove from the oven and allow to cool in the tin for 5 minutes before turning out on to a wire rack. Reserve until cold.

To make the icing, beat together the cream cheese, orange zest, orange juice and vanilla essence. Sift the icing sugar and stir into the cream cheese mixture.

When the cake is cold, discard the lining paper, spread the cream cheese icing over the top and serve cut into squares.

Banana Cake

CUTS IN 8 SLICES

3 medium-size ripe bananas
1 tsp lemon juice
150 g/5 oz soft brown sugar
75 g/3 oz butter or

margarine
250 g/9 oz self-raising flour
2 tsp ground cinnamon
3 medium eggs

50 g/2 oz walnuts, chopped
1 tsp caster sugar,
  to decorate
fresh cream, to serve

Preheat the oven to 190°C/375°F/Gas Mark 5, 10 minutes before baking. Lightly oil and line the bottom of an 18 cm/7 inch deep round cake tin with greaseproof or baking paper.

Mash 2 of the bananas in a small bowl and sprinkle with the lemon juice and a heaped tablespoon of the soft brown sugar. Mix together lightly and reserve.

Gently heat the remaining brown sugar and butter or margarine in a small saucepan until the butter has just melted. Pour into a small bowl, then allow to cool slightly.

Sift the flour and 1 teaspoon of the cinnamon into a large bowl and make a well in the centre. Beat the eggs into the cooled sugar mixture, pour into the well of flour, and mix thoroughly. Gently stir in the mashed banana mixture.

Pour half of the mixture into the prepared tin. Thinly slice the remaining banana and arrange over the cake mixture. Sprinkle over the chopped walnuts, then cover with the remaining cake mixture.

Bake in the preheated oven for 50–55 minutes, or until well risen and golden brown. Allow to cool in the tin, turn out and sprinkle with the remaining teaspoon of ground cinnamon and caster sugar. Serve hot or cold with a jug of fresh cream for pouring.

HELPFUL HINT

The riper the bananas used in this recipe, the better! Look out for reductions in supermarkets and fruit shops, as ripe bananas are often sold very cheaply.

Cappuccino Cakes

MAKES 6

125 g/4 oz butter or margarine	1 tbsp strong black coffee	1 tbsp icing sugar, sifted
125 g/4 oz caster sugar	150 g/5 oz self-raising flour	1 tsp vanilla essence
2 medium eggs	125 g/4 oz mascarpone cheese	sifted cocoa powder, to dust

Preheat the oven to 190°C/375°F/Gas Mark 5, 10 minutes before baking. Arrange six large paper muffin cases in a muffin tin or alternatively place directly on a baking sheet.

Cream together the butter or margarine and the sugar until light and fluffy. Break the eggs into a small bowl and beat lightly with a fork.

Using a wooden spoon, beat the eggs into the butter and sugar mixture a little at a time until they are all incorporated. If the mixture looks curdled, beat in a spoonful of the flour to return the mixture to a smooth consistency. Finally beat in the black coffee.

Sift the flour into the mixture, then with a metal spoon or rubber spatula gently fold in the flour.

Drop spoonfuls of the mixture into the muffin cases. Bake in the preheated oven for 20–25 minutes until risen and springy to the touch. Cool on a wire rack.

In a small bowl, beat together the mascarpone cheese, icing sugar and vanilla essence.

When the cakes are cold, spoon the vanilla mascarpone onto the top of each one. Dust with cocoa powder and serve. Eat within 24 hours and store in the refrigerator.

TASTY TIP

Make sure that you use a good-quality coffee in this recipe. Colombian coffee is generally good and at its best possesses a smooth rounded flavour.

Coffee & Pecan Cake

CUTS INTO 8 SLICES

175 g/6 oz self-raising flour
125 g/4 oz butter or
    margarine
175 g/6 oz golden caster sugar
1 tbsp instant coffee powder
    or granules

2 large eggs
50 g/2 oz pecans,
    roughly chopped

For the icing:
1 tsp instant coffee powder

or granules
1 tsp cocoa powder
75 g/3 oz unsalted
    butter, softened
175 g/6 oz icing sugar, sifted
whole pecans, to decorate

Preheat the oven to 190°C/375°F/Gas Mark 5, 10 minutes before baking. Lightly oil and line the bases of two 18 cm/7 inch sandwich tins with greaseproof or baking paper. Sift the flour and reserve.

Beat together the butter or margarine and the sugar until light and creamy. Dissolve the coffee in 2 tablespoons hot water and allow to cool.

Lightly mix the eggs with the coffee liquid. Gradually beat into the creamed butter and sugar, adding a little of the sifted flour with each addition.

Fold in the pecans, then divide the mixture between the prepared tins and bake in the preheated oven for 20–25 minutes until well risen and firm to the touch. Leave to cool in the tins for 5 minutes before turning out and cooling on a wire rack.

To make the icing, blend together the coffee and cocoa powder with just enough boiling water to make a stiff paste. Beat into the butter and icing sugar.

Sandwich the two cakes together using half of the icing. Spread the remaining icing over the top of the cake and decorate with the whole pecans to serve. Store in an airtight tin.

Index